ITEM 019 387

KT-232-374

# Learning Centre

Park Road, Uxbridge Middlesex UB8 1NQ
Telephone : 01895 853326

UXBRIDGE
COLLEGE

Please return this item to the Learning Centre on or before the last date
stamped below:

2 4 MAR 2014

2 2 APR 2014

- 4 JUN 2014

0 6 JUN 2022

BLAXTER, Loraine et al
How to research          2nd ed.

808· 02

# HOW TO RESEARCH
## SECOND EDITION

Loraine Blaxter,
Christina Hughes and
Malcolm Tight

OPEN UNIVERSITY PRESS
Maidenhead · Philadelphia

UXBRIDGE COLLEGE
LEARNING CENTRE

Open University Press
McGraw-Hill Education
McGraw-Hill House
Shoppenhangers Road
Maidenhead
Berkshire
England
SL6 2QL

email: enquiries@openup.co.uk
world wide web: www.openup.co.uk

and
325 Chestnut Street
Philadelphia, PA 19106, USA

First published 1996
Reprinted 1996, 1997, 1998, 1999, 2000

First published in this second edition 2001
Reprinted 2002 (twice), 2003

Copyright © Loraine Blaxter, Christina Hughes and Malcolm Tight, 2001

All rights reserved. Except for the quotation of short passages for the purpose of criticism and review, no part of this publication may be reproduced, stored in a retrieval system, or transmitted, in any form or by any means, electronic, mechanical, photocopying, recording or otherwise, without the prior written permission of the publisher or a licence from the Copyright Licensing Agency Limited. Details of such licences (for reprographic reproduction) may be obtained from the Copyright Licensing Agency Ltd of 90 Tottenham Court Road, London, W1P 0LP.

A catalogue record for this book is available from the British Library

ISBN   0 335 20903 3 (pb)    0 335 21121 6 (hb)

*Library of Congress Cataloging-in-Publication Data*
Blaxter, Loraine, 1945–
  How to research / by Loraine Blaxter, Christina, Hughes, and Malcolm
Tight. – 2nd ed.
    p.  cm.
  Includes bibliographical references and index.
  ISBN 0–335–20903–3 (pbk.)
  1. Research—Methodology.  I. Hughes, Christina, 1952–  II. Tight, Malcolm.
III. Title.

Q180.55.M4 B59   2001
001.4′2–dc21                                                                00–068920

Typeset by Graphicraft Limited, Hong Kong
Printed in Great Britain by Biddles Ltd, www.biddles.co.uk

# CONTENTS

# LIST OF EXERCISES

# LIST OF BOXES

# ACKNOWLEDGE-MENTS

We would like to acknowledge the continuing contributions made by our students, as well as the many positive and helpful suggestions received from users of the first edition. Particular thanks to marg, Ben at Sage and Shona.

# I

# THINKING ABOUT RESEARCH

## ☐ Introduction

This book is about the practice and experience of doing research. It is aimed at those, particularly the less experienced, who are involved in small-scale research projects. It is intended to be useful to both those doing research, whether for academic credit or not, and those responsible for teaching, supervising or managing new researchers.

The book is written in an accessible and jargon-free style, using a variety of different forms of presentation. The text has been divided into relatively small, linked sections. It is supplemented by a series of exercises, designed to help you progress your research thinking. It has been illustrated by the inclusion of a range of examples, lists, diagrams and tables in 'boxes', as well as through the inclusion of hints and relevant quotations from researchers in the text.

Suggestions for further reading are listed at the end of each chapter, with an indication of their contents. A list of the references used in the text is provided at the end of the book.

The book focuses on process rather than just methods, though these are also considered. It aims to demystify research, recognizing the everyday skills and techniques involved. It presents research as a series of stages, but without suggesting that the research process is either simple or linear.

The book is multidisciplinary in scope. It is designed to be suitable for those undertaking research in the social sciences, as well as in related subjects such as education, business studies and health and social care.

The purpose of this opening chapter is to explore the nature of the research process in the social sciences, to outline the contents of this book and to suggest how you might make use of them. The chapter is organized into the following sections:

- **What is research?** Different understandings of the nature of research, and of who can do it.
- **Why research?** Your motivations for undertaking research.
- **What is original?** Debunking the idea of originality.
- **Truth, power and values.** The context for your research.
- **How to use this book.** What you will find in it, and how to make your way through it.
- **What is different about this edition?** What has changed, and what has been added, since the first edition.

The chapter ends with a summary.

## ☐ What is research?

### The nature of research

We see and hear headlines and stories like those reproduced in Box 1 every day. Research and its results are indeed familiar to us.

You will have had research findings presented to you many times – through books, newspapers and television programmes – in the form of theories, articles or reports. Thus we learn, for example, that the United Kingdom has the highest divorce rate in Europe, or that the price of cars and petrol is also relatively high here. If you are, or have been, a student, you may have written many essays or assignments which 'compare and contrast' or 'critically analyse' the research of others.

We are also continually in contact with research as workers and citizens. Changes in our working practices are justified by the reports of in-house research teams, or those of external consultants. Outside of work, you may have taken part in research through a consumer survey held in a shopping precinct on a Saturday afternoon. You will probably have taken part, whether directly or indirectly, in one of the most extensive research surveys conducted: the national census.

So we may say to you that you are already an expert when it comes to being a recipient of research. You will certainly have opinions. You don't think so? Try Exercise 1: try yourself out!

Now compare your answer to some of the common understandings of research listed in Box 2. Did your view match any of those we selected? If it did, we told you that you were already an expert! If you had a different view, well done!

Do you think 'I could never do research'? Do you feel even the slightest sense of self-identity with this view? If so, read on. Our intention in this book is to

## Box 1: Research in the headlines

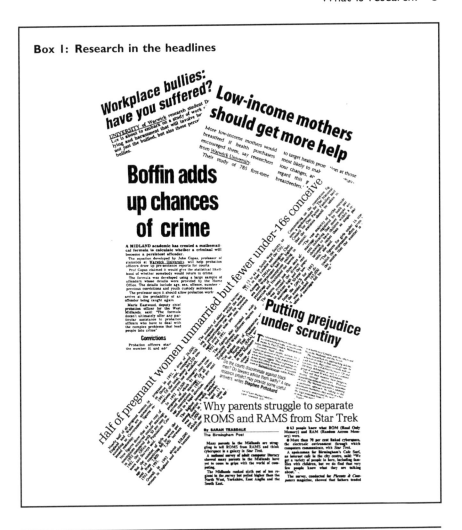

---

**Exercise 1: Your own understanding of research**

How do you view research? Complete the following sentence in no more than 20 words to convey your view of research.

Research is . . .

---

give you the skills and the confidence that you will require to take you successfully from the initial idea to a completed piece of research.

Let us continue by opening up your mind to some of the realities of doing research. In Box 3 you will find a list of some of the things about research which

---

**Box 2: Ten views of research**

1 Research is about proving your pet theory.
2 Research is something done by academics or experts.
3 Research is about establishing the facts.
4 Research is objective.
5 Research is about justifying what your funder wants to do.
6 Research can prove anything you want.
7 Research is time-consuming.
8 Research is scientific.
9 Research is removed from reality.
10 Research cannot change anything.

Note: None of these views is necessarily endorsed by the authors.

---

**Box 3: Ten things you didn't know about research**

1 Research *is* very time-consuming.
2 Research is subjective.
3 Research is often boring, but can also be fun.
4 Research can take over your life.
5 Research can be much more interesting than its results.
6 Research is about being nosey.
7 Research can be done in many ways.
8 Research uses everyday skills.
9 Research gets into your dreams.
10 Research can lead you in unexpected directions.

---

your previous experience may not have told you. You may find it interesting to compare these with the views already listed in Box 2.

Yes, you *can* do research! Many of the skills you need are commonplace and everyday. They include the ability to ask questions, to listen, to make notes and to think.

---

If you doubt this, have a look at the section on **Everyday research skills** in Chapter 3.

---

Yet for many, students and non-students alike, there is no doubt that the very word 'research' can be awe-inspiring. This may be particularly so for the new researcher, who can feel that to conduct and complete even a small-scale research study is well beyond their capabilities.

Let us repeat: you *can* do research! The main lesson to learn is that you need to practice your skills, read and think about research, and to build up your confidence. This book aims to help you in these processes.

## Types of research

Point 7 in Box 3 states that research can be done in many ways. Even a brief review of writings on research will uncover a lengthy and potentially baffling list of types of research. These include, for example:

- pure, applied and strategic research;
- descriptive, explanatory and evaluation research;
- market and academic research;
- exploratory, testing-out and problem-solving research;
- covert, adversarial and collaborative research;
- basic, applied, instrumental, participatory and action research.

The basic characteristics shared by all of these different kinds or views of research are that they are, or aim to be, planned, cautious, systematic and reliable ways of finding out or deepening understanding.

To illustrate further this variety of approach and interest, Box 4 describes a number of examples of research projects in the social sciences. Do any of these have similarities with the research which you are undertaking, or planning to undertake?

---

**Box 4: Examples of research**

1 It took Eileen Barker more than two years from first making contact with the Unification Church to gain permission to undertake her research on her own terms. The decision in favour was 'not because they thought that I would necessarily support them – they did not . . . really know how I regarded the movement – but because I had been prepared to listen to their side of the argument' (Barker 1984: 15). But she was still subjected to a final 'test'. On New Year's Eve 1976, one of the American leaders came to her house with two British moonies. They discussed the research for an hour and left apparently satisfied. But the mystique in which moonies are commonly held led her children to spend 'several exciting but ultimately unrewarded hours searching for the "bugs" which they felt quite certain would have been placed in my study' (*ibid.*: 15).

2 Amer reports an experiment concerned to test whether training in test-taking skills could improve exam performance for English as a foreign language (EFL) students. Experimental and control groups were set up, with the former taught a series of skills: 'read carefully', look for 'clue words', time scheduling etc. The researcher administered two tests to the groups, one before (pre-test) the experimental group received instruction, and one (post-test) after. While the two groups were comparable in the pre-test scores, in the post-test the

experimental group's scores had improved more than the control group's. The experiment was useful, therefore, in indicating that assumptions about, for example, poor linguistic competence being a reason for low test scores might be inaccurate (Amer 1993).

3 Mary, a social work student taking an MA course as part of her professional updating, was required to complete a dissertation of 15,000 words. Her practice experience had suggested that there was little empirical work on the survivors of abuse. She was concerned that asking survivors of abuse to talk about the past would cause further anguish. She was also aware of her own limited time resources, within which she might feel a responsibility to offer some kind of ongoing support to her research participants. Her concerns about these issues led her to undertake a life history approach with a survivor of sexual abuse, whom she gained access to through her contacts in women's support networks. She offered to discuss all of the interview transcripts with her, and to provide her with a copy of the life history document. At the first meeting, she also discussed the likely support the respondent might need, and, on a clear contractual basis, they mutually agreed the parameters for this.

4 Stein's research was based on a review of the literature, where his aim was to indicate that 'refugee behaviour, problems and situations . . . recur in many contexts, times and regions' (Stein 1986: 5). His approach was to survey the literature not to identify gaps, as is common, but to show how much had already been done and was seemingly unrecognized in this area:

> Thus far this chapter has been a lament of unfulfilled refugee research opportunities and needs. It is better, however, to note how much good, even excellent, work has been done. Much of this work is sadly underutilized. The remainder of this chapter will describe some approaches to refugee research and some key resources. In making this survey it will try to follow the stages of the refugee experience.
>
> (*Ibid.*: 8)

5 The study, a multi-centre randomised controlled trial, was set up to investigate the effectiveness and safety of treatments for women with inverted and flat (non-protractile) nipples who want to breastfeed.
(Renfrew and McCandlish 1992: 81)

This research used two networks, one comprised of midwives and one through the National Childbirth Trust, to find volunteers. These were allocated to four trial groups using opaque randomization envelopes.

## Representations of the research process

Just as there are a wide variety of views as to what research consists of, and great differences in actual practices as to what people research and how, so there are alternative perspectives of what the process of undertaking research should look like. A number of diagrammatic representations of the research process have been collected together in Box 5.

## Box 5: Representations of the research process

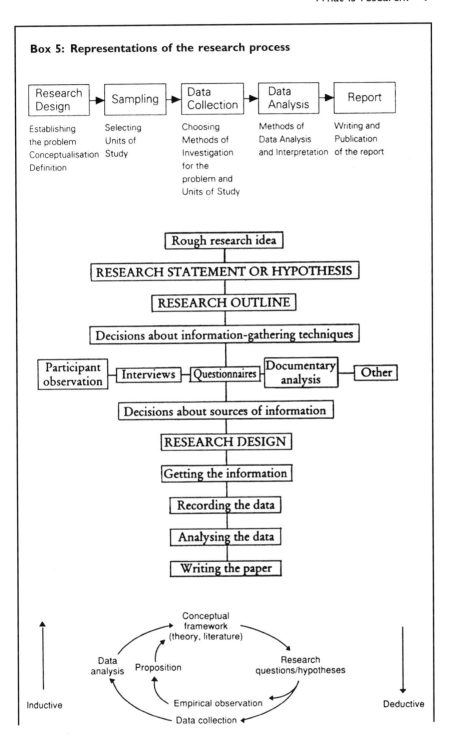

| Research Design | ➤ | Sampling | ➤ | Data Collection | ➤ | Data Analysis | ➤ | Report |
|---|---|---|---|---|---|---|---|---|

Establishing the problem
Conceptualisation
Definition

Selecting Units of Study

Choosing Methods of Investigation for the problem and Units of Study

Methods of Data Analysis and Interpretation

Writing and Publication of the report

Rough research idea

RESEARCH STATEMENT OR HYPOTHESIS

RESEARCH OUTLINE

Decisions about information-gathering techniques

Participant observation — Interviews — Questionnaires — Documentary analysis — Other

Decisions about sources of information

RESEARCH DESIGN

Getting the information

Recording the data

Analysing the data

Writing the paper

Inductive

Conceptual framework (theory, literature)

Data analysis    Proposition

Research questions/hypotheses

Empirical observation

Data collection

Deductive

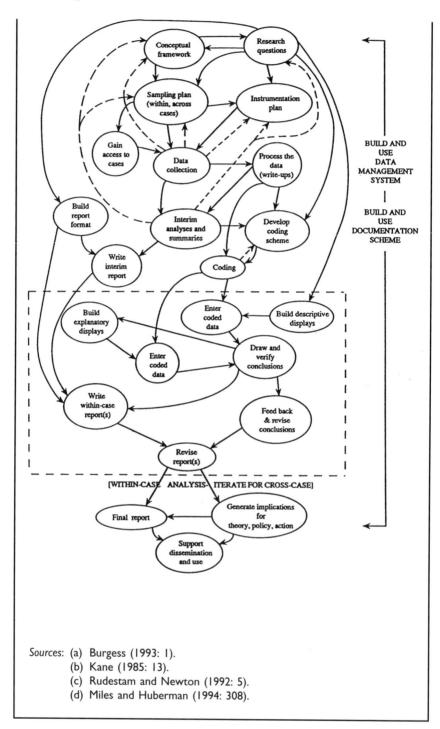

Sources: (a) Burgess (1993: 1).
(b) Kane (1985: 13).
(c) Rudestam and Newton (1992: 5).
(d) Miles and Huberman (1994: 308).

Clearly, all of these diagrams are both simplifications and idealizations of the research process. Real research is inevitably going to be a rather messier process. Nevertheless, Box 5 does suggest at least four common viewpoints:

- Research is often presented as a fixed, linear series of stages, with a clear start and end. You may think, at first glance, that this book is also organized in a linear fashion. Take a closer look! You will find extensive cross-referencing, and different kinds of text and presentation. The book has been designed to make the reader's use of it anything but linear.
- There are also somewhat more complicated presentations of this linear view, which allow for slightly different routes to be taken through the process at particular stages.
- Another common representation portrays research as a circular process, analogous to the more general process of learning. Much the same set of stages is included, and in much the same order, but there is an implication both that the process might be entered at a number of points, and that the experience of later stages might lead to a reinterpretation or revisiting of earlier stages.
- There are also variants to this approach, often associated with action research, which see the research process as cyclical or iterative. Here, the process is shown as going through a number of cycles, the effects of each one impacting upon the way in which successive cycles are approached.

Our preferred view builds on these representations, seeing the research process as a spiral (see Box 6). Seen from this perspective, research:

- is cyclical;
- can be entered at almost any point;
- is a never-ending process;
- will cause you to reconsider your practice;
- will return you to a different starting place.

The nature of the cycle varies between research designs. For example, in most quantitative research, decisions about analysis have to be taken before any fieldwork or data collection is undertaken. This is because the types of statistical techniques that are possible vary with the types of data collected. In the case of qualitative research, by contrast, data collection, sorting, analysis and reading can take place simultaneously.

## ☐ Why research?

### Understanding your motivation and self

So why are you undertaking, or interested in undertaking, research? Think about your reasons and try to complete Exercise 2.

Did you manage to think of six reasons? Did you think of more and run out of space? In our experience, people have at least three reasons for being

**Box 6: The research spiral**

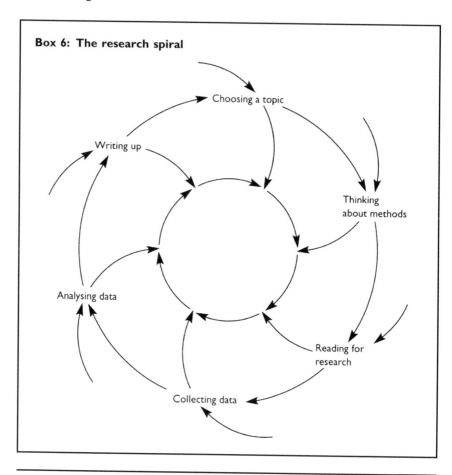

---

**Exercise 2: Reasons for undertaking research**

List your reasons for your current or anticipated involvement in research. List as many as you can think of.

1
2
3
4
5
6

---

involved in research; so, if you could only manage one or two, perhaps you might think again.

Now compare the reasons which you identified with those expressed by experienced researchers. A selection of these is included in Box 7.

---

**Box 7: Reasons for researching**

1  Many of us study aspects of our autobiographies partially disguised as a 'detached' choice of an interesting problem.

(Acker 1981: 96)

2  Edwards quotes Acker and offers herself as an example. Her study of mature women students was not 'motivated by academic concern alone ... While to some extent they statistically noted the stresses that I, along with others, had undergone, they told me nothing satisfactory about what had been going on in my life.'

(Edwards 1993: 12)

3  A few years ago I had some time off work to become a parent. Following this experience of leaving – and returning – I became excited about researching women's experiences of leaving management jobs. I wanted to tell the women's stories from their perspectives ... This seemed like research I personally *had* to do.

(Marshall 1995: 23)

4  My interest in the topic of on-the-job training (OJT) stems from my personal experience. When I worked on vocational training for people from developing countries, and dealt with the comments and requirements from them, one of the most significant points was that there might be a difference between their and our (Japanese) concept of OJT.

(Suzuki 1995: 1)

5  Before university, and some of the way through it, I entertained grand but vague ideas about my future career all in the realm of changing the world dramatically! However, I gradually became reconciled to an academic future. The reconciliation was, of course, accompanied by a bloated sense of the potential for social change of the right kind of research, and in particular of my research project.

(Hammersley 1984: 42)

6  The research project had as its inception my own passage through that decade [the 1980s], and my own despair over the confused mess that white feminist women's response to charges of racism had collectively become by 1983–84 ... as a white feminist, I knew that I had not previously known I was 'being racist' and that I had never set out to 'be racist'.

(Frankenberg 1993: 2–3)

---

As a researcher, you will find it useful to understand why you are involved in research. This will affect how you go about your research, and what you get out of it. If you are in doubt about your motivation, you might ask yourself the following questions:

- Where are you coming from?
- Whose side are you on?
- And where are you intending to get to?
- Do you want to change the world, or to change your world?
- Are you a pragmatist or an idealist?

You may see yourself as a detached researcher, separate from the subjects of your research, an objective bystander who is there to chronicle what happens, find the solutions and make appropriate recommendations. Or you might see yourself as totally enmeshed in the subject of your research, an active participant, committed to improving the circumstances of yourself and your colleagues through your work.

In practice, you are unlikely to be at either of these extremes, but they are useful stereotypes. They suggest the extent to which your motivation may affect your openness to certain approaches to research, and perhaps even influence the kinds of findings you come up with. It is important to you, as a researcher, to be aware of these possible influences. To other people, including those who read and judge the results of your research, these influences may be far more obvious.

Of course, it is possible that you could give no answer to Exercise 2. You may think of yourself as having no particular motivation for undertaking research. Perhaps you are doing it because your boss requires you to, or because it is an essential (but unwanted) part of a course you have signed up for. But even this suggests some motivation, if only to keep your boss happy or to try to get a particular qualification.

But what might you do if you really feel you have no motivation? After all, if you aren't motivated, or are not motivated very strongly, this will affect your drive to finish the research project successfully. The obvious answer to the researcher with no motivation is to get some quickly, or do something else! If the latter is not possible, you might seek motivation in one of the following ways:

- by changing your research project to something you are more interested in;
- by focusing on the skills you will develop through undertaking the research, rather than the output;
- by incorporating within the research some knowledge acquisition of relevance to you;
- by seeing the research project as part of a larger activity, which will have knock-on benefits for your work, your career, your social life or your life in general;
- by finding someone who will support you and push you through until you finish;
- by promising yourself a reward when it is successfully completed.

---

If you are still troubled by your lack of motivation, have a look at the section in Chapter 2 on **What to do if you can't think of a topic.**

---

**Exercise 3: Originality in research**

Complete the following sentence in no more than 20 words:

My research is original in . . .

---

## ☐ What is original?

For many research projects, particularly those carried out for a university degree, there is often a need for some kind or level of originality. This will typically be expressed in regulations or guidance in very general terms: 'an original project', 'an original contribution', 'evidence of original thinking'.

But what is originality? And where can you get some? If you are unsure, and it matters to you in your research, try Exercise 3.

Were you able to answer the question in a way which you found satisfactory?

In Box 8 you will find 15 definitions of originality, collected together by another author. Have a look at them, and see how they compare with your own answer.

---

**Box 8: Fifteen definitions of originality**

Here are 15 definitions of originality, as put together by Phillips and Pugh. The first six are derived from a previous author, Francis, while the other nine derive from interviews with Australian students, supervisors and examiners.

1 Setting down a major piece of new information in writing for the first time.
2 Continuing a previously original piece of work.
3 Carrying out original work designed by the supervisor.
4 Providing a single original technique, observation or result in an otherwise unoriginal but competent piece of research.
5 Having many original ideas, methods and interpretations all performed by others under the direction of the postgraduate.
6 Showing originality in testing someone else's idea.
7 Carrying out empirical work that hasn't been done before.
8 Making a synthesis that hasn't been made before.
9 Using already known material but with a new interpretation.
10 Trying out something in this country that has previously only been done in other countries.
11 Taking a particular technique and applying it in a new area.
12 Bringing new evidence to bear on an old issue.
13 Being cross-disciplinary and using different methodologies.
14 Looking at areas that people in the discipline haven't looked at before.
15 Adding to knowledge in a way that hasn't previously been done before.

*Source:* Phillips and Pugh (2000: 63–4); partly after Francis (1976).

---

As the definitions quoted indicate, it is possible to be original in terms of topic, approach or presentation. The element of originality in your own research is, realistically, likely to very small. Highly original research is very unusual, and you are probably setting your sights far too high if you try aiming for it.

The corollary of this is that your research is almost certainly original in some way, always providing, that is, that you are not slavishly copying someone else's earlier research. So be reassured. But if you are in doubt, check it out with those who will judge the originality of your research as early as possible. This advice also applies if you fear that you may be being too original for comfort. If you want to complete a useful piece of research in a particular context, it would not be sensible to, for example, present it in a way which is unacceptable.

> See also the sub-section in Chapter 2 on **Regulations and expectations**.

## ☐ Truth, power and values

The dominant tradition of the research-policy relationship in Britain sees research as providing objective, factual information which is handed over to policy-makers for their use . . . This approach therefore embodies a clear distinction between facts and values, and sees 'fact-finding' and 'making value judgements' as two separate activities which are pursued sequentially.

(Finch 1986: 195)

The meaning of subjectivity has had distinct power implications in the sense that it has been capable of dismissing many sorts of action and account which are not based on rationality, logic and objective procedure. These forms of action and account are . . . most likely to characterise the 'others' produced as different from white middle-class men: black and Third World people, working-class people and women.

(Hollway 1989: 133)

One memory that I would have sworn was 'the truth and nothing but the truth' concerned a wagon that my brother and I shared as a child. I remembered that we played with this toy only at my grandfather's house, that we shared it, that I would ride it and my brother would push me. Yet one facet of the memory was puzzling, I remembered always returning home with bruises or scratches from this toy. When I called my mother, she said there had never been any wagon, that we had shared a red wheelbarrow, that it had always been at my grandfather's house because there were sidewalks on that part of town.

(hooks 1989: 157)

Many people coming to research for the first time have a tendency to think that they are in the business of establishing 'the truth' about a particular issue or

---

**Exercise 4: The context for your research**

Imagine you are doing research on experiences of training at work, whether within your own company or another.

Would your findings be different if you approached your interviewees through:

- the managing director?
- the personnel manager?
- the shop stewards' committee?
- the unemployed centre?

How might they differ? How might this affect your conclusions? What if you had to write a report of your conclusions for each of these audiences?

You can think about this as an exercise in finding out what is *safe* and what is *risky* in terms of expectations, theory, styles of writing etc.

---

subject. They want to find out 'the facts', or want to 'prove' (or perhaps disprove) a particular argument. They believe that they can be 'objective' in their research, and that others will sit up and take notice when they present their findings.

But research is not a wholly objective activity carried out by detached scientists. It is, as we have suggested, a social activity powerfully affected by the researcher's own motivations and values. It also takes place within a broader social context, within which politics and power relations influence what research is undertaken, how it is carried out and whether and how it is reported and acted upon. If you don't believe this, try Exercise 4.

As Exercise 4 suggests, politics, power and values may be important considerations for your research as well, especially if you carry it out within your own or another organization. Your contacts will affect your access to the subjects of your research, may require you to submit your research proposals for scrutiny, and to revise them, and may exercise some veto over what you can actually write up or publish. If you are unlucky, misread the organizational politics or irritate the researched, you may find cooperation withdrawn part way through your project.

So it is important to understand not just where you are coming from, but also where those you are seeking to research are coming from. Preparatory time spent in learning about this is almost always well spent, as well as being valuable contextual research in its own right.

Rather than expecting to 'find the truth', it is probably better to think of research work in terms of words like rigour, reliability, professionalism and honesty. No one research project can realistically aspire to do more than advance our understanding in some way. Most researchers have to compromise their practices to fit into the time and other resources available for their studies. Doing research is, therefore, about producing something which is 'good enough'.

This does not mean, of course, that such research cannot be pursued with drive, passion and commitment; though it might also be pursued in a more detached fashion. What is important to us as researchers is that research should be as open and transparent as possible in terms of its intentions, methodology, analysis and findings.

### Different audiences and rules

As a researcher, you should also be aware of who you are researching and writing for, and the different rules and expectations which these people may have. You may be researching for a university degree, in which case you will need to produce a dissertation or thesis that will be assessed by academic criteria. Or you may be carrying out a research project for your employer, who will expect a concise report emphasizing the implications of your findings and recommending action. Or you may be balancing both of these roles. While the processes may be broadly similar, the outputs are likely to look very different.

For more advice here, look at the section in Chapter 8 on **Whom am I writing for?**

Your audience may also include those you are researching, whether at work or within a community organization. If the latter, your approach may be to work from the bottom up, gaining consensus and support from all involved throughout the process; and the research may be as much about the change and development engendered in your audience as about any written output.

The important theme which runs through this discussion is your need, as a researcher, to be aware of the context in which you are researching. This manifests itself in rules, whether written or unwritten. You need to be aware of these rules, and to follow them, if you wish to succeed. You cannot hope just to muddle along and not run into any problems.

*Hint:* Open a file on 'Regulations and Expectations'. Include copies of all the written regulations that apply to your research project, and add notes on any unwritten expectations which you may find out about during your work.

### ☐ How to use this book

### The organization of the book

If you have already leafed through this book, or looked at the contents page, you will probably have noticed that it is organized in the kind of sequential, linear fashion which we criticized earlier in this chapter when discussing different representations of the research process. It is difficult to organize a book in any other way.

Thus, there are nine chapters, as follows:

Chapter 1: **Thinking about research**, which considers the nature and context of research.
Chapter 2: **Getting started**, which discusses how to focus your research project.
Chapter 3: **Thinking about methods**, which examines the most common approaches and techniques used in research.
Chapter 4: **Reading for research**, which discusses how and what to read, and reading as a source of data.
Chapter 5: **Managing your project**, which deals with the planning and progressing of the work.
Chapter 6: **Collecting data**, which considers the techniques and issues involved in data collection.
Chapter 7: **Analysing data**, which examines how you can record, analyse and interpret different kinds of data.
Chapter 8: **Writing up**, which deals with the organization and drafting of your report or thesis.
Chapter 9: **Finishing off**, which looks at how to complete your project and what you might do afterwards.

## The elements of the book

In looking at this book, you will probably also have noticed that it does not consist of straightforward text, but is composed of a number of elements. These are:

- the *text* itself, which is designed to offer guidance and lead you through the book;
- a series of 130 *boxes*, which provide summaries, illustrations, examples and lists relevant to the issues discussed in the text;
- a range of 61 *exercises*, which are designed to get you thinking about some of the issues raised in the context of your own research plans and experiences;
- dozens of *quotations*, either in the text or in boxes, exemplifying and illustrating both the experience of other researchers and their insights into researching;
- at the end of each chapter, except this first one, an up-to-date and extensive *annotated bibliography* of relevant books on the topics covered, with an indication of their contents;
- at the end of the book, a complete list of the *references* mentioned in the text;
- within the text, *cross-references* to guide you between parts of the book;
- occasional *hints*, tips and health warnings, designed to keep you on track.

We have adopted this varied presentational form to help you, the reader, to engage with what are rich and complex issues and debates, but without using complicated language. It is also intended to encourage different ways of using the book and its contents.

As social scientists trained in three different disciplines – anthropology, sociology and geography respectively – and now working in a continuing education department, we have tried to include examples and illustrations from across the range of the social sciences. You will, however, find traces of our biographies throughout the book.

### How to find your way through the book

There are many possible ways of using this book. The approach you adopt will depend upon your experience and preferences, the other support you are receiving and the kind of research project you are engaged in. You may, for example, already be well into your research by the time you pick up this book, and be looking for guidance on specific issues; or you may not have started yet, and be scouting around for general advice.

Among the different ways in which you might use this book we can identify the following:

- You could start at the beginning and read through to the end. Though this is commonly perceived as the normal way to read a book, and to conduct research, we do not imagine that many of you will be doing this.
- You could start by reading Chapter 4, **Reading for research**, and then work both backwards and forwards from there.
- You could scan the contents list, read this introductory chapter, flick through the other chapters and sections, and then focus your attention on the pages that are of current interest to you.
- You could use the index to find references to topics that concern you.
- You could use the book as a basis for discussion, dialogue or exchange of ideas between yourself and others engaged in similar research projects.
- If you are involved in teaching or supervising those undertaking research, you might use the book as a source for exercises or ideas.

These are just some of the possibilities. We do not wish to restrict the ways in which you might use the book. Indeed, we would see your use of it as in many ways paralleling the research process itself: starting at any point, jumping from place to place, doing several things simultaneously, returning with renewed understanding to places you have already visited. To help you in this process, we have built in lots of cross-references between the different sections.

---

We would welcome your ideas on and responses to the book. If you would like to make a suggestion, please contact the authors through the publishers.

# What is different about this edition?

In producing this second edition, we have drawn on the many helpful suggestions made by readers, and our own experiences, since the first edition was published in 1996. In particular, we have:

- thoroughly updated the bibliographies and references, to reflect the recent growth in writing and publishing on research methods and processes;
- added new examples and illustrations;
- added some additional textual material, including new sections on **Which method is best?** in Chapter 3, **Using the Internet** in Chapter 4 and **Computer-based analysis** in Chapter 7;
- checked, revised and amended the text, boxes and exercises.

We hope that you find this edition even more useful than the first one!

# Summary

Having read this chapter, you should:

- have some understanding of the variety of activities which may be considered as being 'research';
- appreciate that the research process is not straightforward, predictable or linear;
- have a clearer idea of your own motivations for engaging in research, and of the context for your research;
- be more confident about your own ability to carry out a small-scale research project.

# Further reading

As this is the first chapter in the book, and designed to be introductory, no specific suggestions for further reading will be given here. If you are keen to read more at this stage, however, you might look at the suggestions for the next chapter, or any of the other chapters. In many cases, of course, the books referred to could have been listed in more than one chapter, and contain sections which are relevant to a number of chapters.

We have designed the annotated bibliographies, included in the further reading sections at the end of the following eight chapters, to enable you to:

- browse through and identify texts which are likely to be of particular interest to you;
- identify books which focus on social science research in general, and those which are specific to particular disciplines or subject areas;
- quickly access deeper, more detailed or more theoretical treatments of the social research process.

The bibliographies have been restricted to books.

You will find that the bibliographies vary considerably in length, reflecting the variability in the available literature. Thus, the lists for Chapters 3, 6 and 7, which deal with research methods, and the collection and analysis of data, are substantial; while those for Chapters 2, 4, 5 and 8, which cover starting research, reading, managing your project and writing up, are more limited. The further reading for the final chapter, Chapter 9, is also lengthy, but focuses on more theoretical treatments for those who want to read further into the research literature.

# 2

## GETTING STARTED

## ☐ Introduction

The purpose of this chapter is to help you move from the position of having decided to do a piece of research to having a good idea of what you are going to do.

The chapter looks at six closely related issues:

- **Choosing a topic**. The issues to bear in mind in deciding what you are going to research.
- **What to do if you can't think of a topic**. Some hints and tips on how to develop one.
- **Focusing**. How to get from your initial idea to something that is feasible and relevant.
- **Finding and choosing your supervisor**. How to go about selecting your most important research contact.
- **Individual and group research**. The different factors to bear in mind if you are going to be researching with others.
- **Keeping your research diary**. Make up your mind now to record your feelings, experience, decisions and ideas as you undertake your research project.

> *Remember:* The minute you've decided to do something, you've started your research project. By reading this, you've started.

---

**Box 9: Twelve issues to bear in mind when choosing a research topic**

1 How much choice you have.
2 Your motivation.
3 Regulations and expectations.
4 Your subject or field of study.
5 Previous examples of research projects.
6 The size of your topic.
7 The time you have available.
8 The cost of research.
9 The resources you have available.
10 Your need for support.
11 Access issues.
12 Methods for researching.

---

## ☐ Choosing a topic

> Being selfish is something few adults would, openly at least, admit to. Yet it is central to the sanity of the hard-pressed researcher. At the start of your project you are about to take on a considerable commitment which is probably in addition to many continuing demands on your time . . . So be selfish, focus on what interests you, think about your curriculum vitae and your future professional development as well as the impact your study might have on the workplace, and then step forward with confidence.
>
> (Edwards and Talbot 1994: 4–5)

Choosing your research topic is probably the most important single decision you have to make in doing research. In this section, we discuss 12 points you might bear in mind in making that choice (see Box 9).

### How much choice you have

You may not, of course, have much choice in what you do. The general area for your research, and perhaps the detailed specification, may be determined by your employer or funder. But even in these cases, you will be likely to have some scope for making the project more interesting or relevant to your own concerns. If, for example, you have to do a piece of research which you are not particularly interested in, you might make it more palatable by adding something to it or by focusing on a part of the project which does interest you.

It is quite common for part-time students or researchers, who are registered for degrees which require them to undertake a piece of small-scale research, and who are receiving some support from their employers, to have their choice of research topic at least partly determined by their boss. Their employer will usually then expect to receive a report on the research project, and may also be seeking a more practical result in terms, for example, of improved working practices. In such cases, it is important to be aware of the different expectations of employers and educational institutions, and to plan ahead accordingly.

> More guidance on this is given in the section in Chapter 8 on **Whom am I writing for?** See also Exercise 4 in Chapter 1.

**Your motivation**

> If you have not already read it, you might usefully read the section in Chapter 1 on **Why research?**

If you are in doubt about whether you have the necessary motivation to carry through the piece of research you have in mind, ask yourself:

*Will it get me out of bed early on a wet Monday morning?*

Or, if you are an early morning person:

*Will I want to work on it on Friday evening?*

If your answer is no, you may well have problems ahead, and you might be best advised to change or modify your research topic, if you can, to something which rouses your passion or drive rather more strongly.

**Regulations and expectations**

As we noted in Chapter 1, understanding any and all written regulations and unwritten expectations which apply to your research is of critical importance.

If you are undertaking a research project for, or as part of, a university degree, then you should be provided with a copy of the relevant rules and regulations. If you do not have a copy, ask for one. Read these regulations, question any you are not clear about and follow them.

If you don't follow the regulations – and produce a dissertation or thesis which is too long or too short, in the wrong format or inappropriately written – you are leaving yourself open to problems. It may still get through if the infringements are relatively minor, but don't count on it. You may have to revise substantially and resubmit your work. At best, you are likely to irritate your examiners, whereas, by following the rules, you should immediately create a good impression.

> Further advice on the processes of writing up and presentation is given in Chapters 8 and 9.

Whatever documentation you are given about rules and regulations, however, it is unlikely to deal with 'unwritten rules' or expectations. These you may need to tease out by pertinent questioning of your supervisor, manager, colleagues or fellow researchers.

If you are undertaking research not for a degree, but for your employer, funder or someone else, or just perhaps for personal interest, it is likely there will still be rules and regulations which you have to follow, both written and unwritten. Funders may provide quite precise specifications for the work. Your employer may not be as clear, but will still have expectations which you will need to uncover and address if the process is to be successfully carried through. And, if you wish to publish the results of your research, the publisher will have another set of expectations for you to satisfy.

## Your subject or field of study

Many of the unwritten rules and expectations associated with your research will have to do with the particular discipline or subject area you are working in. It may have preferred styles or conventions for writing, and preferred methodologies for undertaking research. There will certainly be established traditions, and work by 'key thinkers', which you will need to be aware of and perhaps refer to. Your supervisor and department may also have their own preferences or specialisms. You should check on all of these by:

- talking to your supervisor, their colleagues or other researchers in the area;
- looking at other examples of recent research projects carried out in your subject area;
- looking at the research literature for your subject area (books, journals and reports).

## Previous examples of research projects

Whatever subject you are studying, there are likely to be previous examples of similarly sized research projects on similar kinds of topic to which you can get access. If you can't find any in the libraries you have access to, ask a librarian, your supervisor, manager, colleagues or fellow researchers for help.

If you can get hold of some previous examples, don't turn down the chance to do so, because you can learn a lot. This learning will not be so much about the particular subject you are going to research, but about what a completed piece of research looks like, the way it is put together, its scope and its limitations. When you see a completed thesis, dissertation or research report for the first time, you may feel daunted and unable to produce something of that scale. As you become more familiar, however, you should begin to feel that you could write something at least as good.

If you can, get some advice from your supervisor or someone else on which are considered to be better examples of previous research projects, and why. But make your own judgement as well.

---

**Exercise 5: Space and time**

Answer the following questions:

1 How many words or pages are you allowed or expected to write up your research in?
2 How much time (in years, months or weeks) do you have available in which to carry out and write up your research?

---

## The size of your topic

One of the key skills involved in choosing a topic is to be able to pick one of the right size: not too big, not too small, but do-able within the time, space and resources available.

> *Hint:* Think of choosing your research topic in terms of the Goldilocks strategy. You want to select a topic which is not too big, and not too small, but just right (and one which will not break).

If you are new to research you will probably not have developed this skill. Indeed, it is a very common failing, but not necessarily that serious a one, for new researchers to choose topics which are far too big for them to carry out. Hence the need to focus down your study, the theme of another section in this chapter.

As a start, see if you can provide the answers for Exercise 5.

If you are carrying out a research project for a university degree, there will almost certainly be restrictions on both the size and format of your final dissertation or report. In most cases a typewritten or word-processed submission will be required. There will commonly be a maximum number of words allowed, and possibly also a minimum. Appendices or references may be within these totals, or additional to them.

If you don't already know, find out what these restrictions on size are, and keep to them. You may think that the quality of what you write should be more important than its quantity, but think of your readers. Another of the key skills associated with doing research is being able to deliver a 'good enough' product within the time and space allowed. You should be able to write your research up within any reasonable word limit. Over-writing is really just self-indulgence, and it can be more difficult to cut your drafts down in size than expand them.

> Further advice on this is given in the section on **Drafting and redrafting** in Chapter 8.

If you are undertaking research for professional or employment reasons, rather than for a degree, there will almost certainly still be restrictions on the size and format of your report. In business, for example, where you may be writing for very busy people, the need for brevity is paramount. Lengthy and tedious reports will not be read, even by enthusiasts. You need to make it as to the point and interesting as possible; so keep it short and punchy.

### The time you have available

Similar considerations relate to the time you have available for your research study. For a small-scale research study, this will typically be of the order of a few hundred hours in total. You need to make the best use of this time possible. It is unlikely, therefore, that you will be able to do empirical research a long way from your home, university or work. You will also have to limit the extent of any data collection you undertake: there are, for example, only so many interviews or questionnaires you can get completed, or, more importantly, usefully analysed, within a given amount of time.

Of course, time issues vary for different groups of people and different research approaches. For example, if you are a busy professional researching your own practice, you may have a strong temptation to focus on completing your interviews or questionnaire survey, and then hurriedly getting on with the job of analysis and writing. Even though you cannot see the 'products' immediately, it cannot be said too loudly that it is imperative that time and space is given to reflecting on your methods and your data. For those of you who are considering action research approaches, you need to allow sufficient time to progress through the varied cycles involved.

The limitations on your time highlight the importance of planning ahead, scheduling and piloting your work.

See also the sections in Chapter 5 on **Managing time** and **Piloting**.

### The cost of research

Don't forget the cost factor. Unless you have an employer, funder or sponsor who is going to meet absolutely *all* of the costs of your research project, you should be aware of the different costs associated with alternative kinds of research. You will find a list of the kinds of expenses most commonly associated with social science research projects in Box 10.

For even a relatively modest project, the costs which you may have to bear will very easily amount to hundreds of pounds; or, if you have to pay registration fees, a few thousand pounds. Draw up a budget now, and then check whether you are going to be able to afford it. Try Exercise 6

---

**Box 10: The costs of research**

Fees for degree registration or examination.
Travel costs to and from your university or college, and/or your research sites.
The costs of consumables such as paper, tapes and batteries.
Charges for access to certain institutions or individuals.
Equipment purchase or hire costs (e.g. wordprocessor, tape recorder, software).
Book, report and journal purchases.
Photocopying, printing and publication costs.
Postage and telephone costs.
Library fines.

---

**Exercise 6: Costing your research**

Make as complete a list as you can of all the costs you are likely to incur during your research project.

You could use the list given in Box 10 as a basis.

For each item make an estimate of the likely cost. Note which items will be paid for by your sponsor or employer. Note also when these costs are likely to be incurred.

Add a further figure to allow for unexpected costs (perhaps 5 or 10 per cent of your total).

Can you afford it?

---

*Hint:* You may be able to cut your costs in very simple ways. For example, you could reuse the tapes you use for recording interviews. Keep your interviews short. Buy your tape recorder second-hand. You can reduce the costs of photocopying by copying two pages on to one. Buy key texts from previous researchers. Never use first class post. Do your own typing. Print drafts on recycled paper.

### The resources you have available

If you have colleagues or friends to help you with your research, this will clearly allow you to do rather more than if you are on your own. The particular case of group research is considered later in this chapter.

Most people undertaking small-scale research projects will, however, probably be working largely on their own. But this does not mean that you have no resources. These may include, for example, word-processing and computing resources.

UXBRIDGE COLLEGE
LEARNING CENTRE

**Exercise 7: Resources for research**

List below the resources you have access to and those you believe you will need to have access to in order to carry out your research project.

Interpret the idea of 'resources' as widely as possible, to include not just material and financial resources, but also people and skills.

| *Resources available* | *Resources needed* |
| --- | --- |
|  |  |

to a typist and, perhaps most importantly, a good library and access to the Internet. Against these you need to set the resources you will probably need to undertake your research project successfully. Doing Exercise 7 should help you to address these questions.

Once you've completed this exercise, focus on the differences between your two lists. If there is a huge difference between the resources you have available and the resources you think you will need, you might be best advised to start thinking of a research topic or approach which requires fewer resources. If the difference between the two lists is not so great, you could usefully think about how you are going to get access to any additional resources you need.

## Your need for support

One of the key resources you may have identified in Exercise 7 is your need for support. Here we are talking about personal and emotional support, rather than the academic kind. Exercise 8 should help you to identify what support you may need.

> *Health warning:* Undertaking research, or any kind of education, can threaten your personal, family, work or social life. Be aware of the demands which your research project may put on your loved ones, friends and colleagues. See also the discussion of acknowledgements in the section on **Added extras** in Chapter 9.

If you don't have people to fill the kinds of support roles identified in Exercise 8, you may need to find them or develop them, unless, that is, you are an unusually confident, organized and self-aware kind of person. You may think you can go it alone, that you can successfully complete a demanding research project without anyone's support; indeed, even with active opposition. But what if you are mistaken?

**Exercise 8: Seeking support**

Answer the following questions:

1 Who can you 'earbash' about your research?
2 Who will ask you 'How's it going?'
3 Who will make you cups of tea?
4 Who will give you permission not to do things?

## Access issues

Virtually any research project involves questions of access. These are discussed in rather more detail later in this book.

> See the section in Chapter 6 on **Access and ethical issues**.

Here we are primarily concerned with the influence of access on your choice of topic. Access can be seen as relating as much to the resources you have available (e.g. a good library), as discussed in a previous sub-section, as to the subjects of your research.

Obviously, from this point of view, it may make sense to choose a topic for which you believe access will be less problematic. This may suggest doing your research project within your own institution, though that does not guarantee that there will be no problems. Your own institution or employer is likely, for example, to try to exert influence upon, or control, your research strategy and the dissemination of your findings. However, when time is limited, access will be easier than getting permission to research in an organization where you know no one and no one knows you.

> *Hint:* Many small-scale researchers, particularly those who are doing research for academic credit, feel it is simplest (or are pressurized) to study some aspect of their own institution or employer. While this may be a good idea – the research site is readily accessible, you may be able to do some research during work time – it has significant disadvantages. Your employer and colleagues may put you under pressure. There are particular ethical issues connected with researching those over whom you have managerial authority. It can feel like you are always at work. You are likely to learn less than you would if you chose a research topic outside your organization. And what happens if you change your job? Think about other options before you finally decide.

More generally, it is a good idea if you check out the access issues you may run into before you become completely committed to one particular research topic.

**Methods for researching**

When choosing a research topic, it makes sense to think about the methods you will use to collect and analyse data as soon as possible. If you have a choice, consider the methods you will enjoy using or not. For example, if you like talking to people, you might be well advised to make use of interview methods. If you don't like talking to people, on the other hand, you might think about undertaking library or archive-based research. And if you like carrying out statistical or multivariate analyses, you might consider a more quantitative methodology.

The methods you use are a key part of your research, so you need to understand something of the alternatives available to you, and their strengths and weaknesses.

> See Chapter 3, **Thinking about methods**, for a discussion of the main kinds of research methods you might use.

If you enjoy or have a flair for a particular method, this can make your research project more interesting, and help to motivate you to carry it through. Or you might like to use your research project to learn about, or develop your skills in, methods you are not familiar with.

## ☐ What to do if you can't think of a topic

It may be, of course, that you are committed to doing a piece of research, but you just can't think of what to do. This is quite a common problem, and may be associated with your confidence, or lack of it, in undertaking a research project. This section is designed to help you address this problem. It may also help you if you have already thought of a topic, but wish to refine it a bit or consider some alternatives to it; or if you have too many ideas as to what you might research.

This section considers ten suggestions for helping you to brainstorm your ideas for a research project (see Box 11). You should then be in a better position to make a selection and begin to refine your choice down to a workable project.

**Ask your supervisor, manager, friends, colleagues, customers, clients or mother**

You could usefully ask almost anyone for ideas; non-specialists and those who aren't involved, as well as experts and those who are.

---

**Box 11: Ten ways to think of a research topic**

1 Ask your supervisor, manager, friends, colleagues, customers, clients or mother.
2 Look at previous research work.
3 Develop some of your previous research, or your practice at work.
4 Relate it to your other interests.
5 Think of a title.
6 Start from a quote that engages you.
7 Follow your hunches.
8 Draw yourself a picture or a diagram.
9 Just start anywhere.
10 But be prepared to change direction.

---

Your supervisor may have a good deal of advice to offer, and might welcome you researching a topic of interest to them. Or your supervisor might put you in touch with a colleague in a similar position. Similarly, your manager and colleagues at work may have ideas for research which would be of value to your organization. Or your friends and neighbours might have suggestions for research which could help your local community in some way. Talking about your ideas to people who aren't involved with research can be very revealing and helpful.

## Look at previous research work

This is another obvious suggestion, and one which we have already made in the previous section.

> I was desperate for an idea, any idea, so I began by asking around. Surely someone out there in practice would have an exciting question that they felt must be asked but not the knowledge or resources to pursue . . . When it became obvious that no one was going to present a research question to me on a plate I began my search in earnest. I read a lot and went through back copies of journals. I particularly chose the *Journal of Advanced Nursing* and the *International Journal of Nursing Studies* to look through because these were very general in their content, were academic in nature and very often researchers would mention 'implications for further research' at the end of their paper. After leafing through several journals I came across an article about creativity and nursing.
>
> (Miles 1994: 18–19)

There are almost certainly many examples of similar kinds of research projects which you could look at, whether these are presented in the form of published articles or as research reports or theses. You might consider replicating one of these: using the same methods to analyse the same problem, but in a different area or institution. This can be very useful and illuminating, whether you confirm, add to or cast doubt upon the earlier findings.

> See the section in Chapter 1 on **What is original?** if you are worried that developing your project from previous research work is insufficiently original.

### Develop some of your previous research, or your practice at work

You may already have done a piece of small-scale research, or perhaps just researched a particular field of study for an essay or shorter paper. Think about whether it would be possible and interesting to develop this line of thought further. Or, alternatively, you might choose to research a topic which was engaging your attention, and demanding your time, at work. Your own *curiosity* and *desire to learn* is an excellent place to start.

### Relate it to your other interests

You will probably have a range of interests outside of your work or course of study. These might include, for example, family, social, voluntary, community or sporting activities. It is quite possible, depending upon the limitations on the subject area for your research, that you could link your research to one of these interests. Thus, if you are carrying out management research, you might base it, at least partly, on a voluntary or community group you do some work for.

### Think of a title

You may find that thinking of possible titles for research suggests topics of interest to you. After all, a lot of the initial attraction in a book, television programme or film resides in the title. It may be punning, alliterative and/or pithy. It might pose a key research question in a succinct fashion, or suggest a new area for research. For example:

- Training Matters.
- The Empire Strikes Back.
- Women's Ways of Knowing.
- Images of Organization.

Titles need to be as short as possible. Try to think of some you like that will motivate you. A good title should help you to focus your subsequent work.

However, don't feel that you have to keep to the title you originally thought of: the time may come when you need to change it.

### Start from a quote that engages you

Another approach is to extract from the literature you have read one or more quotations which really engage your attention. We are talking here about the kind of statements which draw a strong positive or negative reaction; which make you think that the author really knows their stuff, or, alternatively, doesn't know what they are talking about. These quotations may be comments, interpretations of research data, questions or assertions. They may even directly identify areas needing further research.

### Follow your hunches

You may have a strong instinctive feeling that a particular area or issue needs researching, or will raise interesting questions. This may be because of a critical incident you have experienced. Or it may be that something about it surprises or puzzles you, or just doesn't seem quite right. Don't be afraid to follow such hunches and see where they lead. But, as with all the suggestions given here, don't expend too much time and energy on them if it appears they are not getting you anywhere.

### Draw yourself a picture or diagram

Producing a spider diagram of issues, interests, questions and their possible interconnections is a standard brainstorming technique. It can be undertaken individually or in a group. It might help you to identify or isolate particular areas for research, and suggest how these are related to your general subject area. You might then wish to share your diagram with others, to get their responses and suggestions. An example of such a diagram is given in Box 12.

As an alternative to the spider diagram, depending on your interests and skills, you might draw a picture or a map. The choice is really up to you. The idea is simply to get you thinking about possible areas or questions for research, their relationships and relevance.

### Just start anywhere

Finally, if none of the above engages or appeals to you, you could just start anywhere. Go away and read something, or talk to someone, about some of the issues relevant to your general subject area. Sketch out and begin a research project, any research project of about the right size, even if it feels dull and routine at first. Something better is likely to come out of this activity, perhaps something completely different.

### Be prepared to change direction

This may become necessary if you are denied access to important people or documents, if insufficient people respond to your questions, if you cannot find the data you thought was there, if you change job or move house, if you get bored or for other reasons. Having some in-built flexibility in your research plans – thoughts about alternative approaches to the same question, or about different directions away from your starting point – is a very good idea.

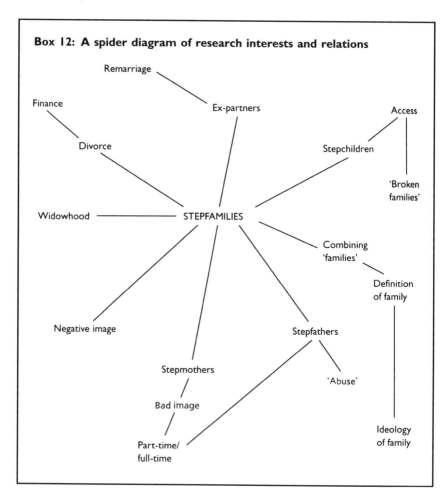

**Box 12: A spider diagram of research interests and relations**

Remember:

- change can be positive;
- it is OK to change;
- lots of people change their research project or focus;
- you always end up at a different place from where you thought you were going anyway.

## ☐ Focusing

Once you have chosen a topic, or perhaps a number of possible alternative topics, you will almost certainly then need to refine it and focus it. Focusing is not an instantaneous process, but takes place over time. During this period you will probably be doing a lot of background reading, thinking about the methods you will use in your research and refining your research design. Indeed, many research projects are not finally focused until the data collection and analysis process is well advanced.

> You may find that working through some of the ideas in Chapter 4, **Reading for research**, helps you to focus your research topic.

You will need to focus your project to ensure that it is relevant to your needs, and to any regulations or expectations you are operating under. Above all, focusing is almost invariably necessary to produce a project that is feasible within the time, space, costs and other practical constraints affecting you. Whatever your chosen research method, you will probably find it useful to address the questions set out by Mason (1996) to help you focus down from your initial idea or ideas to an achievable project (see Box 13).

> For further help in developing your research framework see the section on **Which method is best?** in Chapter 3.

---

**Box 13: Five important focusing questions**

Working from a qualitative research perspective, Mason (1996: 11–18) suggests there are five sets of difficult questions that you need to work through in order to find out what is the essence of your inquiry. These are:

1   What is the nature of the phenomena, entities or social 'reality' which I wish to investigate? For example, are you interested in social actors or behaviours, in feelings, in memories, in policy, in organizational practices?
2   What might represent knowledge or evidence of the entities or social 'reality' which I wish to investigate? For example, what would count as evidence of organizational practices?
3   What topic or broad substantive area is the research concerned with? What would be the generic label for your research?
4   What is the intellectual puzzle? What do I wish to explain? What are my research questions? For example, are you interested in how something works or how and why something has developed? Mason suggests three common intellectual puzzles: (a) developmental puzzles, i.e. how and why did X come about; (b) mechanical puzzles, i.e. how does X work; (c) causal puzzles, i.e. what influence does X have on Y?
5   What is the purpose of my research? What am I doing it for? Mason indicates that this question requires us to consider the political and ethical issues of our research.

---

**Exercise 9: Your research questions**

Write down up to four key questions which your research project seeks to address. Begin each one with a questioning word like how, who, what, when or why.

1

2

3

4

Which of these questions is the most important or central to your research?

---

## Identifying your research questions or hypotheses

An obvious starting point for focusing is to try to set out, loosely at first and then more precisely, the questions you want to answer in your research project. If it suits you, you might express these as hypotheses which you will then seek to prove or disprove. But for most people, straightforward questions will probably be fine. You might like to try Exercise 9 at this point, to see how well you can identify your research questions.

In a small-scale research project you are unlikely to be able to handle more than two or three main research questions. You may only have one, and it might actually be defined for you already. If you have four or more, you should probably be thinking of cutting them down in number and just focusing on a few.

If, or when, you get your research questions right, they should suggest not just the field for study, but also the methods for carrying out the research and the kind of analysis required. If they don't, they are probably pitched at too general a level. Research questions are like objectives, rather than aims: they should contain within themselves the means for assessing their achievement. Box 14 uses two examples to illustrate what is involved in refining your research questions.

## Defining the key concepts, issues and contexts

Defining the key concepts, issues and contexts of your research project should also assist you in focusing your work, as well as being of great help to you later on in your project. They define the territory for your research, indicate the literature you need to consult and suggest the methods and theories you might apply. The nature and meaning of concepts, issues and contexts are explored in Box 15.

Do you already know what the concepts, issues and contexts relating to your research project are? Try Exercise 10.

## Using the doughnut and jam roly-poly models of research

Researchers, particularly those with limited experience, often approach their chosen research topic with considerable enthusiasm, reading widely, checking

---

**Box 14: Refining research questions**

In one case, a student stated that she wanted to do 'something on NVQs' (i.e. National Vocational Qualifications). In the second, the researcher was interested in the 'politics of development'.

Both of these cases, particularly the second, are clearly unfocused and unmanageable subjects for small-scale research. They are the stuff of lifetimes of scholarship or extensive team research. To focus them down to something manageable, issues like the following need to be addressed:

• What NVQ subject areas might I examine? Will I focus on particular institutions or classes? Am I concerned with a given time period? From whose perspective might I examine NVQs: that of the policy-maker, educator, student or funder?
• Am I interested in development in a particular country or area? Over what period of time? Am I talking about economic, political, social or technological development? What level of political analysis am I concerned with: local, regional, national, international or what?

By addressing these kinds of issues, the proposed research project can be refined down in size and appropriate research questions developed. Thus, in the case of 'something on NVQs', the basic question might be:

• How successfully have the NVQs in Accounting been introduced within two colleges of further education in Somerset?

Or, in the case of the 'politics of development', the main research question might be:

• What public subsidies have been attracted to a village in rural France over a ten-year period, and how have these been used?

---

**Exercise 10: Concepts, issues and contexts**

*Concepts:* What are the main concepts of your research? How are they to be defined or operationalized?

*Issues:* Draw a map indicating the key areas of debate that are relevant to your particular research concerns.

*Contexts:* Draw up a genealogy of the key thinkers in your research field to indicate the development of theories, perspectives or methods.

---

sources and contacting experts as appropriate. But their focus can be almost exclusively upon the topic itself, rather narrowly defined, with little reference to how it relates to the broader field of research and study within which it is set. Their desire to explore thoroughly their growing interests in specific areas has to be reconciled with the need for each research project to be focused and

---

**Box 15: Concepts, issues and contexts**

*Concepts:* Dey (1993: 275) defines the term concept as 'a general idea which stands for a class of objects'. Concepts are 'umbrella' terms. For example, the concept of class refers both to the classification of people according to, say, income or employment, and to judgements that we might make about others (or of course ourselves). Examples of concepts include truth, beauty, evil, time, hunger, love, destiny, ethnicity, gender, class and space. In quantitative research it is very important to define the meanings of your key concepts in advance in order to measure them systematically. This requires you to be clear about the *indicators* that you are going to use that will stand in for the concept. For example, if your research is concerned with poverty you might define poverty in terms of income or benefit groups, housing size and so forth. For some qualitative researchers, generating conceptual categories at the analysis stage will be much more common, because such researchers are interested in the perceptions of their respondents. This does not, however, mean that if you are planning to conduct qualitative research you need give no initial thought to defining concepts. You still need to be explicit and aware of how you are defining concepts in the research questions that you formulate, and in the observations and interviews you conduct. The way you define concepts will shape the data you collect.

*Issues:* These refer to the broad questions that underlie and direct disciplines, sub-disciplines or subject areas, as well as public affairs. They are the subject of continuing debate and study from a range of perspectives. Examples of issues include the links between educational participation and economic development, the effects of television programmes on people's behaviour and the relationship between road building and traffic congestion. It is often the case in small-scale research, particularly for undergraduate or MA projects, that the focus on a particular issue leads to a neglect of the wider disciplinary and sub-disciplinary issues and theories.

*Context:* This relates to the background of existing research, knowledge and understanding that informs new and ongoing research projects. Research seldom, if ever, breaks wholly new ground. It builds on an extensive history of other people's work. You will need to have some familiarity with this if you are to make the most of your own research work. Your work might, for example, ask similar questions, replicate a study in another area or seek to modify existing findings. Your research context will include many studies that are not specifically relevant to your particular research questions, but are illustrative of broader issues in your disciplinary field, applications of your methodological approach or comparative studies in other countries.

---

contextualized within a more general framework. Some examples of this tendency are discussed in Box 16.

We would argue that a balanced research project should consist of a detailed study set within, and linked to, an understanding of the broader context of the subject field. It is possible to put rough proportions on this balance. Thus, while the bulk of the time available for the research, say 70–80 per cent, will usually

---

**Box 16: All focus and no context**

- Edward wanted to examine the impact that fitness training might have on his colleagues. He believed that if they all undertook such training, their performance on the job would be improved, there would be less absenteeism, long-term sickness and early retirement, with consequent improvements in cost-effectiveness for the organisation.
- Audrey wanted to look at the incidence of post-traumatic stress among her colleagues, the consequences for their work and the implications for their training. As her organization was an emergency service, her expectation was that most of those questioned would have suffered such stress, though they might feel under pressure to minimize or deny it. She believed that pre-training was necessary to help people to cope with the stresses they would have to face in their work.
- Tessa wanted to understand the processes involved in decision-making within organizations. Her concern was with learning how employees could be kept sufficiently up to date with developments in their job area. She believed that new practices should be introduced to facilitate this.

In each of these three cases, the students initially chose far too big a field to research and write up successfully in a year of spare-time commitment. Their ambitions had to be gradually pared down during the research study period. In each case, the students' focus was almost exclusively upon the topic itself, rather narrowly defined, with little reference to how it related to the broader field of training and human resource development which they were studying.

Thus, Edward became very concerned with measures of human fitness, alternative fitness regimes and the practices of comparable professional organizations in other countries. Audrey concentrated on measures of stress, critical incidents and their effects, and alternative counselling approaches. And Tessa focused on different organizational models and systems, and the psychology of decision-making.

---

be devoted to the specific research question or questions, a substantial chunk, 20–30 per cent, would be spent on the contextual issues and connections. A similar proportioning would probably apply in writing up the research.

The allocation and organization of space in writing up your research is discussed in the section on **How to argue** in Chapter 8.

We have called this balance of context and focus the doughnut model of research (we are referring here to the British jam doughnut rather than the American ring doughnut: see Hughes and Tight 1996). It is illustrated in Box 17.

In practice, however, novice and small-scale researchers often tend towards two other patterns. Both of these over-focus on the details of the particular research project being undertaken. In one pattern, the positions of the study and

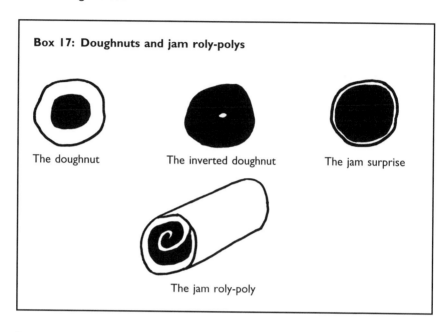

**Box 17: Doughnuts and jam roly-polys**

The doughnut            The inverted doughnut            The jam surprise

The jam roly-poly

its context are reversed, so that limited reference to the wider field is found embedded within the details of the research. In the other pattern, often presented as an initial response to criticism, the detailed study is placed within its context, but the latter is far too thinly presented. We call these two patterns the inverted doughnut, clearly a structure which could not sustain itself, and the jam surprise, something rather sickly and only to be eaten if lots of tissues are available.

There is a danger, of course, in over-extending the use of any metaphor; and the image of the doughnut may also seem rather too simplistic. We have already argued that it is more realistic to present the research process as a spiral, which is cyclical, can be entered at almost any point, is a never-ending process, will cause you to reconsider your practice and will return you to a different starting place.

See the section in Chapter 1 on **What is research?**, particularly Box 6.

The doughnut provides a static image, a beginning or end point, and does not convey much about the process of research. As such, while it offers a good starting point for using metaphors in this context, it needs further development. Hence the jam roly-poly or Swiss roll.

This alternative image expresses the continual interleaving of context and specifics, as well as the multiple possibilities for interconnections between them. Thus, the jam roly-poly can be sliced at any point to give a stratified mixture of jam and pastry, or, by analogy, research data and theory or context. These relationships hold throughout the length of the jam roly-poly, suggesting

**Exercise 11: Metaphors of the research process**

Do the metaphors of the doughnut and the jam roly-poly bear any relation to your thinking about your own research? And what about the research spiral?

Are there other metaphors which you can think of, or which you prefer? Are these metaphors visual? If so, you might care to draw an illustration.

We would like to hear from you if you have thought of a good metaphor!

---

a thematic approach to research, running from beginning to end. And the image allows for different conceptualizations: there could be different proportions of jam and roly-poly, different flavours of jam and different colourings used.

If you like the idea of using metaphors to explore the research process, try Exercise 11.

### Sketching a research outline or proposal

Another technique which should help you to focus your research ideas is to try to sketch out a proposal or outline of your research project and plans. This may well be required of you if you are studying for a degree, or if you need to get the approval of your manager for your project. It will be essential if you are trying to get some funding from somewhere to support your research.

You may already have drafted your research questions, and have a good idea of the key concepts, issues and contexts involved, but do you have a clear notion of what the whole project might look like? Can you sketch out a summary of how your eventual research report, dissertation or thesis might be organized? This is the theme of Exercise 12.

A parallel approach is to draft a schedule for the research work itself. Knowing you will have only so much time in which to do the work, sketch out what you will be doing, month by month or week by week, in order to achieve your ends. Remember to leave yourself some flexibility and some 'free time', to allow for when things don't go exactly as planned.

> This approach is discussed in more detail in Chapter 5, in the section on **Mapping your project**.

These exercises should help you to highlight just how realistic your proposals actually are. Look at your proposed chapter or section contents, and at your monthly or weekly plans. Do you really think you will be able to squeeze that much into the time and space available?

---

**Exercise 12: Producing a research outline**

Note down the prospective contents of your eventual dissertation, thesis or report. You can do this chapter by chapter, or section by section, but should include sub-headings and details.

Once you've done this, you could try to set yourself word limits for the various sections or chapters you envisage including.

---

## Trying it out on a non-specialist: explaining your topic in simple language

It is important that you are able to explain your research project in simple, everyday terms. You need to be able to render the strange familiar, as well as, at other times, the familiar strange.

There will not be many people who will understand, or want to understand, the details of your theoretical framework, methodology, sampling strategy or analytical approach. This may be the case even if you are carrying out your research within a university department or research institute, if only because research outside the sciences tends to be both a specialized and an individualized activity.

Yet you may have to deal with many people in the course of your research, to whom you will need to give some explanation of just what it is you are doing. These may include people in organizations you are researching, and contacts who can enable you to access sources or information. They will also be likely to be fellow researchers or colleagues with whom you wish to share or exchange experiences, and all your other day-to-day social and family contacts who are interested in what you are up to.

You will need, therefore, to be able to summarize what you are doing both briefly and in non-technical language. In doing so, you may clarify your thoughts and avoid some of the jargon and humbug within which researchers can find themselves immersed. And the non-specialists you talk to may also have useful suggestions to make.

So try explaining your research plans to your grandma, or your neighbour, or the person standing next to you in the bar, or your babysitter. They could be invaluable in helping you to focus your work.

## Informal piloting

One final suggestion in this section is to start your research project with some 'informal' pilot activity. We are using the term informal here to distinguish this from the pilot surveys which are commonly built into research projects. An informal pilot could turn into a pilot, but is meant as an early initial try-out, through which you can judge the feasibility of your overall research plans, and then make modifications as necessary. By doing it, you are not committing yourself, but checking and focusing your ideas.

See also the section on **Piloting** in Chapter 5.

If you like the idea of informal piloting, try to carry out a couple of interviews, or get some friends to fill in a few questionnaires, or go and observe some organizational activities – or whatever else it was that you had in mind. You will almost certainly learn a great deal from the activity, not least an idea of the amount of time collecting data can take. If you do it early, it should enable you to alter your strategy, if necessary, to something more effective and feasible.

Having done some informal piloting, you might like to look at, and consider the questions in, Exercise 22 in Chapter 3.

### ☐ Finding and choosing your supervisor

Much has been written, and a lot more spoken, about the varied relationships between researchers and their supervisors. If you doubt this, talk to some more experienced researchers: they will probably all have horror stories, even if only second- or third-hand, to relate. If you are a novice or small-scale researcher, the sort of person whom this book is aimed at, you will most probably have or need a supervisor, though you may not use that term.

Your relationship with your supervisor is of critical importance for you and your research. This is not to say that you can't get through the job without having a good supervisor and a wonderful supervisory relationship, but you will probably find it a lot easier, more stimulating and more rewarding if you do.

### What is a supervisor?

'Supervisor' is the term most commonly used within universities and colleges for academics who have personal responsibility for overseeing the progress of individual students' research projects. The term 'tutor' is sometimes used in a similar way. Ideally, such supervisors should have both some knowledge of the specialist areas in which their students are researching and a general understanding of the research process and the various strategies possible. They should have an inside knowledge of the rules and regulations, both written and unwritten, affecting your research project. They should have some skill in conducting the kind of in-depth, but partial and discontinuous, relationships required for successful supervision. And they should help to keep you focused on your research.

There are, however, significant differences in the ways in which supervision is organized in different universities and subjects. While many students in the social sciences are supervised on an individual basis by a single supervisor, other patterns are common. You may have two supervisors, who meet you separately or together, or you may be supervised by a small committee of academics. You may find yourself as part of a small research group that has shared supervisions. Each of these arrangements has different implications for power, attention and dynamics.

You may, of course, not be doing your research in a university or as part of a degree, but it is still probable that you will have or need a supervisor. If you are carrying out research within and/or for your own organization, your supervisor might be called your mentor, or perhaps just your manager or boss. If you are researching outside an organization, or within the community, your supervisor might be a colleague.

Whatever they are called, there is little doubt that the great majority of researchers can benefit from having a supervisor of some kind. So if you haven't got one, or think you can do well enough without one, think again. Perhaps you could at least ask a friend or colleague, or a fellow student or researcher, to be your informal mentor or supporter, because you will need someone to talk to about your research from time to time. You should, however, be prepared to negotiate the terms of the relationship. Supervisors, like researchers, need to have some idea of what they are getting themselves into.

These issues are discussed further in the section on **Dealing with key figures and institutions** in Chapter 5.

### What to look for in your supervisor

Whatever the nature of, or context for, your research, you may have little or no choice in who is your supervisor. Supervisors may come with the job, or they may be chosen for you by someone else, or they may appear to be the only ones with the specialist knowledge who are available. Nevertheless, you should still see yourself as having some say in this most important matter. If you think there is someone more suitable who might be available, or would prefer a different kind of arrangement, do what you can to arrange for this either formally or informally. Even if this is not possible, you should be able to affect the nature of the supervisory relationship.

Before you get this far, however, it might be as well to ask yourself just what you want, and by implication what you don't want, from your supervisor. Try Exercise 13.

In Box 18 you will find two lists:

- nine qualities that research students expect from their supervisors;
- six qualities that supervisors expect from their students.

It does seem significant that the supervisors appear to have fewer expectations than the students. You might like to compare these lists with your answers to Exercise 13.

---

**Exercise 13: What do you want from your supervisor(s)?**

Identify and list the qualities you are looking for in your supervisor(s):

1
2
3
4
5
6
7
8

You may, of course, be able to identify more than eight, but don't be too demanding! Supervisors are human beings too, and will have many other responsibilities, some of them of higher priority, than looking after you.

---

**Box 18: Students' and supervisors' expectations**

What students expect of their supervisors:

- to be supervised;
- to read their work well in advance;
- to be available when needed;
- to be friendly, open and supportive;
- to be constructively critical;
- to have a good knowledge of their research area;
- to structure the tutorial so that it is relatively easy to exchange ideas;
- to have sufficient interest in their research to put more information in the student's path;
- to be sufficiently involved in their success to help them get a good job at the end of it all.

What supervisors expect of their students:

- to be independent;
- to produce written work that is not just a first draft;
- to have regular meetings;
- to be honest when reporting upon their progress;
- to follow the advice that they give, when it has been given at their request;
- to be excited about their work, able to surprise them and fun to be with.

*Source*: Phillips and Pugh (2000: Chapters 8 and 11).

---

On reflection, do you think any of the qualities which you listed, or which were identified in Box 18, were unrealistic? You would be very lucky indeed to find all these qualities in one person. In practice, you will probably have to settle for someone who has some of the qualities identified – perhaps those you regard as the most essential – or use a number of people to address your different expectations. In our judgement, there is only one quality which is essential for a successful supervisor–researcher relationship: that both you and your supervisor are committed to you successfully completing your research.

## ☐ Individual and group research

> As Totter once said: when you are swinging helplessly at the end of a hundred-foot rope it is important to know that the man [sic] at the other end is a friend.
>
> (Bowman 1992: 21)

The small-scale research exercise which you are engaged in may be a group effort rather than your responsibility alone. This may be a matter of choice, may be dictated to some extent by the nature of the research itself or may be a formal requirement of your degree programme or employment. While many of the issues affecting the processes of group research are in essence the same as those for individual research, there are some key differences. These are the subject of this section.

> *Hint:* If group processes are important to your learning programme, you may want to ask your supervisor or manager for references, guidance or training on group dynamics.

### Individual versus group research

What are the advantages and disadvantages of doing group research? This is the theme of Exercise 14.

Our own assessment of the pros and cons of individual and group research is summarized in Box 19. You may find it interesting to compare your answers to Exercise 14 with our assessment, and to see what similarities and differences there are.

Like many aspects of researching, your choice of whether to do individual or group research should be informed by your awareness of yourself. What are your strengths and weaknesses, preferences and hates? Would they be better accommodated within the support network of a group, or would you be better advised to work largely on your own?

If you have no choice about engaging in group research, you will have to make the best of it. If you do have a choice, however, it should be informed.

### Managing the group

If you are involved in a small-scale group research activity, much depends, of course, on the size and composition of the group undertaking the research, and on the existing power relationships among these people. Unless you are all of much the same age, from the same kind of backgrounds, on the same wavelengths

**Exercise 14: Advantages and disadvantages of group research**

What do you consider to be the chief advantages of doing group research?

1

2

3

4

What do you consider to be the chief disadvantages?

1

2

3

4

If you had a free choice, which would you prefer to do?

---

**Box 19: Individual or group research?**

Group research:

- enables you to share responsibility;
- lets you specialize in those aspects of the work to which you are best suited;
- provides you with useful experience of team working;
- allows you to take on larger-scale topics than you could otherwise manage;
- provides you with a ready made support network;
- may be essential for certain kinds of research.

Individual research:

- gives you sole ownership of the research;
- means that you are wholly responsible for its progress and success;
- may result in a more focused project;
- is of an overall quality determined by you alone;
- means that you have to carry out all elements of the research process.

---

and with similar motivations, you will need to work out ways of resolving differences, planning ahead and implementing the research project. This will almost certainly involve some division of responsibilities, regular discussion of progress and probably also some leadership.

Box 20 summarizes the key issues for those involved in group research projects. If you cannot satisfactorily answer these, you should address them at your next group meeting. If you do not, individually and collectively, know who is doing what and how the research will be progressed, you are heading for problems. If your group is lacking in individuals with key skills, you will need either to develop them quickly or to recruit additional members.

---

**Box 20: Key issues for group researchers**

- Does the group need and have a leader?
- Who is responsible for:
  - organizing meetings;
  - keeping records;
  - chasing progress?
- What are the strengths and weaknesses of the group for carrying out the research project?
- How are the different roles and tasks required for the successful completion of the research project shared among the group?
- Will everyone in the group have a role in each phase of the research, or will some specialize in particular phases?
- Does every member of the group have a clear idea of their tasks and responsibilities?
- Do you each feel able to respect differences between group members?
- Are there individuals or sub-groups within the group who are not happy with the task or organization of the group?
- Will the results of the research be reported on and written up individually, collectively or both?

---

See also the section in Chapter 5 on **Sharing responsibility**.

## Producing the finished product

When undertaking any piece of research, it is always good to have an idea of what the finished product might look like. This is particularly true for group research. Here, as indicated in Box 20, the issue arises as to whether the final report or dissertation (and its assessment) is going to be a truly joint effort, or whether separate reports are going to be produced by the different individuals involved in the group.

You may formally need not just to produce a separate individual product, but to demonstrate clearly what your own contribution has been and how you have carved out something of your own from the overall group research. If this is the case, you should plan your work within the group accordingly so that you are not disadvantaged.

## ☐ Keeping your research diary

Quite early on, my notes became such a mess that I bought a loose-leaf binder, and divided it into sections . . . Very soon the sections disappeared . . . it was impossible to separate 'me' from 'theoretical ideas' from 'field notes'. I gave up making notes separately on index cards while I was reading, because an idea from a quotation would spark off an idea about the significance of something I had experienced, and the note would develop into an analysis of that experience. I had endless talks with friends, both women and men, and would write notes on these afterwards if it was relevant. I called these my field notes.

(Hollway 1989: 9)

A journal also allows one to grapple with the deep and lasting effect that field-work produces . . . which is often more evident when analysing the data than when collecting it. During the months I spent transcribing 27 lengthy taped life-history interviews of members of Jews for Jesus, I was forced to continually examine my own relationship to Judaism and religion in general. While I could put off my informants' questions about my 'position with God' by saying 'I'm not ready to consider this commitment', alone with my typewriter and those convincing tapes I asked this kind of question many times: 'Why not me? Sarah is so like me in background and abilities. She has found such peace, purpose, growth, and understanding in life because of her commitment. What am I afraid of?'

(Lipson 1991: 85)

Whatever kind of research project you are engaged in, and regardless of the methodology you are using, you may find it a good idea to keep a research diary. In this diary, you might record your progress, feelings, thoughts, insecurities and insights, day by day, as your research continues. A variety of formats are possible. While most diaries will probably be kept on paper, there is no reason why you shouldn't keep one on tape or on a wordprocessor.

One school of thought recommends that you should organize your research diary in terms of observational notes, methodological notes, theoretical notes and analytic memos (see Box 21). This is just one strategy, however, and you might opt to use a different format, perhaps more akin to the literary notion of the diary. Box 22 includes two examples of what actual research diaries look like, one hand written, one typed.

---

**Box 21: The four sections of the research diary according to Schatzman and Strauss**

- *Observational notes.* These record 'events experienced principally through watching and listening. They contain as little interpretation as possible and are as reliable as the observer can construct them.'
- *Methodological notes.* 'A statement that reflects an operational act completed or planned: an instruction to oneself, a reminder, a critique of one's own tactics. It notes timing, sequencing, stationing, stage setting or manouvering. Methodological notes might be thought of as observational notes on the researcher himself [*sic*] and upon the methodological process itself.'
- *Theoretical notes.* 'Self-conscious, controlled attempts to derive meaning from any one of several obervational notes.'
- *Analytic memos.* The analytic memo enables the researcher to 'elaborate upon the inference or to tie up several inferences in a more abstract statement.'

*Source:* Schatzman and Strauss (1973: 146, 101, 104).

---

# Box 22: Examples of research diaries

I walked the back road towards the chapel and the church, banking on
not meeting anyone there, and 'c s it was on the rough hill slope below
the chapel,

Then walked down towards the church to face the walk home down the
main street. On a bit of green outside the church, a man I recognised
as the curé was playing a very hectic ball game with about 20 children.
Opp. on my side of the road, three oldish men sat watching. They commented
on the flowers, saying they were pretty but old. I asked the name of the
teasle -forgot it except for the 'c' but looked it up cardère. The three
men would have chatted if I could. On a bench in the street three old
women sat, with some young children round. They commented on something
jolie, so I smiled and wished I could reply.

Returned here to check the surruptisious lines I8d drwn on the back of
the newspaper, and decided that I was a lousy map maker. Still. I have a
an idea of the layout, and can do it slowly, bit by bit.

**ON** I walked into the nursery and couldn't
find anyone. I was early. It seemed quite
a large place with various rooms and no. one
seemed to be about. Eventually I found someone
and asked for LN. I then found her. She
showed me into her office and I sat down.
She asked me if I'd like a drink and I followed
her into the staff room. There were few
staff members there, one pregnant. I was introduced
and one lady talked to me easily. The others

**MN** I lost her a couple of times in the interview –
our toothball my q's either didn't make sense,
or she was thrown by the q. A couple of
times I lost concentration. I don't know
if the info is there or whether – I'm still worried
about the quan... of it. Didn't get through it all.

**TN** How interesting thing is that h/t
actually spoke clearly about the fears
that they have about the use of this
research [nb. it was a primary h/t
who was more keen at first meeting!].
Particularly that it will be used against
them to shut the nurseries, have the
building here for family centre work,
and shifted nursery work to the primaries.

See also the section in Chapter 6 on **Recording your progress.**

Your research diary should prove to be an invaluable resource in filling in the context for your research, and reminding you of critical incidents and particular aspects of data collection or fieldwork. It will also give you regular practice in distilling your ideas and in writing. It could be a support, in which you can confide and work out your concerns and fears. And, as it builds up during the project, it will serve as a trigger for reflection and a physical (but we hope not too embarrassing) reminder of just how far you have progressed.

## ☐ Summary

Having read this chapter, you should:

- be better able to choose a research topic which is feasible and motivates you;
- have an understanding of how you may focus your original ideas into something more achievable;
- be aware of the issues involved in choosing a supervisor;
- have a clearer idea of the advantages and disadvantages of group research;
- be ready to get on with the actual research work!

## ☐ Further reading

In this section, we list a limited selection of books which are of particular relevance to the topics discussed in this chapter, together with an indication of their contents.

Bailey, C. (1995) *A Guide to Field Research*. London: Pine Forge.
This text takes the student through the main elements of conducting a field research project.
Bell, J. (1999) *Doing Your Research Project: A Guide to First-time Researchers in Education and Social Science*, 3rd edn. Buckingham: Open University Press.
This introductory text reviews the stages of implementing a research project. It is divided into three parts. Part 1, 'Preparing the ground', includes reviewing the literature and negotiating access. Part 2, 'Selecting methods of data collection', includes designing questionnaires and keeping diaries. Part 3, 'Interpreting the evidence and reporting the findings', includes writing up a research project.
Booth, W. C., Colomb, G. G. and Williams, J. M. (1995) *The Craft of Research*. Chicago: University of Chicago Press.
Designed to help the reader to plan, carry out and report on research in any field and at any level. Covers the research process from finding a topic to shaping a question to making an argument.

Burgess, R. G. (1993) *Research Methods*. Walton-on-Thames: Thomas Nelson.
An introductory text which contains questions for students and further reading. The chapters include discussion of experiments, surveys, ethnography, historical research, ethical issues, analysis and writing.

Burton, D. (ed.) (2000) *Research Training for Social Scientists: A Handbook for Postgraduate Researchers*. London: Sage.
Eight main sections consider philosophical issues; ethical and legal issues; getting started; qualitative research design, data collection and analysis; qualitative software; survey research design and data collection; quantitative data analysis; and finishing off.

Cryer, P. (1996) *The Research Student's Guide to Success*. Buckingham: Open University Press.
From registering and settling in, through interacting with your supervisor, managing yourself and cooperating with others, to dealing with flagging, producing your thesis and conducting yourself in the examination.

Denscombe, M. (1998) *The Good Research Guide for Small-scale Social Research Projects*. Buckingham: Open University Press.
The three parts of the book focus on strategies (surveys, case studies, experiments, action research, ethnography), methods (questionnaires, interviews, observation, documents) and analysis (quantitative, qualitative, writing up).

Fitzpatrick, J., Secrist, J. and Wright, D. J. (1998) *Secrets for a Successful Dissertation*. Thousand Oaks, CA: Sage.
Useful American guide which includes chapters on writing the proposal, choosing a methodology, developing a support group, using technology and defending the dissertation. The 'emergency appendectomies' include a list of 'action words to introduce quotes'.

Graves, N. and Varma, V. (eds) (1997) *Working for a Doctorate: A Guide for the Humanities and Social Sciences*. London: Routledge.
Ten chapters focus on a range of relevant issues, including funding, time management, supervision problems, writing, the student experience, intercultural and gender issues and the British PhD in comparative perspective.

Murray, L. and Lawrence, B. (2000) *Practitioner-based Enquiry: Principles and Practices for Postgraduate Research*. London: Routledge.
Designed for postgraduate students undertaking small-scale research projects in or around their work environments and/or as part of a higher education programme.

Pittman, V. (1997) *Surviving Graduate School Part Time*. Thousand Oaks, CA: Sage.
American text containing much useful advice on programme selection, distance study, planning, finance and coping with problems along the way.

Preece, R. (1994) *Starting Research*. London: Pinter.
Written for the student who has to write a dissertation, this text focuses mainly on surveys and experimental design. The chapters begin by asking 'What is research?' and continue to discuss 'Elements of scientific method', 'Logic of scientific method', 'Information in research', 'Method of primary information collection', 'Organization and analysis of surveys', 'You can understand statistics', 'The research question' and 'The research dissertation'. Further reading is included at the end of the chapters.

Robson, C. (1993) *Real World Research: A Resource for Social Scientists and Practitioner Researchers*. Oxford: Blackwell.
The text has been written for those who cannot or do not wish to undertake research in the 'controlled' conditions of a laboratory but in the 'real world' settings of applied fields. Comprehensive in scope, the text includes discussion of surveys, case studies, experimental design outside the laboratory, observation, interviews, questionnaires, analysis of quantitative and qualitative data, dissemination and the practitioner-researcher role.

# 3

# THINKING ABOUT METHODS

## ☐ Introduction

Many, perhaps most, introductory books on doing research pay a great deal of attention to the extensive variety of research methods which are available and in use. If you are already well into your research project, detailed guidance on the use of particular methods may, of course, be invaluable. If, on the other hand, you are just beginning research, or lack confidence, such detail and its associated jargon can be both discouraging and demotivating.

The approach we have taken in this chapter is to present your choice and use of research methods as an integral part of the whole process of doing research, and to relate this to the rest of your life. From this perspective, we would argue not just that you can do research, but that you already possess many useful research skills.

If you have not already done so, you might usefully read the section in Chapter 1 on **What is research?** at this point.

The chapter is organized into the following sections:

- **Everyday research skills**. Applying life skills and experience to research.
- **Which method is best?** Thinking about research philosophy and design.
- **Families, approaches and techniques**. Alternative approaches to thinking about research methods.

- **Action research**. Using your research project to study and change something you care about.
- **Case studies**. Focusing your research project on a particular example or examples.
- **Experiments**. Testing your research hypotheses through controlled studies.
- **Surveys**. Collecting data from people, materials and artefacts.
- **Which methods suit?** Different ways to think about your choice.
- **Deciding about methods**. Issues to bear in mind when deciding upon your research design.

## ☐ Everyday research skills

As we said in Chapter 1, you are already a researcher. If you doubt this, try Exercise 15.

---

**Exercise 15: Looking at your life**

Recall a recent incident from your life, or a conversation, or a television or radio programme you have watched or listened to, or a newspaper or magazine article you have read, or a journey you have made.

Summarize the event, source or experience you have chosen in one sentence.

---

In doing Exercise 15, you will have made use of a variety of everyday skills which are also important research skills:

- You will have chosen a particular event, source or experience to write about. You will have had to be very selective, as the possible range from which you could have made a choice will have been immense. In other words, you will have drawn a sample of one from a very large population.
- You will have performed, whether you were consciously aware of it or not, an examination of the event, source or experience you chose. This examination will, of course, have been conducted from your own perspective, though it may have involved an awareness of the perspectives of others. In other words, you will have collected and analysed a set of data.
- You will have summarized the event, source or experience chosen, and presented this summary in a brief written form. In other words, you will have written up your analysis.

In completing this ostensibly simple exercise, therefore, you will have demonstrated your familiarity with some or all of the everyday skills listed in Box 23. These are all skills which most adults have developed to some extent and use on a day-to-day basis. Within the educational system, they are commonly referred to as core, key, generic or transferable skills. They are also important research skills, used continually by academics and other researchers.

---

**Box 23: Everyday life skills for research**

- Reading
- Listening
- Watching
- Choosing
- Questioning
- Summarizing
- Organizing
- Writing
- Presenting
- Reflecting

---

Researchers use these skills for the collection, selection, analysis and presentation of data. Researchers, however, make use of these taken-for-granted skills in a conscious, considered and systematic fashion, and aim to be rigorous, critical and analytical. Research involves the professionalization of everyday skills. And it also requires the researcher to pay particular attention to alternative values, views, meanings and explanations, while remaining alert to biases and distortions. In essence, though, research skills remain everyday skills, and your experience and understanding of the latter provide a ready route into thinking about research design and methods.

## Reading

We regularly read from a wide variety of sources: books, newspapers, magazines, instruction manuals and so on. We are not only literate, but also familiar with the particular conventions involved in reading different sorts of materials. Thus we are likely to be critical in reading election literature or double glazing publicity material, but more relaxed when reading popular novels or magazines. You will have developed many skills through reading, not least how to understand and relate to what you are reading.

---

Chapter 4 focuses on **Reading for research**. If you have not looked at it yet, you might usefully scan it now.

---

## Listening

Unless we have a hearing impairment, we will spend much or all of our time, consciously or subconsciously, listening: to friends and members of our families, to our colleagues and associates, to the people we meet in the street or in the shops, to radio and television programmes, to records, tapes or compact discs, to the 'background' sounds of our environment. Through this constant listening, you will have developed skills in identifying different people's voices, their attitudes and emotions, their openness and honesty. You will have learned how to extract useful information from listening, and how to relate this information to that coming to you from other sources.

> The issues involved in listening for research are considered further in the section on **Interviews** in Chapter 6.

## Watching

We watch our children, pets and those we care for at home; we watch the behaviour of our colleagues at work; we watch what we are doing ourselves as we cross the street or negotiate our way through a crowded room; we watch television for information, entertainment or relaxation; we watch sporting or cultural events in our leisure time. Through watching, you will have learnt to identify a wide range of visual signals, indicative of, for example, friendliness, unease or danger. Watching, like listening and reading, involves categorizing.

> The issues involved in watching for research are considered further in the section on **Observation** in Chapter 6.

## Choosing

Every day of our lives we make many deliberate choices. These range from the fairly trivial – which breakfast cereal to have, which route to take to work, when to go to bed – to the momentous – whether to move house or change our job, whether to get married, split up or have a child. In making choices, we are aware that there are a variety of options open to us, each with different implications. Through choosing, you will have developed skills of relevance to selecting topics for research, methods to be used in research and the subjects or objects to be sampled during the research.

> **Sampling and selection** are considered in Chapter 6.

## Questioning

In performing everyday skills, we are implicitly questioning the information we receive through our senses, placing this within acceptable frameworks, critically assessing its relevance and challenging it when we find it wanting. You will have built up considerable skill in questioning, both directly, through asking questions of others, and indirectly, through reviewing the information you have gathered from various sources. These skills are particularly relevant when you are using documentary sources and questionnaire techniques.

> The use of **Documents** and **Questionnaires** for data collection is considered further in Chapter 6.

## Summarizing

We do not treat all the information we constantly receive in everyday life as being of equal value, but reject most of it as being of little or no value, and critically question much of the rest. What we choose to retain in our memories for future application will typically be in summary form. Thus, if a colleague asks us what happened at a meeting yesterday, we will provide a summary response: we are highly unlikely to give, or be able to give, a verbatim report. Through such everyday actions, you will have learnt a great deal about summarizing information: what to leave out, what to stress, what is of key importance.

> The issues involved in summarizing data are considered in the section on **Managing your data** in Chapter 7.

## Organizing

In addition to summarizing the information you receive in everyday life, you will have become quite adept at organizing it. Thus, in recounting what happened to your colleague at a meeting, you will organize your account in a particular way. You might do this by giving the key points first, and then filling in the detail; or by focusing on the most momentous events; or by telling your story in its historical sequence.

> The techniques involved in organizing your research project are the subject of Chapter 5, **Managing your project**, while the organization of your writing is considered in the section on **How to argue** in Chapter 8.

## Writing

Adults' experiences of writing, as of reading, vary quite considerably. Some of you will have recent experience of extended pieces of writing, such as reports or essays, perhaps even books. Others will be more familiar with shorter and more immediate forms of writing, such as letters or memos. Or you may have done very little writing at all since your school days, having a job and a lifestyle which does not require much written communication.

---

Writing for research purposes is the subject of Chapter 8, **Writing up**.

---

**Presenting**

Presentation may be seen as related to writing. However, while you may have little current day-to-day experience of writing at any length, you are highly likely to have some experience of presenting your ideas in non-written forms. You will probably have had to do this to your colleagues, to your fellow students, to your family and friends. Presenting forms part of the general process of discussion and argument. It is a key way in which you exert your influence on others and establish your place in the world.

---

The presentation of your research is considered further in the section on **What do I do now?** in Chapter 9.

---

**Reflecting**

The final everyday skill to be considered here, reflection, is perhaps the most researcherly. It has to do with the ability to stand back from, and think carefully about, what you have done or are doing. You will almost certainly have done this many times, in reflecting on, for example, how the day at work went, or whether, had you said or done something differently, things might have worked out better. In research terms, it is particularly important to reflect upon your own role in the research process.

---

The issues of reflection and reflexivity are considered further in the sub-section on **How will you affect your research?** later in this chapter.

---

In carrying out your research project, you will probably make use of all the everyday skills we have identified in this section. You will use them in conjunction as well as individually, and you will devote a lot of conscious thought to your use and development of them.

## ☐ **Which method is best?**

> You can never empirically or logically determine the best approach. This can only be done reflectively by considering a situation to be studied and your own opinion of life. This also means that even if you believe that one approach is more interesting or rewarding than another, we as authors of this book do not want to rank one approach above another. In fact, we cannot *on any general ground*. The only thing we can do is to try to make explicit the special characteristics on which the various approaches are based.
>
> (Arbnor and Bjerke 1997: 5; emphasis in original)

There are many ways of thinking about, and categorizing, the wide variety of methods available for designing, carrying out and analysing the results of research. As we have already noted, there are numerous texts available that either attempt to provide a comprehensive overview of these methods or focus on a smaller selection or just one method. Understandably, then, for those new to research a key question is: which method is best? It is easy to be confused.

You may ask 'why can't we "just" collect data and make statements?' (Arbnor and Bjerke 1997: 3). However, the choice of the 'best' method is not simply the technical or practical question that it might at first appear. Different kinds of research approaches produce different kinds of knowledge about the phenomena under study. The question 'which method is best?' is not solely about whether, for example, to use interviews, questionnaires or observations. Underpinning these research tools are more general philosophical questions about how we understand social reality, and what are the most appropriate ways of studying it.

A key distinction can be made here between *method* and *methodology*. The term *method* can be understood to relate principally to the tools of data collection: techniques such as questionnaires and interviews. *Methodology* has a more philosophical meaning, and usually refers to the approach or paradigm that underpins the research. Thus, an interview that is conducted within, say, a qualitative approach or paradigm will have a different underlying purpose and produce broadly different data from one conducted within a quantitative paradigm.

> See the section in this chapter on **Families, approaches and techniques** for a discussion of quantitative and qualitative research paradigms.

An awareness of the implications of methodological issues and their impact on the kinds of knowledge that research produces, and of what kinds of knowledge it is possible to produce, is an important but often neglected issue in small-scale research. Our purposes here are to draw your attention to the broader philosophical issues associated with researching social reality. We aim to do this in two ways:

- by providing some guidance about how you can develop an understanding of the underlying philosophical issues that impact on your research;
- by indicating the main issues that you should consider in the initial design of your research.

In Chapter 2 (see Box 13) we set out five questions as a way of helping you to focus your research. We want to build on these questions here by encouraging you to explore more fully your own, and others', assumptions about social reality and how knowledge is produced about that reality. We all have theories about how the world works, what the nature of humankind is and what it is possible to know and not know. In social science, these issues are often categorized and referred to as paradigms. The usefulness of the term paradigm is that it offers a way of categorizing a body of complex beliefs and world views.

The most common paradigms that new researchers are introduced to are those termed *quantitative* and *qualitative* (see the following section). These terms are often presented as competing alternatives, and this should alert you to the political and contested nature of knowledge construction. As Oakley (1999: 155) comments, paradigms:

> are ways of breaking down the complexity of the real world that tell their adherents what to do. Paradigms are essentially intellectual *cultures*, and as such they are fundamentally embedded in the socialization of their adherents: a way of life rather than simply a set of technical and procedural differences.

Because of the degree of adherence such socialization can produce about the 'correct' way of researching the social world, discussion about the relative merits of quantitative or qualitative approaches has at times become a veritable war zone.

The quantitative and qualitative paradigms offer a basic framework for dividing up knowledge camps. Yet within these two broad camps there are debates about how social research should proceed, and about what forms of knowledge are perceived to be valid and invalid. The difficulty for all of us is that these debates are complex and often invoke the use of very inaccessible language. It is no wonder, then, that students ask what is wrong with simply focusing on the collection of data, as this involves using a set of technical skills that can be fairly easily learnt. Moreover, these are the skills with which students are most familiar in terms of their prior experience.

Our advice to those who are new to these paradigm debates is twofold. First, you might begin by focusing on the following four paradigms: positivist and post-positivist; intrepretive; critical; and postmodern. The first three of these are the most common in social research. More recently, there has been a growth of interest in the potential and limitations of research that operates within postmodern assumptions. Box 24 provides definitions of these paradigms.

Second, to aid your understanding of the relevancy of broader issues of methodology to your own research, particularly at the research design stage, Exercise 16 sets out some questions to illustrate the distinctions and similarities between key research paradigms. This exercise should cause you to reflect on some of the

**Box 24: Social research paradigms: some definitions**

*Positivism*. This is the view that social science procedures should mirror, as near as possible, those of the natural sciences. The researcher should be objective and detached from the objects of research. It is possible to capture 'reality' through the use of research instruments such as experiments and questionnaires. The aims of positivist research are to offer explanations leading to control and pre-dictability. Positivism is a very predominant way of knowing the social world; what Guba and Lincoln (1994) refer to as the 'received view'. This can be seen by the ways in which many perceive positivist approaches to be simply a commonsensical way of conducting research. While there are many varieties of positivism (see Crotty 1998), quantitative approaches that use statistics and experiments are seen as classic examples.

*Post-positivism*. This is a response to the criticisms that have been made about positivism. As its name suggests, post-positivism maintains the same set of basic beliefs as positivism. However, post-positivists argue that we can only know social reality imperfectly and probabilistically. While objectivity remains an ideal, there is an increased use of qualitative techniques in order to 'check' the validity of findings. 'Postpositivism holds that only partially objective accounts of the world can be produced, because all methods are flawed' (Denzin and Lincoln 1994: 15).

*Interpretivism*. Interpretivist approaches to social research see interpretations of the social world as culturally derived and historically situated. Interpretivism is often linked to the work of Max Weber (1864–1920), who suggested that the social sciences are concerned with *verstehen* (understanding). This is compared to *erklaren* (explaining), which forms the basis of seeking causal explanations and is the hallmark of the natural sciences. The distinction between *verstehen* and *erklaren* underlies that (often exaggerated) between qualitative and quantitative research approaches. Interpretivism has many variants. These include hermeneutics, phe-nomenology and symbolic interactionism.

*Critical*. As you might expect, critical social paradigms critique both positivism and interpretivism as ways of understanding the social world. 'Critical inquiry . . . [is not] a research that seeks merely to understand . . . [it is] a research that challenges . . . that [takes up a view] of conflict and oppression . . . that seeks to bring about change' (Crotty 1998: 112). Included in this category would be femin-ist, neo-Marxist, anti-racist and participatory approaches.

*Postmodern*. While the other paradigms offer grand theories for understanding the social world, 'advocates of postmodernism have argued that the era of big narratives and theories is over: locally, temporally and situationally limited nar-ratives are now required' (Flick 1998: 2). Postmodernist approaches seek to over-come the boundaries that are placed between art and social science. Postmodern approaches do not offer a view of rational progression to a better world. All we might expect is that social life will be in some ways different. As with the other paradigms, there are a variety of positions within the broad label of postmodernism. These would include post-structuralism.

---

**Exercise 16: Thinking methodologically about research design**

1 What are the main purposes of your research? For example, are you trying to change injustices in the world, or are you trying to understand how social reality is perceived through the perspectives of the researched?

2 What is your role in the research? For example, are you an 'expert' or a change agent?

3 What is the nature of knowledge? For example, do you believe that there are facts or laws that can be known, or is knowledge informed historically through insights that occur from time to time and replace ignorance and misapprehensions?

4 What are the criteria that you are bringing to judge the quality of your research? For example, should the research be objective and generalizable, or should it contribute to a fundamental change in social life?

5 Do you think your values should affect your research?

6 What is the place of ethics in your research? For example, do you consider it sufficient to abide by a code of professional ethics, or should the way the research is conducted closely match your own ethical frameworks?

7 What 'voice' do you adopt (or are you encouraged to adopt) when writing a research report? For example, do you write as a disinterested scientist, a transformative intellectual or a passionate participant?

8 What do you (and your teachers, managers and/or colleagues) think are the essential issues that you need research training in? For example, should you be trained primarily in technical knowledge about measurement, design and quantitative methods, in this and qualitative approaches, or do you need to be resocialized away from your existing assumptions about the nature of research?

9 Can you accommodate several methodologies in your research?

10 Who is the audience for your research? For example, are you hoping to persuade government administrators, funders and policy committees, feminists and Marxists or your colleagues and fellow researchers?

Adapted from Guba and Lincoln 1994

---

methodological issues associated with the design, conduct and knowledge generation implicit in your own research.

## ☐ Families, approaches and techniques

In this section, we take a simpler and more straightforward way into the discussion of methods and methodologies, by looking at three successive levels:

- two research *families*, or general strategies for doing research (two alternative formulations are offered).
- four *approaches* to designing your research project.
- four *techniques* for collecting data.

These families, approaches and techniques are summarized in Box 25. The two alternative sets of two families are discussed in this section, while the four

---

**Box 25: Research families, approaches and techniques**

*Research families*
• Quantitative or qualitative
• Deskwork or fieldwork

*Research approaches*
• Action research
• Case studies
• Experiments
• Surveys

*Research techniques*
• Documents
• Interviews
• Observation
• Questionnaires

---

approaches are the subject of the following four sections. The four techniques are separately considered in Chapter 6, **Collecting data**.

## Families

Research is a systematic investigation to find answers to a problem. Research in professional social science areas, like research in other subjects, has generally followed the traditional objective scientific method. Since the 1960s, however, a strong move towards a more qualitative, naturalistic and subjective approach has left social scientists divided between two competing methods: the scientific empirical tradition, and the naturalistic phenomenological mode. In the scientific method, quantitative research methods are employed in an attempt to establish general laws or principles. Such a scientific approach is often termed nomothetic and assumes social reality is objective and external to the individual. The naturalistic approach to research emphasises the importance of the subjective experience of individuals, with a focus on qualitative analysis. Social reality is regarded as a creation of individual consciousness, with meaning and the evaluation of events seen as a personal and subjective construction. Such a focus on the individual case rather than general law-making is termed an ideographic approach.

(Burns 2000: 3)

As the above quotation indicates, researchers are adept at classifying themselves and their peers into two groups: us and them. In this sub-section we consider two alternative research dichotomies: qualitative/quantitative and deskwork/fieldwork. The first of these distinctions has been the subject of much debate. The second distinction is much more pragmatic, and hence less debated, and has to do with the individual researcher's preferences and opportunities for going out to do their research (fieldwork) or staying in the office, library or laboratory (deskwork).

## Qualitative or quantitative?

> Quantitative research is empirical research where the data are in the form of numbers. Qualitative research is empirical research where the data are not in the form of numbers.
>
> (Punch 1998: 4)

> 'Qualitative' implies a direct concern with experience as it is 'lived' or 'felt' or 'undergone'. (In contrast, 'quantitative' research, often taken to be the opposite idea, is indirect and abstracts and treats experiences as similar, adding or multiplying them together, or 'quantifying' them.)
>
> (Sherman and Webb 1988: 7)

As Punch indicates, quantitative research is, as the term suggests, concerned with the collection and analysis of data in numeric form. It tends to emphasize relatively large-scale and representative sets of data, and is often, falsely in our view, presented or perceived as being about the gathering of 'facts'. Qualitative research, on the other hand, is concerned with collecting and analysing information in as many forms, chiefly non-numeric, as possible. It tends to focus on exploring, in as much detail as possible, smaller numbers of instances or examples which are seen as being interesting or illuminating, and aims to achieve 'depth' rather than 'breadth'.

There has been widespread debate in recent years within many of the social sciences regarding the relative merits of quantitative and qualitative strategies for research. The positions taken by individual researchers vary considerably, from those who see the two strategies as entirely separate and based on alternative views of the world, to those who are happy to mix these strategies within their research projects. Because quantitative strategies have been seen as more scientific or 'objective', qualitative researchers have felt the need to argue their case strongly. Qualitative research has become increasingly popular over the past two decades. The continuing debate over its relative merits can be seen more broadly as being about the status and politics of different kinds of research.

How distinctive are qualitative and quantitative forms of research? On first consideration, the use of questionnaires as a research technique might be seen as a quantitative strategy, whereas interviews and observations might be thought of as qualitative techniques. In practice, however, it is often more complicated than that. Thus, interviews may be structured and analysed in a quantitative manner, as when numeric data are collected or when non-numeric answers are categorized and coded in numeric form. Similarly, surveys may allow for open-ended responses and lead to the in-depth study of individual cases.

Box 26 sets out the perceived differences between the qualitative and quantitative research families, while Box 27 sets out their similarities.

## Fieldwork or deskwork?

The distinction between deskwork and fieldwork offers an alternative way of thinking about basic research strategies.

**Box 26: The differences between qualitative and quantitative research**

*Qualitative paradigms*

- Concerned with understanding behaviour from actors' own frames of reference
- Naturalistic and uncontrolled observation
- Subjective
- Close to the data: the 'insider' perspective
- Grounded, discovery-oriented, exploratory, expansionist, descriptive, inductive
- Process-oriented
- Valid: real, rich, deep data
- Ungeneralizable: single case studies
- Holistic
- Assume a dynamic reality

*Quantitative paradigms*

- Seek the facts/causes of social phenomena
- Obtrusive and controlled measurement
- Objective
- Removed from the data: the 'outsider' perspective
- Ungrounded, verification oriented, reductionist, hypothetico-deductive
- Outcome-oriented
- Reliable: hard and replicable data
- Generalizable: multiple case studies
- Particularistic
- Assume a stable reality

*Source*: Adapted from Oakley (1999: 156).

**Box 27: The similarities between qualitative and quantitative research**

- While quantitative research may be mostly used for testing theory, it can also be used for exploring an area and generating hypotheses and theory.
- Similarly, qualitative research can be used for testing hypotheses and theories, even though it is mostly used for theory generation.
- Qualitative data often include quantification (e.g. statements such as more than, less than, most, as well as specific numbers).
- Quantitative approaches (e.g. large-scale surveys) can collect qualitative (non-numeric) data through open-ended questions.
- The underlying philosophical positions are not necessarily as distinct as the stereotypes suggest.

Fieldwork refers to the process of going out to collect research data. Such data may be described as original or empirical, and cannot be accessed without the researcher engaging in some kind of expedition. The fieldwork might, for example, involve visiting an institution to interview members of staff, or standing on a street corner administering questionnaires to passers-by, or sitting in on a meeting to observe what takes place. In some disciplines, such as anthropology and sociology, fieldwork assumes particular importance.

Deskwork, on the other hand, consists of those research processes which do not necessitate going into the field. It consists, literally, of those things which can be done while sitting at a desk. These may include, for example, the administration, collection and analysis of postal surveys, the analysis of data collected by others, certain kinds of experimental or laboratory work, literature searches in the library and, of course, writing.

As in the case of the qualitative–quantitative divide, the fieldwork–deskwork distinction is also something of a false dichotomy, since most, if not all, research projects will make use of both sets of approaches. No matter how much time a researcher spends in the field, it is difficult to avoid some deskwork, even if this only consists of writing up results. Similarly, though it is possible to carry out useful research without ever leaving an office environment, information is usually still being accessed somehow.

The distinction between fieldwork and deskwork is, obviously, also not clear-cut. It is debatable, for example, into which category one would place telephone or email interviews, which can be conducted at the desk but effectively take the researcher, at least electronically, into the field. And how would you categorize using your laptop while out in the field collecting data? The development of information and communication technologies, in particular the growth of the Internet, is undoubtedly blurring the fieldwork–deskwork distinction.

From the perspective of practice, however, this distinction may be more significant to researchers than that between qualitative and quantitative methods. An appreciation of it may help you in planning and implementing your research project. Your opportunities and preference for either fieldwork or deskwork – and you will be most likely to prefer one or the other – may help you in choosing, where this is possible, not just the topic of your research but the kinds of methods you use.

## Approaches

Box 25 identifies four basic approaches to, or designs for, research in the social sciences: action research, case studies, experiments and surveys. These are discussed individually in more detail in the following four sections of this chapter.

It should be said at once that this classification is not meant to be either definitive or exclusive. It simply recognizes the most common approaches used by those carrying out small-scale research projects. Individual projects may, of course – as the examples given later in this chapter illustrate – involve more than one of these approaches; thus, a case study may be carried out through action research, while particular projects may involve both experiments and surveys.

## Techniques

Box 25 also identifies four basic social science research techniques: the study of documents, interviews, observations or questionnaires. These techniques are considered in more detail in Chapter 6, where the focus is on **Collecting data**.

## Linking families, approaches and techniques

It should be stressed that the various families, approaches and techniques identified here do not map simply on to each other. Thus, it is possible to use action research, case study or survey approaches within either a qualitative or a quantitative research strategy, though experiments tend to be quantitative in nature. Similarly, case studies, experiments and survey approaches might be employed as part of desk-based or field-based research strategies; but action research tends to imply some fieldwork. Documents, interviews, observations and questionnaires may be used as part of all the research strategies and approaches identified, though the way in which they are used and analysed will vary.

In other words, the families, approaches and techniques represent dimensions of the research process. The researcher may use alternatives from the different dimensions in combination as appropriate to study a particular set of research questions. You may focus on specific approaches or techniques, and concentrate on either deskwork or fieldwork, or a qualitative or quantitative strategy; or you might mix or vary your usage. It is up to you, given your preferences, the resources you have available, the constraints you are operating under and the particular issues which you wish to research.

## ☐ Action research

AR [action research] is a complex, dynamic activity involving the best efforts of both members of communities or organizations and professional researchers. It simultaneously involves the co-generation of new information and analysis together with actions aimed at transforming the situation in democratic directions. AR is holistic and also context bound, producing practical solutions and new knowledge as part of an integrated set of activities . . . AR is a way of producing tangible and desired results for the people involved, and it is a knowledge-generation process that produces insights both for researchers and the participants. It is a complex action–knowledge generation process . . . the immense importance of insider knowledge and initiatives is evident, marking a clear distinction from orthodox research that systematically distrusts insider knowledge as co-opted.
(Greenwood and Levin 1998: 50)

The purpose of action research is, always and explicitly, to improve practice.
(Griffiths 1998: 21)

Action research is an increasingly popular approach among small-scale researchers in the social sciences, particularly for those working in professional areas such as education, health and social care. It is well suited to the needs of people conducting research in their workplaces, and who have a focus on improving aspects of their own and their colleagues' practices. For example, the teacher who is concerned to improve performance in the classroom may find action research useful because it offers a systematic approach to the definition, solution and evaluation of problems and concerns.

---

**Box 28: Two examples of action research projects**

Slim and Thompson (1993) report on participatory action research that was designed to increase the value given to the knowledge, experience, culture and priorities of local people. To achieve this a major strategy of this research was to help development workers to improve their listening and learning skills. This meant that the research had to reverse common expert–novice relations between development workers and those who should be benefiting from this work. This reversal meant that development workers needed to become novices who seek to learn and listen. Those whose lives it is the intention to value become teachers and experts. At the heart of this reversal is the need for effective dialogue. This dialogue, of course, is likely to be primarily oral. In seeking to help development workers manage this reversal, Slim and Thompson outline the necessary listening skills that need to be developed. They note that those using oral testimony techniques need to 'allow people to speak on their own terms' (p. 63). Different forms of oral testimony were collected. These included family tree, diary, group and community interviews, single issue testimonies and the recording of songs, legends, stories, plays, traditional accounts of community or family history passed from one generation to another, personal life stories, recollections and memories.

This project was based within the Xerox Corporation in the United States in the 1990s. Xerox had lost its monopoly in the photocopying business, and its market position was declining. Management studies suggested that substantial savings could be made by 'outsourcing' some work processes. Rather than simply implement these findings, a cost study team was set up to consider the problem, with representatives of labour and management working together. This eight-person team worked together full-time for six months. Its research suggested anticipated cost savings of $3.6 million, as compared to the estimated savings from outsourcing of $3.2 million.

*Source:* Whyte *et al.* (1991).

---

Yet action research is also an important approach for those with wider concerns for social justice. It lends itself to the direct involvement and collaboration of those whom it is designed to benefit. This is particularly the case for participatory action research, which is not designed and undertaken by research 'experts', but by those community members who are involved in the issues that the research is addressing. Box 28 summarizes two contrasting examples of action research, one from the community development literature the other from a large commercial company. Box 29 lists seven criteria distinguishing action research from other approaches.

From these descriptions, you may have formed the impression that action research can be a very demanding, but also very rewarding, research approach. For this reason, it should not be lightly engaged in, and is probably inappropriate for most small-scale research projects. Box 30 identifies a number of inappropriate uses of action research.

---

**Box 29: Criteria distinguishing action research**

'We have selected seven criteria to distinguish different types of action research, and would argue that these seven, in dynamic interaction, distinguish action research from other methodologies . . .

Action research:

1 is educative;
2 deals with individuals as members of social groups;
3 is problem-focused, context-specific and future-orientated;
4 involves a change intervention;
5 aims at improvement and involvement;
6 involves a cyclic process in which research, action and evaluation are interlinked;
7 is founded on a research relationship in which those involved are participants in the change process.'

*Source*: Hart and Bond (1995: 37–8).

---

**Box 30: Inappropriate uses of action research**

Never use action research to:

1 Drive an unpopular policy or initiative through.
2 Experiment with different solutions without thinking through very carefully their soundness and the ethics involved.
3 Manipulate employees or practitioners into thinking they have contributed to a policy decision when it has already been made.
4 Try to bring a dysfunctional team or workgroup together (whether or not they actually are dysfunctional, any doubts you may have suggest you need to examine your 'systems' first, before engaging in a time-consuming and potentially disruptive project).
5 Bolster a flagging career. Action research will expose any weaknesses you may have extremely quickly!

*Source*: Adapted from Morton-Cooper (2000: 24–5).

---

In terms of the discussion in Chapter 1, action research is clearly a very applied approach, one which could also be seen as experimental. It offers a research design which links the research process closely to its context, and is predicated upon the idea of research having a practical purpose in view and leading to change. As the diagram in Box 31 indicates, it also fits well with the idea of the research process as a spiral activity, going through repeated cycles and changing each time.

---

See the section on **What is research?** in Chapter 1.

---

**Box 31: The participatory action research spiral**

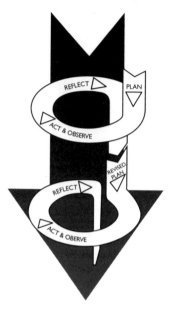

*Source:* Atweh *et al.* (1998: 22).

---

For these reasons, action research would be most likely to involve an extensive component of fieldwork, as opposed to deskwork. How might it be located, however, with reference to the distinction between quantitative and qualitative strategies? Try Exercise 17.

If you have concluded that action research is chiefly or necessarily qualitative, you might like to look again at the second example of action research given in Box 28. Would you say that this project, with its overt focus on saving production costs, adopted a qualitative strategy, either wholly or in part?

---

**Exercise 17: Is action research qualitative research?**

Compare the characteristics of qualitative and action research, as outlined in Boxes 26, 27 and 29.

What similarities and differences can you detect?

Would you say that action research was primarily or necessarily a qualitative research strategy? Give reasons for your conclusions.

Does action research fit into any of the paradigms discussed in Box 24?

---

# ☐ Case studies

> The case study is the method of choice when the phenomenon under study is not readily distinguishable from its context.
>
> (Yin 1993: 3)

> Unlike the experimenter who manipulates variables to determine their causal significance or the surveyor who asks standardized questions of large, representative samples of individuals, the case study researcher typically observes the characteristics of an individual unit – a child, a clique, a class, a school or a community. The purpose of such observation is to probe deeply and to analyse intensively the multifarious phenomena that constitute the life cycle of the unit with a view to establishing generalizations about the wider population to which that unit belongs.
>
> (Cohen and Manion 1995: 106–7)

> Life histories, oral or written stories [can function] as in-depth case studies of households, of groups and of events. To serve as a foundation for generalizations, case studies should be related to a theoretical framework which in turn may be adjusted as case study results provide new evidence. The social analyst gives clear guidance to the story teller or informants on how to structure the story, if structuring is at all desired. Case studies, as the name indicates, concentrate on special cases. Generalizations from case studies must be handled with care.
>
> (Mikkelsen 1995: 80)

The case study is, in many ways, ideally suited to the needs and resources of the small-scale researcher. It allows, indeed endorses, a focus on just one example, or perhaps just two or three. This might be the researcher's place of work, or another institution or organization with which they have a connection: a company, a voluntary organization, a school, a ship or a prison. Or it might be just one element of such an organization: a class, a work team, a community group or a football team. Or the focus might be on one individual, or a small number of individuals, as in life history studies or analyses of how top managers have reached their positions.

Many of you may be familiar with case studies, and their analysis, through their use as examples on courses. In this sense, case studies are often used to illustrate problems or indicate good practices. The distinction between this usage of case studies and case study as a social research method lies in the explicit recognition, in the latter usage, of an underlying methodological philosophy about how we know the social world, and its linkage to a body of theory and practice in the literature.

Box 32 summarizes two contrasting examples of case study research. One involved the study of 20 cases, the other just four. While the latter was explicitly qualitative in approach, the former showed concerns with representativeness, and might also have been described as a survey. Each study paid explicit attention to sampling and selection issues, and used a range of data collection techniques, including interviews, observation and documents.

---

**Box 32: Two examples of case study research**

A   This report is based on a final sample of 20 case study firms. 6–10
people were typically interviewed in each case . . . These interviews were
conducted with the aid of a detailed pro-forma and recorded in hand-
written notes directly on the pro-forma. In every case, the managing
director or equivalent was interviewed (often more than once), along
with a cross-section of people by function and organisational level . . .
The case study sample was constructed to capture what we believe are
the important factors bearing upon skill supply, HRM [human resource
management], training and development in the SME [small and medium-
sized enterprise]. The decision rules for selecting firms were as follows:

1   Size . . .
2   Stages of development . . .
3   Sector . . .
4   Local labour markets . . .
5   Ownership . . .
6   Firms showing a high level of concern for, and activity in, training,
HRD [human resource development] and HRM (progressives), and
firms showing low concern/activity (laggards).

(Hendry *et al.* 1991: 3)

B   A case study method was used to explore circumstances which facilitate or
inhibit progress towards sex equality at work.

Four organisational case studies were involved in the research, each
taking four months to complete . . . This was qualitative research. That
is to say its legitimacy does not spring from numbers, either of
organisations studied or of people interviewed. Rather it gains what
authority it has from the depth of insight made available . . . The cases
were selected to provide a panel of varying experiences to which similar
questions might be addressed.

The author provides information on how data were collected (observation,
reading files, interviews), and on how people were selected for interview.
Analysis of the case study material was undertaken by theme. The author is
explicit that she offers only one reading of the social situations and relationships in the organizations she studied. That reading 'is specific to my own
subject position: as a white middle-class heterosexual woman operating in an
academic mode, age fifty-five, mother of two adult daughters.'

(Cockburn 1991: 3–4, 13)

---

Restricting your research to a detailed study of one or a small number of cases
does not, however, mean that the context for those cases can be ignored. It is a
temptation, as it is with action research, for researchers to immerse themselves
wholly in the details of the case. This is a tendency which should be guarded
against. Box 33 identifies this tendency, alongside other advantages and disadvantages of this research approach.

**Box 33: Advantages and disadvantages of case studies**

*Advantages*

1 Case study data are drawn from people's experiences and practices and so are seen to be strong in reality.
2 Case studies allow for generalizations from a specific instance to a more general issue.
3 Case studies allow the researcher to show the complexity of social life. Good case studies build on this to explore alternative meanings and interpretations.
4 Case studies can provide a data source from which further analysis can be made. They can, therefore, be archived for further research work.
5 Because case studies build on actual practices and experiences, they can be linked to action and their insights contribute to changing practice. Indeed, case study may be a subset of a broader action research project.
6 Because the data contained in case studies are close to people's experiences, they can be more persuasive and more accessible.

*Source*: Adapted from Cohen and Manion (1995: 123).

*Disadvantages*

The disadvantages of case studies are linked to their advantages. In particular:

1 The very complexity of a case can make analysis difficult. This is particularly so because the holistic nature of case study means that the researcher is often very aware of the connections between various events, variables and out-comes. Accordingly, *everything* appears relevant. It is not, however, and to write up your case as if it is does not make for good research. You might think about this in terms of a 'Russian doll' metaphor, where each piece of data rests inside another, separate but related. You need to show the connections but not lose sight of the whole.
2 While the contextualization of aspects of the case strengthen this form of research, it is difficult to know where 'context' begins and ends.

You might like at this point to look again at the section on **Focusing** in Chapter 2, and particularly at Box 16.

One other caution about adopting a case study approach to your research project has already been mentioned in this book. It also applies to action research, as well as to other research approaches. This concerns the tendency for small-scale researchers, particularly those in employment who are receiving support from their employers, to base their research projects within their places of employment. While you may in practice have little or no choice about this, if you do have some choice, you should consider other alternatives.

Case studies may be progressed in a variety of ways. Yin (1993) identifies six types of case study, defined along two dimensions:

- in terms of the number of cases – single or multiple;
- in terms of the purpose of the study – exploratory, descriptive or explanatory.

Thus, we can talk in terms of single descriptive case studies, multiple exploratory case studies and so forth. Exercise 18 explores these categorizations a little further.

---

**Exercise 18: Types of case studies**

Consider the two examples of case studies outlined in Box 32 in terms of the typology suggested by Yin (1993).

How would you categorize each of the examples?

Do you think that Yin's typology is useful?

---

## ☐ Experiments

> In the social sciences, there are two broad traditions of research: experimental and nonexperimental. While both seek to explain human behaviour, they differ critically in the amount of control they have over the data. Simply put, experimentalists manipulate variables suspected of producing an effect, while nonexperimentalists observe them.
>
> (Lewis-Beck 1993: ix)

> The experiment is a situation in which the *independent variable* (also known as the exposure, the intervention, the experimental or predictor variable) is carefully manipulated by the investigator under known, tightly defined and controlled conditions, or by natural occurrence. At its most basic, the experiment consists of an *experimental group* which is exposed to the intervention under investigation and a control group which is not exposed. The experimental and control groups should be equivalent, and investigated systematically under conditions that are identical (apart from the exposure of the experimental group), in order to minimize variation between them.
>
> (Bowling 1997: 191; emphasis in original)

For many people undertaking small-scale research in the social sciences, the idea of conducting experiments may seem rather strange. The experimental method is particularly associated with the physical sciences, where materials and non-human life forms are more amenable to experimentation. Indeed, experiments are at the heart of what is known as the scientific method, with its practice of formulating and testing hypotheses through carefully designed and controlled tests. The associated terminology, repeated in the quotations above – e.g. subjects, independent, dependent and extraneous variables, control – appears very precise and suggestive.

Experiments are, however, widely used as a research approach in a number of the social sciences, particularly psychology (which is often classified as a science

---

**Box 34: Two examples of experimental research**

A Piaget's experiments on child cognition have recently been replicated and extended. An experiment was designed to obtain data about the process whereby children learn to solve large set number conservation problems. The experiment involved randomly assigning children to one of three experimental groups. Each group received the same problems to solve in the same order. The only difference was in the feedback they got to their answers, and in the experimenter's interest in their reasoning.

*Source*: Siegler (1995).

B The disciplinary practices used by mothers to control their children in four ethnic groups in Australia are compared from a developmental perspective. A vignette approach was used in which each mother was asked to say how she would deal with 12 situations involving her oldest child at 8 years of age and at 4 years of age. The responses were coded as power assertion, love withdrawal, induction and permissiveness. Twenty mothers from each of the ethnic groups, Greek, Lebanese, Vietnamese and Anglo, from the same socioeconomic level and geographic area were randomly chosen from lists of families that met the criteria for inclusion in the study.

*Source*: Papps *et al.* (1995: 49).

---

rather than a social science), but also economics, health care and education. Box 34 summarizes two contrasting examples of experimental research in the social sciences.

There are good reasons, though, for more caution in the use of experiments as a research approach in the social sciences. As already indicated, the social sciences are concerned with human behaviour and perspectives. A strict application of an experimental approach to research in these areas would suggest exposing one group of individuals to the experiment – which might be beneficial or disadvantageous, and difficult to judge in advance – while denying it to others. There are, in other words, ethical issues around the use of experiments involving people. Yet, while they appear particularly evident in the case of experiments, these issues are just as strong for other research approaches. They apply to action research, to case studies and to surveys as well.

---

These issues are discussed further in the section on **Access and ethical issues** in Chapter 6.

---

Some of the considerations to be borne in mind when designing a useful social experiment are addressed in Exercise 19. The advantages and disadvantages of experiments are listed in Box 35.

---

### Exercise 19: Designing social experiments

Suppose you are a headteacher, and you have been told that your school is to be part of a national pilot study concerned with the introduction of a new curriculum and examination.

The pilot requires that a given year group is split into two classes, with one group following the new curriculum and taking the new examination, and the other continuing with the previous curriculum and examination.

How would you go about designing this experiment so that it gave valid results?

What resources and authority would you need in order to implement it? What could such an experiment tell you about the usefulness or suitability of the new curriculum and examination?

How would such an experiment differ from an action research project?

---

### Box 35: Advantages and disadvantages of experiments

*Advantages*

1 Because of the random assignment of people to intervention and control (i.e. randomization of extraneous variables) the risk of extraneous variables confounding the results is minimized.
2 Control over the introduction and variation of the 'predictor' variables clarifies the direction of cause and effect.
3 If both pre- and post-testing is conducted this controls for time-related threats to validity.
4 The modern design of experiments permits greater flexibility, efficiency and powerful statistical manipulation.
5 The experiment is the only research design which can, in principle, yield causal relationships.

*Disadvantages*

1 It is difficult to design experiments so as to represent a specified population.
2 It is often difficult to choose the 'control' variables so as to exclude all confounding variables.
3 With a large number of uncontrolled, extraneous variables it is impossible to isolate the one variable that is hypothesized as the cause of the other; hence the possibility always exists of alternative explanations.
4 Contriving the desired 'natural setting' in experiments is often not possible.
5 The experiment is an unnatural social situation with a differentiation of roles. The participant's role involves obedience to the experimenter (an unusual role).
6 Experiments cannot capture the diversity of goals, objectives and service inputs which may contribute to . . . outcomes in natural settings.

*Source:* Bowling (1997: 193).

# ☐ Surveys

*Survey research . . .* is the *method* of *collecting information* by asking a set of preformulated *questions* in a predetermined sequence in a structured *questionnaire* to a *sample* of individuals drawn so as to be *representative* of a defined *population.*

(Hutton 1990: 8)

Survey research in education involves the collection of information from members of a group of students, teachers, or other persons associated with the educational process, and the analysis of this information to illuminate important educational issues. Most surveys are based on samples of a speci-fied target population – the group of persons in whom interest is expressed. The researcher often wishes to generalize the results obtained from the samples to the populations from which the samples were drawn.

(Rosier 1988: 107)

As these quotations indicate, surveys are usually associated as a research approach with the idea of asking groups of people questions. There is, however, a related meaning of survey which is also relevant to the social sciences. This is when the subjects which are being questioned by the researcher are really objects: mater-ials or artefacts rather than people. Thus, most small-scale research projects will involve some kind of literature survey; but in some cases, as when documentary analysis is extensively used, this may be the basis for the whole project.

> The issues involved in conducting a literature survey are considered in the section on **Coping with the research literature** in Chapter 4. The analysis of documents is discussed in the section on **Documents** in Chapter 6.

Box 36 summarizes two contrasting examples of survey research, one a smaller-scale literature survey, the other a larger-scale questionnaire survey. Note the common concern with sampling strategy. The advantages and disadvantages of surveys are considered in Box 37. Like experiments, surveys have their own peculiar terminology or jargon, which includes terms like census, population, sample, case and variable.

Exercise 20 asks you to consider the value of questionnaire surveys in the light of the previous discussion of alternative research strategies and approaches.

Questionnaires and interviews, the techniques which are at the heart of one type of survey research, occupy a major place in small-scale social science research projects. This is the case to such an extent that, when students or employees are asked to carry out a research study, they almost automat-ically think of using these techniques, usually both at once. Interviews and questionnaires can also, of course, play a part in action research, case studies

---

**Box 36: Two examples of survey research**

A This survey focused on published literature on employment and family life. Two criteria were used in selecting material:

- only literature published in the 1980s or 1990s was considered;
- only UK material was used.

Survey findings were referred to more than research using case study or qualitative techniques. Two key demographic trends were used to guide the research: the increasing number of mothers in paid employment, and the growing population of older people.

The researchers conducted their survey largely through academic libraries in London. They used a range of databases, including PAIS, PsycLit, EconLit, SocioFile, the Family Resources Index and ASSIA. National and international published statistics, and the researchers' own specialist knowledge, were the other main sources used.

*Source*: Brannen *et al.* (1994).

B This national survey was carried out for the National Institute of Adult Continuing Education by a market research company. A sample of 4,608 adults aged 17 years and over living in England, Scotland and Wales were interviewed using a detailed schedule of questions. An additional sample of adults living in inner London was also included at the request of the Inner London Education Authority. All interviews were conducted in the respondents' own homes.

The research set out to record the 'nature and level of participation in learning among adults'. A particular interest was to 'consider what impact the high level of public investment in adult learning in London had on adults' private learning projects.'

*Source*: Sargant (1991, quotes from p. 26).

---

**Exercise 20: Using the survey approach**

Consider the advantages of surveys for collecting information, as outlined in Box 37.

How realistic do you think it is for surveys to meet the expectations which are set out?

Does this mean that the results of survey research are necessarily more accurate than those arrived at through other approaches?

Do surveys lend themselves to qualitative as much as quantitative research strategies?

---

---

**Box 37: Advantages and disadvantages of surveys**

*Advantages*

- Questions are designed so that answers from individual interviews can be added together to produce results which apply to the whole sample . . .
- The research is based on interviews with a representative sample of respondents . . .
- The questions are designed to be unbiased . . .
- Surveys lend themselves to future replication . . .
- Large surveys can often be broken down.

*Source*: Hutton (1990: 11–13).

*Disadvantages*

1 The data, in the form of tables, pie charts and statistics, become the main focus of the research report, with a loss of linkage to wider theories and issues.
2 The data provide snapshots of points in time rather than a focus on the underlying processes and changes.
3 The researcher is often not in a position to check first hand the understandings of the respondents to the questions asked. Issues of truthfulness and accuracy are thereby raised.
4 The survey relies on breadth rather than depth for its validity. This is a crucial issue for small-scale researchers.

---

and experimental approaches to social science research. Yet they are not the only techniques available, with the use of documents and observations also widespread.

## ☐ Which methods suit?

> The question 'quantitative or qualitative?' is commonly asked, especially by beginning researchers. Often, they are putting the 'methods cart' before the 'content horse'. The best advice in those cases is to step back from questions of method [and tools], and give further consideration to the purposes and research questions, bearing in mind that the way questions are asked influences what needs to be done to answer them.
>
> (Punch 1998: 245)

As this quote reminds us, you need to consider some of the broader issues of research design and philosophy before focusing on the tools and techniques for data collection. Box 38 poses some further questions to help you revise, reflect upon and reformulate your plans. In addition, there are further issues which you may need or wish to consider to help you in reaching your decision. Eight are considered in this section.

---

**Box 38: Which method to choose**

1 *Research questions.* What exactly are you trying to find out? Focus on the 'exactly' as this can lead you into either the quantitative or qualitative direction.
2 *Are you interested in making standardized and systematic comparisons or do you really want to study this phenomenon or situation in detail?*
3 *The literature.* How have other researchers dealt with this topic? To what extent do you wish to align your own research with standard approaches to the topic?
4 *Practical considerations.* Issues of time, money, availability of samples and data, familiarity with the subject under study, access to situations, gaining cooperation.
5 *Knowledge payoff.* Will you learn more about this topic using quantitative or qualitative forms of research? Which approach will produce more useful knowledge? Which will do more good?
6 *Style.* Some people prefer one approach to another. This may involve paradigm and philosophical issues or different images about what a good piece of research looks like.

*Source:* Adapted from Punch (1998: 244–5).

---

### What do you need or want to find out?

One of the key determinants of the approach you might use in your research is undeniably the nature of the research proposed. You may want, or need, to answer a particular question or set of questions. This may immediately suggest a method or technique to you. For example, if you want to find out what members of the general public think about a given issue, an obvious way forward is to ask some of them. Or if you need to understand why a traffic management plan does not appear to have reduced traffic congestion, observing traffic behaviour in the relevant area may seem appropriate.

In the research literature, it is sometimes suggested that if your research questions are well enough focused or refined, they will effectively determine the methods you use to answer them. In practice, however, in almost every case there will be alternative techniques which could be used, either instead of or in conjunction with the one(s) you first think of. Thus, to follow up the two examples just given, you might observe the public's actual behaviour, where this impacts upon the issue under consideration, or you might attempt to model traffic behaviour using a computer programme.

The words 'want' and 'need' in the title of this sub-section also suggest an important distinction, one which has to do with focusing as well as method. Here, as when considering your research plans in general, you need to think about which methods are practicable given the time and other resources you have available.

### What skills do you have?

As we suggested in the opening section of this chapter, on **Everyday research skills**, one of the key resources you have available for your research is yourself.

**Exercise 21: Everyday and research skills**

Refer back to the discussion in the section on **Everyday research skills** (see also Box 23). Ten such skills were identified:

- Reading
- Listening
- Watching
- Choosing
- Questioning
- Summarizing
- Organizing
- Writing
- Presenting
- Reflecting

For each of these skills, give yourself a grading on a scale from 1 (low) to 10 (high). Which of these skills do you consider yourself to be best at? What research approaches or techniques does that suggest to you that you might be best advised to adopt? Would these fit in with your existing research plans?

You will have many skills as an adult which have been developed through everyday life. So you might find it useful to think about what skills you are best at and what skills you like using.

Do you like talking to people? Do you like watching people? Would you prefer to sit at a desk and read documents? Or work on data stored on a computer? Each of these preferences suggests that you might be most comfortable using a particular technique: interviews, observation or documentary analysis. You might, therefore, find it easiest, where possible, to research an area which allows you to use the skills you have best developed, or which you are most comfortable with. Use Exercise 21 to help you to decide.

Alternatively, you might, in carrying out an audit of your everyday and research skills, decide that you want to use your research project deliberately to develop skills which you feel you lack, but which could be useful to you. This might be a good way of adding interest or personal benefit to a research project which could otherwise be rather boring or limiting. Be careful, however, not to overreach yourself if this might affect the likelihood of you successfully completing your project.

**Will your methodological preferences answer your questions?**

Bearing the two previous questions in mind, you now need to consider whether the everyday research skills you wish to use are actually suited to the issues you are going to investigate.

To return to the two examples used above, if you like talking to people, and feel that you are reasonably good at it, you will probably be comfortable with the idea of researching public opinion by talking to people. Or, if you are experienced with computer modelling, you may be engaged by the prospect of researching traffic management options using these techniques. If the circumstances were reversed, however, you might have some qualms.

There may, as has already been suggested, be ways around such problems, short of changing your research topic. In the latter case, if computers turn you off and you would much rather talk to people, you might research traffic management by questioning a number of drivers and pedestrians, perhaps referring to existing computer-based studies as necessary. Or, in the former case, you might approach the study of public opinion by re-examining some of the many sources of published information, rather than by questioning people directly.

In many cases, however, particularly where you do not have an entirely free choice over the subject of your research, you will find yourself needing to use methods you may not feel entirely happy with.

### How will your methods affect the answers you get?

Just as it is sometimes argued that your research questions should determine your approach and techniques, so, in an analogous fashion, it is often suggested that the methods you use will significantly affect the answers you get. There is, of course, a good deal of sense in this argument.

If you carry out a questionnaire survey, the information you collect will be rather different from what you would get if you used in-depth interviews, though there might be a good deal of overlap. The questions, and thus the nature and scope of the answers, in a questionnaire are determined in advance by the researcher. Interviews, by contrast, even when highly structured, allow for more flexibility in asking and answering questions. While the responses to the former tend to be brief, those to the latter may be very lengthy, so fewer interviews may be carried out in the same time.

It is also the case, of course, that the choice of the subjects or objects of your research – people, classes, traffic, books etc. – assuming that you are not able to study every possible subject or object of relevance to your questions, will influence your findings. This issue is discussed further in the section on **Sampling and selection** in Chapter 6.

### How will you affect your research?

Reflexivity demands a type of emotional literacy on the part of the researcher, who can sensitively engage with the research study while/because s/he is aware of her/his own responses, values, beliefs and prejudices.

(Morley 1996: 139)

Researchers are themselves a powerful, and often under-recognized, influence on their research and their findings. This influence extends beyond the choice of the research topic itself and the methods used to explore it. As a researcher, you will have certain opinions and views about a wide range of issues, and these are likely to find some expression in your research and your reporting of it. Thus, as

---

**Exercise 22: Developing reflexivity: ten questions to ask yourself**

Think about a situation you have been in, preferably in piloting your research.

1  What was my role in this situation?
2  Did I feel comfortable or uncomfortable and why?
3  What actions did I take? How did I and others act?
4  Was it appropriate? How could I have improved the situation for myself, and others?
5  What can I change in future?
6  Do I feel as if I've learned anything new about myself or my research?
7  Has it changed my way of thinking in any way?
8  What knowledge, from theories, practices and other aspects of my own and others' research, can I apply to this situation?
9  What broader issues – for example, ethical, political or social – arise from this situation?
10  Have I recorded these thoughts in my research diary?

---

well as having a set of research questions to ask, you may already have a view on the likely answers. This will affect the way in which you ask questions, of people or of documents, and the significance you attach to their answers. It will also affect who you ask, using your contacts or networks, and the ways in which your questions are answered.

As an adult, you also have a range of individual demographic characteristics, including your sex, age, class, race and size. These will impact upon your research in more or less complex ways, and will raise issues related to the contexts of your research. For example, if you are a white, middle-class male, conducting field-work in a women's refuge, or in inner-city areas with large black populations, you will need to consider the ways in which your sex, class and ethnicity contribute to your research findings. While such clear differences between the researcher and the researched throw these issues into relief, they are relevant in other cases as well.

If someone else carried out your research, using the same approach, techniques and sample, the results would be, at the very least, subtly different. There is no easy way in which the affect of the researcher on the research can be minimized. You cannot be wholly objective and, in many ways, it is foolish to try to be so. The play of emotions between researcher, researched and research is often something to be welcomed and celebrated. Yet there is a need to be aware of your influence on your research, and to be as open as you can in recording and recognizing these effects. Exercise 22 lists ten questions to ask yourself to help develop your reflexivity.

## Which methods are acceptable?

Another key issue in deciding about your approach to your research is the question of which methods may be acceptable. You may be working under direction or in collaboration with others, for example, and these people may have an influence on your choice of methods. Your research may be funded by an organization which has very definite views on the value of alternative techniques, or has produced a research brief which limits or directs your choice. Or you may be working within a subject or disciplinary tradition which expects you to take a given methodological perspective.

In all these cases, however, it should be useful to you to be able to reach a considered opinion on the advantages and disadvantages of using particular approaches or techniques. You may also be able to go a little further, and modify or add to the choice of methods.

### Using more than one method

It is common, of course, for researchers to use more than one method. This is even more likely if you are carrying out your research project as part of a group, rather than on your own. Your main method might, for example, be a questionnaire survey, a set of interviews or a series of observations, but this is likely to be complemented, at the very least, by some documentary analysis to enable you to explore relevant literature or policy. Most research projects in the social sciences are, therefore, in a general sense multimethod.

There are, however, good reasons for deliberately seeking to use more than one method in the main body of your research. You may follow up a survey with some interviews, in order to get a more detailed perspective on some of the issues raised. The telling anecdote may be much more revealing and influential than almost any amount of figures. You might follow the reverse process, using interviews in order to identify the key issues about which you would then ask questions in your survey. You might complement interviews within an institution with the analysis of available documents, in order to compare written and spoken versions.

Where two or more methods are used in this way, to try to verify the validity of the information being collected, the process is referred to as triangulation. This kind of approach should be carefully considered if your resources allow. Box 39 suggests eleven ways in which qualitative and quantitative research approaches may be productively combined.

### Allowing for changes of direction

Another reason for not restricting yourself in your planning to just one method or technique is to allow for possible changes of direction in the research project. You may find, for example, that you are not getting sufficient responses to your postal survey, or that it is not being answered satisfactorily. Or you may be unable to get access to many of the people you were planning to interview, or to the sites where you were going to carry out observations. Or, as you read the literature, you may find that your research questions have already been addressed thoroughly by others. In such cases, which are not uncommon, having planned to use more than one method should allow you to change your approach and direction more easily.

---

**Box 39: Eleven ways to combine qualitative and quantitative research**

1 *Logic of triangulation.* The findings from one type of study can be checked against the findings derived from another type. For example, the results of a qualitative investigation might be checked against a quantitative study.
2 *Qualitative research facilitates quantitative research.* Qualitative research may help to provide background information on context and subjects; act as a source of hypotheses; aid scale construction.
3 *Quantitative research facilitates qualitative research.* Usually this means quantitative research helping with the choice of subjects for a qualitative investigation.
4 *Quantitative and qualitative research are combined in order to provide a general picture.* Quantitative research may be employed to plug the gaps in a qualitative study that arise because, for example, the researcher cannot be in more than one place at any one time, or not all issues are amenable solely to a quantitative or a qualitative investigation.
5 *Structure and process.* Quantitative research is especially efficient at getting at the structural features of social life, while qualitative studies are usually stronger on process aspects.
6 *Researchers' and subjects' perspectives.* Quantitative research is usually driven by the researcher's concerns, whereas qualitative research takes the subject's perspective.
7 *Problem of generality.* The addition of some quantitative evidence may help generalizability.
8 *Qualitative research may facilitate the interpretation of relationships between variables.* Quantitative research readily allows the researcher to establish relationships among variables, but is often weak when it comes to exploring the reasons for those relationships. A qualitative study can be used to explain the factors underlying the broad relationships.
9 *Relationship between macro and micro levels.* Employing both quantitative and qualitative research may provide a means of bridging the macro–micro gulf. Quantitative research can tap large-scale structural features of social life, while qualitative research tends to address small-scale behavioural aspects.
10 *Stage in the research process.* Used at different stages of a longitudinal study.
11 *Hybrids.* Use of qualitative research in a quasi-experimental quantitative study.

*Source:* Adapted from Punch (1998: 247).

---

## ☐ Deciding about methods

By now, you may have a fairly clear answer to the following questions:

- How are you going to do the research?
- What is your strategy and approach?
- What techniques or methods are you going to use?

Or you may still be pretty vague. If you are in the latter position, you might wish to read around your subject more, and return to this point later. If you do have

---

**Exercise 23: Your research methods**

How are you going to do your research? Note down your present ideas or intentions.

---

---

**Exercise 24: Your research methodology**

What are the advantages of the methods you have chosen?

What are their disadvantages?

What other methods might you use as alternatives?

---

some ideas, think about them for a few minutes, and then try to summarize your intended research design using Exercise 23.

In reflecting on your plans, think about the details of what you are going to do for your research project. You may have said, for example, that you are going to read so many books or articles, complete a certain number of interviews, administer so many questionnaires or observe a group of people over a given period; or you may have mentioned more than one of these. Can you, however, say why you have chosen these particular methods? In other words, do you have a methodological perspective?

As we have already argued, thinking methodologically is an important, but often neglected, part of doing research. Exercise 24 is designed to help you to think methodologically about your research plans.

If you can answer the kinds of questions posed in Exercise 24, you already have, or are well on the way to having, a methodological perspective on your research. If you have some understanding of the range of possible research strategies, approaches and techniques available to you in undertaking research, you are going to be in a much better position to make an informed choice about which methods to use yourself, and how best to apply them.

## ☐ Summary

Having read this chapter, you should:

- appreciate that you already have many everyday skills which will be of use to you in your research;
- have a good understanding of the different approaches, techniques and methods which are available to you as a small-scale researcher in the social sciences;
- have decided, or be closer to deciding, which methods you are going to use, and be able to justify that choice;
- have a clearer idea of your own methodological preferences.

# ☐ Further reading

In this section, we list a selection of books which are of particular relevance to the topics discussed in this chapter, together with an indication of their contents. The list is extensive because a large number of books have been written on the subject of alternative research methods, their uses, advantages and disadvantages.

The listing has been organized into two sections: general texts and discipline-based texts.

## General texts

Ader, H. J. and Mellenbergh, G. J. (eds) (1999) *Research Methodology in the Life, Behavioural and Social Sciences.* London: Sage.

The focus is exclusively on quantitative methods. Topics covered include experimental design, clinical trials, cross-sectional research, longitudinal analysis, measurement models, graphical modelling, structural equation modelling and meta-analysis.

Bechhofer, F. and Paterson, L. (2000) *Principles of Research Design in the Social Sciences.* London: Routledge.

Designed for researchers who know what they want to study, but have yet to decide how best to study it. Chapters discuss experiments, representativeness, choice of locale and group, interviews, questionnaires, fieldwork, time, policy analysis, journalism and literature.

Black, T. R. (1999) *Doing Quantitative Research in the Social Sciences: An Integrated Approach to Research Design, Measurement and Statistics.* London: Sage.

This book is organized into six parts, covering research design, measurement design, the use of statistics, ex post facto, experimental and quasi-experimental designs, non-parametric tests and non-causal relationships.

Brewer, J. D. (2000) *Ethnography.* Buckingham: Open University Press.

Offers guidelines for good practice, and advice on the collection, analysis, interpretation and presentation of ethnographic data.

Browning, G., Halcli, A. and Webster, F. (eds) (2000) *Understanding Contemporary Society: Theories of the Present.* London: Sage.

Thirty-three chapters discuss contemporary social theories (including postmodernism, post-feminism, narrative and rational choice theory) and themes (from globalization through restructuring and nationalism to environmentalism).

Burns, R. B. (2000) *Introduction to Research Methods,* 4th edn. London: Sage.

Organized into four parts, which focus on general issues, quantitative methods, qualitative methods and survey methods. Includes many self-testing questions for the reader to check their understanding.

Cresswell, J. W. (1994) *Research Design: Qualitative and Quantitative Approaches.* London: Sage.

Which do you choose: qualitative or quantitative approaches? How do you write a journal article? These are two of the issues addressed in this text.

Davies, C. A. (1998) *Reflexive Ethnography.* London: Routledge.

A practical and comprehensive guide to ethnographic methods. Engages with significant issues associated with modernism/postmodernism, subjectivity/objectivity and self/other.

Fetterman, D. M. (1998) *Ethnography: Step by Step,* 2nd edn. Thousand Oaks, CA: Sage.

How does one manage a mountain of data and make meaningful statements? These are the key questions addressed by this book. Chapters cover anthropological concepts, methods and techniques, ethnographic equipment, analysis, writing and ethics.

Flick, U. (1998) *An Introduction to Qualitative Research*. London: Sage.
Deals with how to construct and interpret verbal, visual and observational data, with practical guidance on documentation, analysis, coding and categorization. Lots of examples, summaries and suggestions for further reading.

Frankfort-Nachmias, C. and Nachmias, D. (1996) *Research Methods in the Social Sciences*, 5th edn. London: Arnold.
Provides a non-technical introduction to the principal research methods employed in the social sciences. Covers theory, design, data collection and analysis, and computer applications. Appendices deal with report writing and using SPSS.

Goldblatt, D. (2000) *Knowledge and the Social Sciences*. London: Routledge.
Provides an introduction to key philosophical and epistemological issues in the social sciences. Addresses both positivist and interpretive methodologies through a comparison of contemporary debates about social change.

Greenfield, T. (ed.) (1996) *Research Methods: Guidance for Postgraduates*. London: Arnold.
Thirty-two chapters covering a wide range of topics, including research proposals, ethics, reviewing the literature, using computers, sampling, interviewing, statistics, models, writing, presenting and career opportunities.

Greenwood, D. J. and Levin, M. (1998) *Introduction to Action Research: Social Research for Social Change*. Thousand Oaks, CA: Sage.
The three parts of the book consider the nature of action research, science, epistemology and practice, and varieties of action research praxis.

Hakim, C. (2000) *Research Design*. London: Routledge.
A practical overview of the issues involved in the design of social and economic research, covering both theoretical and policy-related research.

Hammersley, M. and Atkinson, P. (1995) *Ethnography: Principles in Practice*, 2nd edn. London: Routledge.
An introductory text to ethnographic methodology. The chapters discuss access, recording data, analysis and writing.

Hantrais, L. and Mangen, S. (eds) (1996) *Cross-national Research Methods in the Social Sciences*. London: Pinter.
Examines critically the methodological and managerial issues arising from comparative research, with a particular focus on the economic and social policy agenda of the European Union. The book is organized in four parts, covering quantitative and qualitative methods, accessing information and evaluation.

Herzog, T. (1996) *Research Methods and Data Analysis in the Social Sciences*. New York: HarperCollins.
An introductory text, focusing on observational, survey and experimental methods, and the kinds of data which they produce. Includes chapters on scientific method, measurement, ethics and critical thinking.

Horn, R. V. (1993) *Statistical Indicators for the Economic and Social Sciences*. Cambridge: Cambridge University Press.
This text has been written to illuminate the connections between the production of statistics and the indicators used in their production. The examples are drawn from economics, sociology, social policy and planning. The contents include 'Indicator techniques' and 'Economic and social application of indicators'. The indicators discussed relate to the measurement of health, education, culture, war and peace, the labour market and productivity.

Krueger, R. K. (1994) *Focus Groups: A Practical Guide for Applied Research*, 2nd edn. Thousand Oaks, CA: Sage.

For those interested in marketing and gauging public opinion, this text takes the reader through the processes of conducting focus group interviews and analysing the results.

Kumar, R. (1999) *Research Methodology: A Step-by-step Guide for Beginners.* London: Sage.
Organized in terms of eight organizational steps: formulating a research problem, conceptualizing a research design, constructing an instrument for data collection, selecting a sample, writing a research proposal, collecting data, processing data and writing a research report.

Lavraka, P. J. (1993) *Telephone Survey Methods: Sampling, Selection and Supervision*, 2nd edn. London: Sage.
Outlines the processes involved in conducting telephone surveys. The book includes discussion of generating random telephone numbers, mixed mode surveys, new tele-communications technologies and on-the-job training of interviewers.

Lee, R. M. (2000) *Unobtrusive Methods in Social Research.* Buckingham: Open University Press.
Focuses on research methods other than surveys and interviews, including found data, captured data (i.e. observation), running records, personal documents and the Internet.

Linkogle, S. and Lee-Treweek, G. (2000) *Danger in the Field.* London: Routledge.
An analysis of the potential pitfalls in qualitative research in a variety of research settings.

McKenzie, G., Powell, J. and Usher, R. (eds) (1997) *Understanding Social Research: Perspectives on Methodology and Practice.* London: Falmer Press.
Three parts deal with the nature of enquiry, the nature of disciplines and research practice. Emphasizes that there is no single practice or correct methodology.

McNiff, J., Whitehead, J. and Lomax, P. (1998) *You and Your Action Research Project.* London: Routledge.
Offers practical guidance on doing an action research project as part of an award-bearing course.

Marshall, C. and Rossman, G. (1999) *Designing Qualitative Research*, 3rd edn. Thousand Oaks, CA: Sage.
Introduces students to the processes of qualitative research. Includes sections on data collection, data management, analysis and resource allocation decisions.

Mason, J. (1996) *Qualitative Researching.* London: Sage.
Focuses on the practice and process of qualitative research. Chapters consider research design, the generation of data through interviewing, observation and documents, sampling and selection, and the organization and analysis of data.

Maxim, P. S. (1999) *Quantitative Research Methods in the Social Sciences.* New York: Oxford University Press.
Reviews general statistical theory and methods, and explores the problems that quantitative social scientists face in conducting research. Topics discussed include scientific method, theory formalization, causality, statistical inference, sampling, experimental design, measurement theory and errors, and hypothesis testing.

May, T. (1997) *Social Research: Issues, Methods and Process*, 2nd edn. Buckingham: Open University Press.
The text does not assume considerable prior knowledge of social research and explores issues of perspective, social theory, values and ethics. Data collection methods such as official statistics, questionnaires, interviewing, participant observation, documentary sources and comparative research are included. Questions at the end of each chapter are designed to deepen understanding and reflection.

May, T. and Williams, M. (eds) (1998) *Knowing the Social World.* Buckingham: Open University Press.

Ten contributions examine the relations between philosophy, social theory and empirical research, how we can claim to 'know' the social world and what the properties of the social world and their implications might be.

Mikkelsen, B. (1995) *Methods for Development Work and Research: A Guide for Practitioners*. New Delhi: Sage.

A research methods text designed for those working in development settings. Particular attention is given to participatory approaches, poverty and gender analysis, monitoring and evaluation, and ethics and interventions.

Moser, C. A. and Kalton, G. (1993) *Survey Methods in Social Investigation*. Aldershot: Dartmouth (reprint).

A classic text in survey methods: all stages are included. These are planning, sampling, experiments, documentary evidence, observation, questionnaires, interviewing, scaling, response errors, analysis and presentation of results.

Neuman, W. L. (2000) *Social Research Methods: Qualitative and Quantitative Approaches*, 4th edn. Boston: Allyn and Bacon.

Comprehensive introduction organized into five parts: foundations, planning and preparation, quantitative data collection and analysis, qualitative data collection and analysis, and social research and communication with others. Appendices include the American Sociological Association Code of Ethics and a glossary of terms.

Oppenheim, A. N. (1992) *Questionnaire Design, Interviewing and Attitude Measurement*, 2nd edn. London: Pinter.

An introduction to survey design, questionnaire construction and attitude scaling methods. The text includes examples and exercises, with further readings indicated at the end of each chapter. Piloting, exploratory work, data processing and statistical analysis are also discussed.

Plummer, K. (2000) *Documents of Life 2: An Invitation to Critical Humanism*, 2nd edn. London: Sage.

This revised edition considers recent developments in the use of life stories and other personal documents in social research. Issues examined include the emergence of an auto/biographical society, writing and narrative, memory and truth, and humanism.

Punch, K. F. (1998) *Introduction to Social Research: Quantitative and Qualitative Approaches*. London: Sage.

Comprehensive introduction, which covers developing models for empirical research, the logic of quantitative and qualitative research (design, data collection and analysis), mixing methods, evaluation and writing.

Richardson, J. T. E. (ed.) (1996) *Handbook of Qualitative Research Methods for Psychology and the Social Sciences*. Leicester: British Psychological Society.

Fourteen contributions organized into three parts: introducing, using and evaluating qualitative research methods. Methods covered include protocol analysis, grounded theory, ethnography and discourse analysis.

Robson, C. (2000) *Small-scale Evaluation: Principles and Practice*. London: Sage.

Designed for those undertaking small-scale evaluations for the first time. Chapters deal with the nature and purpose of evaluation, collaboration, ethical and political issues, design, analysis, practicalities and communicating findings.

Sapsford, R. (1999) *Survey Research*. London: Sage.

Considers the nature of survey research, sampling, methods of data collection, tabular analysis, correlation, regression and factor analysis, analysis of variance, using existing data sources and reporting results.

Seale, C. (ed.) (1998) *Researching Society and Culture*. London: Sage.

Three sections cover: philosophy, methodology and history; beginning research (policy, theory, research proposals); and doing research (including chapters on social surveys, using official statistics, doing ethnography, analysing discourse and reading and writing research).

Silverman, D. (ed.) (1997) *Qualitative Research: Theory, Method and Practice*. London: Sage.

Fifteen chapters examine many of the issues involved in observational and interview approaches, and in the analysis of text, audio and video sources. Reliability and validity, and the use of qualitative research to address social problems, are also considered.

Sommer, B. and Sommer, R. (1997) *A Practical Guide to Behavioral Research: Tools and Techniques*, 4th edn. New York: Oxford University Press.

An introduction to the research techniques and tools used in psychology, sociology, anthropology and related subjects. Covers observation, interviewing, questionnaires, experiments, content analyses, case studies, and the use of personal and archival documents. New chapter on the use of the Internet.

Stake, R. E. (1995) *The Art of Case Study Research*. Thousand Oaks, CA: Sage.

A review of case study approaches written for students at undergraduate level. The text explores the ways in which a case can be selected, how issues can be applied to other cases and interpretation of evidence. Naturalistic, holistic, ethnographic, phenomenologic and biographic research philosophies are drawn on.

Strauss, A. L. and Corbin, J. (1998) *Basics of Qualitative Research*, 2nd edn. London: Sage.

Written for students, and located within the 'grounded theory' school, this text includings coding, theoretical sampling, using the literature and writing a thesis.

Tashakkori, A. and Teddlie, C. (1998) *Mixed Methodology: Combining Qualitative and Quantitative Approaches*. Thousand Oaks, CA: Sage.

The three sections of this book focus on the paradigms and politics of research (positivism versus constructivism, research design), methods and strategies, and applications, examples and future directions.

Vaus, D. A. de (1995) *Surveys in Social Research*, 4th edn. Sydney: Allen & Unwin.

With the novice researcher mainly in mind, this text discusses how to plan, conduct and analyse social surveys. Combines questionnaire construction and administration, sampling and formulating research questions, with techniques for coding, and developing indicators and statistical methods.

Whyte, W. F. (ed.) (1991) *Participatory Action Research*. Newbury Park, CA: Sage.

A range of papers which aim to make the case for participatory action research. Divided into two main sections, the book focuses first on those papers related to industry and second on those related to agriculture.

Williams, M. and May, T. (1996) *An Introduction to the Philosophy of Social Research*. London: UCL Press.

An introductory text, linking philosophy to actual research practices. Uses illustrations from the United Kingdom, Europe and the United States.

Yin, R. K. (1989) *Case Study Research: Design and Methods*. Newbury Park, CA: Sage.

Seen as a 'classic' text, Yin considers design, data collection, analysis and writing up a case study. The text includes exercises at the end of each chapter.

Yin, R. K. (1993) *Applications of Case Study Research*. Newbury Park, CA: Sage.

Aimed to provide guidance for those who wish to carry out a case study, the text uses examples from actual research. The text is organized into three parts: theory of case study; design and analysis; evaluation. The contexts used for illustration include education, management information systems, youth programmes and community-based prevention programmes.

## Discipline-based texts

Abbott, P. and Sapsford, R. (1998) *Research Methods for Nurses and the Caring Professions*, 2nd edn. Buckingham: Open University Press.
Aimed at readers who wish to evaluate and contribute to professional practice. Includes practical exercises and examples. Methods covered include interviews, observations, controlled trials, surveys and secondary sources. Also discusses reading and writing research.

Altrichter, H., Posch, P. and Somekh, B. (1993) *Teachers Investigate Their Work: An Introduction to the Methods of Action Research.* London: Routledge.
Designed for the professional development of teachers, this text includes exercises and strategies. The contents include discussion of the research diary, starting research, data collection, analysis and dissemination.

Anderson, G. and Arsenault, N. (1998) *Fundamentals of Educational Research*, 2nd edn. London: Falmer Press.
An introductory text to the methods and sources of educational research. Contents include literature surveys, research design, historical, descriptive, experimental, correlational, ethnographic, case study, policy research and programme evaluation issues. Advice is given on surveys, questionnaire construction, interviewing and focus groups.

Atweh, B., Kemmis, S. and Weeks, P. (eds) (1998) *Action Research in Practice: Partnership for Social Justice in Education.* London: Routledge.
A collection of stories from action research projects in schools and a university.

Bassey, M. (1999) *Case Study Research in Educational Settings.* Buckingham: Open University Press.
Suggests how case study research can be a prime strategy for developing educational theory which illuminates policy and enhances practice.

Bernard, H. R. (1994) *Research Methods in Anthropology: Qualitative and Quantitative Approaches.* London: Sage.
A comprehensive review of methodological approaches and techniques in anthropology. Includes ethics, focus groups, theory development, using computers for managing fieldnotes, doing library searches and analysis.

Bowling, A. (1997) *Research Methods in Health: Investigating Health and Health Services.* Buckingham: Open University Press.
Five sections examine the scope of health research; the philosophy, theory and practice of research; quantitative research (two sections); and qualitative and combined research methods.

Breakwell, G. M., Hammond, S. and Fife-Shaw, C. (eds) (1995) *Research Methods in Psychology.* London: Sage.
An edited collection comprised of four sections. These are concerned with the relationship between psychological theory and methodology; design and philosophy of research; data collection; and data analysis.

Broad, B. and Fletcher, C. (eds) (1993) *Practitioner Social Work Research in Action.* London: Whiting and Birch.
Written primarily for students and practitioners in social work and social policy, and particularly those concerned with CCETSW's post-qualifying guidelines, the emphasis is on practitioner research. Contents include women in management, working with children with learning difficulties, work in children's assessment centres and the probation service. A range of techniques used in social research are discussed, including repertory grid analysis, life history, Delphi panels and observation.

Burgess, R. G. (ed.) (1993) *Educational Research and Evaluation for Policy and Practice?* London: Falmer.
Written for students, researchers, academics, policy-makers and practitioners, this collection of papers aims to identify the key processes involved in educational research and evaluation. The book is divided into two parts: issues in policy focused research and evaluation; educational research and evaluation for policy and practice – some empirical studies. Discussion includes the relationship between contractors and customers, educational evaluations for the US Congress, local and national evaluation and professional development.

Cassell, C. and Symon, G. (eds) (1994) *Qualitative Methods in Organizational Research: A Practical Guide.* London: Sage.
With a focus on issues connected to studying organizations, this edited collection includes discussions of interviewing, discourse analysis, tracer studies, stakeholder analysis and case studies.

Cohen, L. and Manion, L. (2000) *Research Methods in Education*, 5th edn. London: Routledge.
Covering the range of methodological approaches in social research, this text draws on examples from predominantly school-based education. Chapters include discussion of triangulation, role-playing, interviewing, personal constructs, action research, case study, developmental research, ex post facto research and experimental designs.

Davidson, J. O. and Layder, D. (1994) *Methods, Sex and Madness.* London: Routledge.
An exploration of methods through research on sex and madness. Contents include discussion of using official statistics, the survey method, interviewing, observation in laboratories, ethnography and documentary sources.

Edwards, A. and Talbot, R. (1994) *The Hard Pressed Researcher: A Research Handbook for the Caring Professions.* Harlow: Longman.
A guide to practitioner research for those in health, education, community and social work. Includes the major types of research, such as experimental design, survey, case study, interpretive and action research.

Field, D., Clark, D., Corner, J. and Davis, C. (eds) (2000) *Researching Palliative Care.* Buckingham: Open University Press.
Aimed at those involved in palliative care who wish to pursue research, this book identifies key methods, provides examples of issues and practices, and discusses related methodological and ethical issues.

Fuller, R. and Petch, A. (1995) *Practitioner Research: The Reflexive Social Worker.* Buckingham: Open University Press.
Designed with the busy practitioner in mind, this book offers advice on realistic ways for studying one's own agency. Illustrated with many real life examples, there is a particular focus on how research skills can be married to insights from practice.

Halpin, D. and Troyna, B. (eds) (1994) *Researching Education Policy: Ethical and Methodological Issues.* London: Falmer.
This edited collection is concerned to explore three dimensions of policy-related research. These are issues of sponsorship and contract, ethics and methodological perspectives. The papers discuss the Education Reform Act 1988, school governance, parents and policy elites.

Hart, E. and Bond, M. (1995) *Action Research for Health and Social Care: A Guide to Practice.* Buckingham: Open University Press.
Designed as a core text for students in higher education and practitioners on professional training courses, the text is composed of three parts. Part 1, 'Action research in context, process and practice', traces the history of action research and its linkages to

education, management, community development and nursing research. Part 2, 'Action research case studies', includes both successful examples and those which, as the authors describe, indicate 'instructive failure'. Part 3, 'Working from a project perspective', provides a 'toolkit' for researchers.

Hastrup, K. and Hervick, P. (eds) (1994) *Social Experience and Anthropological Knowledge*. London: Routledge.
Traces the research process from fieldwork to data analysis. It shows how an ethnographer arrives at an understanding of 'culture' and 'society', and of how they change. Topics covered vary from ageing in rural France to reflexivity and moral judgement in Greece.

Haworth, J. (ed.) (1995) *Psychological Research*. London: Routledge.
Intended as a practical guide for new researchers. A range of authors explain research strategies and theories as exemplified in their own work.

Hawtin, M., Hughes, G. and Percey-Smith, J., with Foreman, A. (1994) *Community Profiling: Auditing Social Needs*. Buckingham: Open University Press.
With an emphasis on 'practical' research projects, this text has been written for those with an interest in housing, community care, community health, urban regeneration and local economic development. The text includes the analysis of concepts such as community and needs assessment. Using secondary data sets, conducting surveys, analysis and presenting the data are also outlined. Chapters on community involvement and related dissemination issues are also included.

Hayes, N. (2000) *Doing Psychological Research: Gathering and Analysing Data*. Buckingham: Open University Press.
Organized into two parts. 'Gathering data' addresses techniques such as experiments, observational studies, questionnaires, interviews, case studies and documentary analysis. 'Making sense of data' examines different methods of qualitative and quantitative analysis.

Hek, G., Judd, M. and Moule, P. (1996) *Making Sense of Research: An Introduction for Nurses*. London: Cassell.
Aims to demystify research for nurses by explaining its role, providing an overview of the research process and outlining the main approaches to research.

Hertz, R. and Imber, J. B. (eds) (1995) *Studying Elites Using Qualitative Methods*. London: Sage.
First-hand accounts of studying elites, including discussions of access, interview strategies and writing up the research.

Jupp, V., Davies, P. and Francis, P. (eds) (2000) *Doing Criminological Research*. London: Sage.
Thirteen chapters examine issues in planning, doing and experiencing research in criminology. Topics covered include interviews with female prisoners, realistic evaluation of criminal justice, the measurement of crime and understanding the politics of criminological research.

Lee, R. M. (1994) *Dangerous Fieldwork*. London: Sage.
For those whose research may place them in dangerous situations, this text offers strategies and information. Includes research related to sexual harassment, drug-related violence and the study of gangs.

Lindlof, T. R. (1994) *Qualitative Communication Research Methods*. London: Sage.
Designed for communication studies students, this book offers a review of work in the area.

McLeod, J. (1994) *Doing Counselling Research*. London: Sage.

For those interested in researching counselling and psychotherapy, this text explores quantitative and qualitative methodologies. Included in the discussion are aspects related to literature reviews, evaluating outcomes and ethical issues.

Mertens, D. M. and McLaughlin, J. A. (1995) *Research Methods in Special Education.* Thousand Oaks, CA: Sage.

Offers a framework for critically analysing and conducting research on individuals with disabilities. Topics covered include literature reviews, quantitative and qualitative methods, identification and selection of subjects, information collection, data analysis, interpretation and reporting.

Morton-Cooper, A. (2000) *Action Research in Health Care.* Oxford: Blackwell Science.

Considers the ethos and principles of action research, strategies and advice for practitioners and researchers, giving support to those engaged in action research and critiques of action research.

Padgett, D. K. (1998) *Qualitative Methods in Social Work Research: Challenges and Rewards.* Thousand Oaks, CA: Sage.

Covers research design, ethical issues, sampling strategies, data collection and analysis methods, questions of rigour and relevance, writing up and combining qualitative with quantitative methods.

Reinharz, S. (1992) *Feminist Methods in Social Research.* New York: Oxford University Press.

With a focus on feminist research practice, this text offers a comprehensive review of the field. The text argues for the plurality of methods employed by feminist researchers, indicated by over one thousand books cited in the bibliography.

Remenyi, D., Williams, B., Money, A. and Swartz, E. (1998) *Doing Research in Business and Management: An Introduction to Process and Method.* London: Sage.

This book is organised in three parts, focusing on the context and process of business/management research, the most common methodologies and methods applied, and the reporting of research.

Robinson, V. (1993) *Problem-based Methodology: Research for the Improvement of Practice.* Oxford: Pergamon.

Focusing on applied research in education, this text argues that a 'problem-based' methodology needs to be adopted if research is to have an impact. The purpose of this text is to outline the processes involved in such an approach.

Rossi, P. H. and Freeman, H. E. (1993) *Evaluation: A Systematic Approach*, 5th edn. Newbury Park, CA: Sage.

For those concerned with the utility and effectiveness of social intervention programmes, this text is designed to outline appropriate methods of data collection, analysis and interpretation. The text contains discussion of diagnosis, measurement and monitoring, with numerous examples from evaluation research.

Schostak, J. F. (2001) *Understanding, Designing and Conducting Qualitative Research in Education.* Buckingham: Open University Press.

Offers a strategy focusing on the project as the organizing framework that ensures that the methods chosen are appropriate to the subject of study.

Stevens, P. J. M., Schade, A. L., Chalk, B. and Slevin, O. D'A. (1993) *Understanding Research: A Scientific Approach for Health Care Professionals.* Edinburgh: Campion Press.

Designed with Project 2000 students particularly in mind, this text provides an overview of research methods and methodologies. Chapters include: The scientific perspective; The research process; Qualitative research; The research problem; The literature review; Research design; Data collection; Reliability and validity; Data analysis; Interpretation and presentation of results; Evaluating research. The text includes study activities.

Stronach, I. and Maclure, M. (1997) *Educational Research Undone: the Postmodern Embrace*. Buckingham: Open University Press.
Postmodernism and deconstruction are connected to issues in philosophy, research methodology and policy critique. Literary theory, anthropology and sociology are drawn upon to construct alternative ways of reading and writing social research.

Thomas, A., Chataway, J. and Wuyts, M. (eds) (1998) *Finding Out Fast: Investigative Skills for Policy and Development*. London: Sage.
Focuses on key skills and approaches for research designed to inform policies, particularly on development. The four parts deal with conceptual issues, the use of documents and literature surveys, working with people and organizations, and data analysis.

Verma, G. and Mallick, K. (1998) *Researching Education: Perspectives and Techniques*. London: Routledge.
Aims to help the reader to understand the concepts and terminology used in educational research, and to provide guidance on initiating and implementing research studies.

# 4

## READING FOR RESEARCH

### ☐ Introduction

Carrying out a research project in the social sciences will almost invariably involve the researcher in a significant amount of reading, particularly if they are not already well read in the subject area. The work and skills associated with reading for research – how to read, what to read, how to make sense of your reading – can be a major worry and barrier for the relatively inexperienced researcher. The purpose of this chapter, therefore, is to support you in developing and using your research reading skills.

The chapter is organized into the following sections:

- **Why read?** The importance of reading for research.
- **Coping with the research literature**. Dealing with the volume and variety of reading available.
- **Basic reading strategies**. Guidance on what and where to read.
- **Using libraries**. How to get the best out of them.
- **Using the Internet**. Navigating the universe of information.
- **Good enough reading**. How to read.
- **Reading about method as well as subject**. The importance of understanding and exploring research approaches and techniques.
- **Recording your reading**. Being meticulous.
- **The literature review**. How to put it together.
- **Issues in reading**. Problems with too much or too little literature.

---

**Box 40: Ten reasons for reading for research**

1 Because it will give you ideas.
2 Because you need to understand what other researchers have done in your area.
3 To broaden your perspectives and set your work in context.
4 Because direct personal experience can never be enough.
5 To legitimate your arguments.
6 Because it may cause you to change your mind.
7 Because writers (and you will be one) need readers.
8 So that you can effectively criticize what others have done.
9 To learn more about research methods and their application in practice.
10 In order to spot areas which have not been researched.

---

## ☐ Why read?

It is possible to carry out research without engaging in much direct reading, though it would be unusual to do so without any new reading. This may happen, for example, where the constraints on the time available do not allow for much reading, where the method and context are familiar or where the researchers involved are being employed simply to administer questionnaires or carry out interviews for someone else.

We would argue strongly, however, especially where the research has an academic connection, that it is highly desirable, if not essential, to engage in related reading while carrying out a research project. Your research project needs to be informed and stimulated by your developing knowledge as you carry it out. Box 40 gives ten reasons for reading for research.

As you look through Box 40 you may recognize many of the reasons given. You may be able to add others as well. You should also see, however, that a mixture of positive and negative reasons is given. You may read both for the delight of discovery and to cover your back. You may read in order to contextualize what you are doing or to impress your own readers with your knowledge of the literature.

Box 40 also suggests two other important points about reading for research. Thus, it is essential not just to read, but to read at different stages of the research project and to read for a variety of purposes (see Box 41). For the committed researcher, reading becomes a continuing and wide-ranging activity.

## ☐ Coping with the research literature

To the novice researcher, it can seem like there is so much that needs reading, and that it is so difficult to get on top of or make sense of it. More experienced researchers, you may or may not be relieved to know, can have much the same

---

**Box 41: Reading at different stages and for different purposes**

*Stages*

- At the beginning of your research, in order to check what other research has been done, to focus your ideas and to explore the context for your project.
- During your research, to keep you interested and up to date with developments, to help you better to understand the methods you are using and the field you are researching, and as a source of data.
- After your research, to see what impact your own work has had and to help you to develop ideas for further research projects.

*Purposes*

- Accounts of research on similar topics to your own.
- Accounts of research methods being applied in ways which are similar to your own plans.
- Accounts of the context relating to your project.

---

concerns. But the new researcher may feel overwhelmed by the magnitude of these demands for quite a long time.

You may be concerned about:

- *The volume of literature.* The amount of material written on most subjects is already huge, and expanding at an ever increasing rate. How does the researcher get to grips with this?
- *The variety of literature.* There are so many kinds of literature (e.g. textbooks, journals, magazines, newspapers, policy documents, academic papers, conference papers, Internet materials, internal reports, novels) that may be relevant. How does the researcher use this range of sources?
- *Lack of boundaries.* Unless a project is very tightly defined, it may be impossible to judge which areas of the literature are relevant. How does the researcher avoid reading too widely or aimlessly?
- *Conflicting arguments.* As soon as you start reading, you are likely to be confronted by different opinions, arguments and interpretations. It may seem that no two writers agree about even the most basic issues. How do researchers assess these arguments, and place themselves within them?

---

*Hint:* If you find very conflicting arguments in your reading around, you may well have identified an issue or debate which would be worth exploring in your research project.

---

If you recognize these problems, and are not sure where to start in reading the research literature or what to do with it when you have read it, try Exercise 25.

---

### Exercise 25: Starting reading

Find half a dozen books, papers, articles, reports or other materials which seem relevant to your proposed area of research. Don't take very long over your selection. Then produce a brief, annotated bibliography of the chosen materials. Take no more than 30 minutes to do this, and write no more than a short paragraph on each book.

When you have completed your bibliography, think about what you had to do in order to complete this exercise.

---

If you found this exercise relatively easy to do, you may not need to read this chapter in detail. If you found it difficult, don't despair, as there are lots of helpful suggestions in the remainder of the chapter. Whatever you do, don't worry too much now: you don't have to do it all at once! If you can, allow yourself some time, especially at the beginning of your project, to be baffled and enthralled by the scope and variety of the literature available.

## ☐ Basic reading strategies

This section offers some basic guidance on four related questions:

- where to read;
- what to read;
- whom to read;
- how to find what you need to read.

### Where to read

The obvious place to read – at least, until the past few years – may seem to be the library, particularly if you are doing a research project in an academic setting. Libraries come, of course, in different guises. They may be wide-ranging or specialized resources, general or academic in function, for reference only or available for borrowing. This last distinction highlights a critical point, that of access. While public libraries are available to everyone, and university libraries normally allow access to all bona fide researchers, some may impose restrictions on borrowing or charge fees, and others may prohibit access altogether.

> **Using libraries** is the subject of the next section in this chapter.

The other obvious place to read, nowadays, is on your computer, making use of some of the vast range of materials now available through the Internet. Compared to libraries, the material available on the Internet is much more variable in quality. You do, of course, need to have, or have access to, a computer and Internet connection. Given this, access is easy, though at times it may be frustrating and can be expensive.

> **Using the Internet** is the subject of the next but one section in this chapter.

Beyond these sources, however, there are many other places in which you might read. Bookshops are an underused resource from this point of view. They have the advantage of being up-to-date, but may be restricted to certain kinds of material (e.g. just books) and will usually have little that is out of print. You don't have to buy the books on display, but will be restricted in what you can do if you don't buy them.

Your employer, colleagues, supervisors, friends, fellow students and research subjects may have access to relevant materials which they may be willing to share with you. A key strategy here for the researcher, particularly one working in fields where written resources are restricted, is to exploit as many possible sources and venues for reading as are feasible. Books which are unavailable in your main library may turn up unexpectedly elsewhere, while your colleagues or the subjects of your research may have access to materials of which you are completely unaware. So, where possible, use a variety of sources for your reading.

### What to read

The short answer to the question of what to read has to be to read as much, and as many different kinds or sources of texts, as possible (see Box 42). This will enable you to encounter a range of views and forms of presentation within the different kinds of writing appropriate to your topic.

The kinds of things you might read could include:

- *Books*: of all kinds.
- *Journals*: local, national and international, home and overseas, practitioner-oriented or research-based, popular and academic, abstracting journals.
- *Reports*: produced by institutions or organizations of different kinds, including employers, representative associations, political parties, trade unions, voluntary bodies, community groups, central and local government and international bodies.
- *Popular media*: the daily and weekly press, magazines, radio and television broadcasts.
- *Computer-based materials*: an increasingly important source, which may include both textbook and journal materials as well as discussion groups and websites.
- *Memos, minutes, internal reports*: produced by organizations you are studying, or which are relevant to your research topic.
- *Letters, diaries* and other personal documents produced by individuals of interest.

---

**Box 42: Sources, types and kinds of research literature**

• Books
• Journals
• Reports
• Popular media
• Computer-based materials
• Memos, minutes, internal reports
• Letters, diaries

• Published and unpublished papers
• Contemporary and classic works
• Introductory and overview texts
• Edited collections and literature reviews
• Methodological and confessional writings

• Primary sources
• Secondary sources
• Tertiary sources

---

In using these different kinds of written sources, it will be useful to bear in mind a number of other distinctions between types of material for reading:

• *Published and unpublished literature.* Much that is of relevance to your research, perhaps because it is a relatively new field, may not be published. Unpublished material (e.g. committee minutes), though more difficult to access as an outsider, may be of critical importance to your research.

• *Contemporary and classic works.* While it is important to be as up-to-date as possible, this does not mean that you should ignore older materials. There may be key classic texts in your discipline which you should refer to. Or you may find that much the same issues which you are addressing have been tackled by others quite some time ago.

• *Introductory and overview texts.* All disciplines have produced one or more basic texts which summarize the development and current state of thinking. Typically designed for sixth form or undergraduate audiences, these texts can be very useful means for reading quickly into a new or unfamiliar subject area, or for refreshing your understanding.

• *Edited collections and literature reviews.* These may also be of particular use to you when starting your research, particularly if they have been recently published. Edited collections, including those published by the Open University as course materials, can be an excellent introduction to a given topic. Literature reviews may be invaluable as well, but do not place too much reliance on their opinions or selection. Wherever possible, refer to the original materials as well so that you can form your own views.

• *Methodological and confessional accounts.* In addition to reading books and papers which relate directly to the issues you are researching, you should also consider reading material on the approaches, techniques and methods you are using in your research project. These may focus on the methods themselves or on other people's experience of applying them. More guidance on this is given in the section on **Reading about method as well as subject** later in this chapter.

Finally, in your reading you should be aware of the extent to which texts present and make use of original data:

> Some texts contain mostly data. Others contain discussions and interpretations of data, in which the author is arguing for a particular point of view. A third kind of text contains relatively little argument, much presentation of information and few references to the sources of that information. We call these three kinds of texts primary, secondary and tertiary sources.
>
> (Taylor 1989: 56)

You would be unwise to restrict your reading mainly to tertiary sources, which tend to be of a journalistic or polemical character, though these can be valuable and may be central to your research.

## Whom to read

Faced with a bookshelf containing 20 or 30 books on the same topic, or decades or dozens of journals, it can be very difficult to decide where to start. You might choose one volume at random, or take a more considered view, perhaps selecting the most recent book written and published in your country.

In doing so, it is important to be aware of whom you are reading, where they are coming from, how authoritative a voice they have and what their motivations in writing might be. In part, your aim should be to read a range of views, exploring both the founding thinkers or the great names of your field and the diversity of current opinions. Remember, however, that everyone is capable of being mistaken in opinions or interpretations. That is, after all, the purpose of research writing: to stimulate further thinking.

You should be able to get plenty of guidance on whom to read, at least to start with, from your supervisor, manager, colleagues or fellow researchers. Some of the kinds of sources mentioned above, particularly literature reviews, are also excellent places to go for suggestions on whom to read. As you read more and more literature, you will begin to build up a view of the most quoted or cited authors, and the classic texts; but you should also follow your own hunches and seek out less-read materials.

> *Hint:* Take some time to just browse – serendipity is a wonderful thing.

## How to find what you need to read

If you are a researcher tackling an unfamiliar field of study for the first time, you need to be able to get to grips with the relevant literature as quickly as possible.

---

**Box 43: Eight stages in finding what you need to read**

1  Take advice from available sources: your supervisor, manager, fellow researchers or students.
2  Locate books, journals or other materials that appear relevant by asking advice, browsing around or using a library catalogue or Internet search engine (see the following two sections on **Using libraries** and **Using the Internet** for further advice). You will find that keyword searches can be particularly useful.
3  Once you have identified relevant shelf or Internet locations, look at other sources there which are relevant to your topic.
4  Once you have identified relevant journals, look through recent issues to find the most up-to-date writing on your topic.
5  Read outwards from your original sources by following up interesting-looking references.
6  Identify key texts by noting those that are referred to again and again. Make sure that you read the most popular or relevant of these. Seek out the latest editions.
7  As you develop a feeling for the literature relevant to your field, try to ensure that you have some understanding of, and have done some reading within, its different areas.
8  Use the time and resources you have available to do as much pertinent reading as possible.

---

Your aim should be to become familiar with the key texts on your subject area, and to supplement this understanding with a broader and more selective reading around the topic.

> You might find it useful at this point to look at the section on **Focusing** in Chapter 2.

Box 43 presents an eight-stage approach to finding what you need to read. For advice on how to read it, see the later section on **Good enough reading**.

## ☐ Using libraries

Almost any library, and particularly academic libraries, will have a wide range of facilities and resources available to support you in your research. They are not just about books! If you doubt this, or haven't been in a good library for a while, try Exercise 26.

You may have identified a wide variety of potential sources of information or advice, depending on your experience of using libraries. Box 44 details six main sources with which you will probably need to be familiar if you are going to do a reasonable amount of reading and you wish to be up to date.

---

**Exercise 26: Using your library**

Pay a visit to a library you envisage using for your research project. This may be a university or college library, a library attached to a specialist organization or your main local public library.

Look around the library and identify the different sources of information or advice which might be of use to you in your research. Find out about Internet access, electronic information sources and bibiliographic services. If you have time, familiarize yourself with these sources, and assess their varied advantages and disadvantages. Make a list of your findings.

---

Note that we have started this list with librarians themselves, and ended it with what is perhaps the most obvious source, the shelves of books and journals themselves.

*Hint:* Remember that all the books on one topic, and with the same class mark, may not be gathered together on the same shelf or shelves. Oversize books and pamphlets are often separately shelved, some older books may be kept in store, while very popular books may be in a reserve section. You need to be able to identify and use all these locations.

There are a number of other points which you should bear in mind when using your library, particularly if you are conducting your research at least partly for academic credit.

**Reading journals as well as books**

Don't neglect to read the journals relevant to your topic. These are the only reasonably up-to-date guide to thinking in your subject area, and will include much material that has not yet made it, and may never make it, into books.

**Accessing materials not in the library**

You may run up against the problem of identifying materials which look of interest and then finding that they are not available in the library you are in. Two obvious strategies for responding to this problem are the use of alternative libraries or sources, and accessing materials through the inter-library loan system. Each of these has associated costs. Practically, there are limits on what can be expected of any individual library and on how much reading a researcher can be expected to do.

---

**Box 44: Sources of information in the library**

- *Librarians.* These are an endangered species, yet are usually keen and interested to help. Researchers owe a duty to librarians to make good use of them, and there is much that a librarian may be able to advise you on or help you with, if approached in the right way.
- *Catalogues.* Whether in the form of the traditional card index, housed on microfiche or on a computer, you need to understand how a library is catalogued if you are going to make best use of it. Once you know how your subject interests are coded, you should be able to search for other materials sharing these codes. Or, with computer-based catalogues, you can usually search using key words, subject titles or authors' names.
- *Databases and computers.* Larger libraries will often have computer-based sources which go beyond the materials they house themselves. They will usually be linked up to the Internet. A variety of databases (e.g. ERIC, BIDS) allow the reader to search for relevant materials using key words, and to scroll through summary or detailed information on these texts. Practice may be needed to make full use of the range of facilities available.
- *Abstracts and reviews.* Two other specialist sources are of considerable use to the researcher if they are available. Abstracts are published in book, journal or on-line form on an increasing variety of subjects, and contain up-to-date summary material on recent publications in their fields. Reviews are contained in a wide variety of popular or specialist periodicals, and can be an invaluable guide to what has been recently published that might be worth reading or is influential.
- *Dictionaries and encyclopedias.* Larger general and any specialist dictionaries and encyclopedias can also be a useful starting point, though they typically will not go far enough into any particular topic to be of continuing use.
- *Open shelves.* Finally, and perhaps most obviously, most libraries have a considerable area of open shelving, containing both books and journals (bound and current issues). Browsing these can guide you to which areas of the library are likely to be of most use, and indicate the scope of the library's holdings in particular areas. Many key texts are unlikely to be on the shelves at any one time, of course, as they will be on loan or in use, so this method should only be used in conjunction with other, more comprehensive forms of searching. Recall books on loan immediately if you think they may be of interest.

---

The question of how much to read is considered in the section on **Issues in reading** later in this chapter.

Before you do try to access materials which are not in your library, make sure you have checked what is in them using available databases, abstracts or digests.

**Photocopying**

Where you cannot borrow materials, or do not have the time to bring them back, you may wish to photocopy selected items. Cost will probably be a limiting factor here, as will the legal restrictions on copyright. Nevertheless, many researchers make considerable use of photocopying facilities, spending limited time in the library and then reading what they have copied as and when convenient.

> *Hint:* When using a photocopier, you may find that it saves you money and time, as long as your eyesight is good enough, to use the 'reduce' button, printing two pages at half size on one. It is also a good idea to photocopy materials starting from the last page and working backwards: that way they come out of the copier in the correct order.

## ☐ Using the Internet

> In the last few years the increase in the amount of information that can be found on-line has been enormous. Many bibliographic sources are available in several formats – as hard copy, on CD-ROM, and on-line via the Internet. If you have on-line access via a computer it is possible to search for the details of books, journal articles and conference proceedings, as well as for data such as statistics, maps, contacts in organizations, email addresses and so on. You may also be able to access on-line the full text of many of the primary sources you need, particularly journal articles. The number of periodical titles that are available electronically is growing rapidly.
>
> (Baker 1999: 64)

There is no doubt that the opportunities for searching for information via the Internet are enormous. Indeed, the accessibility of this information makes it a very attractive source for research. However, having the world's library at your fingertips can also be bewildering and time-consuming, as one link leads you on to the next. This is why a search using the Internet needs to be systematic and carefully managed, and requires you to keep an eye on the quality of the information you are accessing.

> See the section later in this chapter on **The literature review** for further advice on systematic searching.

Box 45 illustrates some of the Internet resources that will be useful for social science and humanities researchers. We would draw your attention to four of the categories listed. These are *search engines, metasearch engines, directories* and *Internet gateways*. For many students, a first step on the Internet is to use a

---

**Box 45: Key sites for social science researchers**

*Examples of Internet gateways*

http://sosig.ac.uk/
The Social Science Information Gateway (SOSIG) provides access to key sites. Coverage includes business and management, economics, education, environmental sciences and issues, ethnology, ethnography, anthropology, geography, government and public administration, law, philosophy, politics, psychology, social science policy and methodology, social welfare, sociology, statistics, women's studies.

http://www.niss.ac.uk
The National Information Systems and Services (NISS) gateway provides key information resources on the UK education sector.

http://portico.bl.uk/gabriel/en/countries.html
Gabriel provides a gateway to Europe's national libraries.

http://www.ciolek.com/WWWVL-InfoQuality.html
The Information Quality WWW Virtual Library. This site gives information relating to the use of net-based sources of information in academic research.

*Examples of specific sites for reports of research, bibliographic databases or research databases*

http://www.esrc.ac.uk
This is the site for the Economic and Social Research Council (ESRC), the key funding body for social science research and postgraduate studentships in the UK. It offers links to other research councils, funding organizations, government departments, media, political parties, learned societies and European research councils.

http://www.regard.ac.uk
REGARD is a fully searchable database of research funded by the ESRC. It comes with a set of handy hints and tips for Internet searching (see Box 47).

http://www.data-archive.ac.uk/
Also funded by the ESRC, this data archive is based at the University of Essex and houses the largest collection of accessible computer-readable data in the social sciences and humanities in the UK. The archive can provide data to help in masters and PhD research, especially for those working in the fields of economics, statistics, politics, sociology, accountancy, business studies, public health, welfare and history. It offers links to a range of other relevant information resources.

http://www.essex.ac.uk/qualidata/
Also funded by the ESRC and housed at the University of Essex, this is an archive of qualitative research data, mainly arising from ESRC funded projects. One of the aims of the site is to encourage the secondary use of archived qualitative data. Links to a range of other relevant information sources.

http://caqdas.soc.surrey.ac.uk/
This is the Computer Assisted Qualitative Data Analysis Software site, again set up by the ESRC. Its aims are to disseminate information needed to choose and use a range of software programs that have been designed to assist with qualitative data analysis. It has an exceptionally useful bibliography with hot-links to actual articles and other sites. There is also an advisory help-line.

http://www.statistics.gov.uk/
This is the site of the UK Office for National Statistics. On this you will find
StatBase, which is an on-line encyclopaedia of official statistics.

http://www.bl.uk/
This is the British Library site, including information on 16 million books and
periodicals, 660,000 newspaper titles, 295,000 manuscripts, 4 million maps,
1.4 million music scores and 205,000 photographs.

*Examples of search engines*

http://www/excite.co.uk/

http://www.ukplus.co.uk/

*Examples of metasearch engines*

http://www.allonesearch.com/
All-in-One houses over 500 of the Internet's search engines, databases, indexes
and directories in a single site.

http://www.BigHub.com/
Formerly called iSleuth and now renamed BigHub.com. Using this site will enable you
to search multiple engines, web directories and news databases simultaneously.

*Examples of directories*

http://www.dir.yahoo.com/Social-Science/
Classifies information into categories that enable you to restrict the search and so
improve the quality of returned information. Categories include African studies,
American studies, anthropology, area studies, Asian studies, economics, political
science, psychology, science, technology and society, social work, sociology, urban
studies, women's studies.

http://www.ipl.org/ref/
The Internet Public Library offers directories and research facilities for academics.

*Web training*

http://www.vts.rdn.ac.uk/
The RDN Virtual Training Suite is provided by the Institute of Learning, Research
and Teaching at Bristol University. It offers a set of free 'teach yourself' tutorials
in a growing number of social science subject areas for students, lecturers and
researchers who want to find out what the Internet can offer.

http://tramss.data-archive.ac.uk/
This is the website of the Teaching Resources and Materials for Social Scientists
(TRAMSS) at the Institute of Education, London. The aim of the site is to extend the
use of large and complex social science data sets and appropriate analytical tools.

*search engine*, such as Excite, Lycos or UKPlus. One of these should help you
to locate the various sites that would be relevant to your topic. The search
engine identifies these sites by using the key word or words that you enter.
These key words are matched against, literally, millions of documents catalogued on the web to produce an index of sites of likely relevance.

However, the web is a huge resource, and the information it contains is placed on it by a huge variety of institutions and individuals. It is, therefore, absolutely essential to be able to distinguish between useful and useless information, and to assess the varied quality of the information found. Search engines use a scattergun approach, selecting *any* site that fits your key words, regardless of the source or quality. *Metasearch engines* can be more useful, because they search using several engines and bring information back to you in a more integrated way. *Directories* classify the information into specific categories, and can help you to restrict your search within a specific field.

> *Health warning:* Searches need careful refining if you are not to be inundated with lots of useless information.

Because of concerns about quality and the sheer amount of information, attempts have been made to classify material on the web into useful categories. This is done through what are called *Internet gateways*. These are sites that edit sources of information, so they can direct you more immediately to what is relevant and appropriate. A key gateway for social scientists is the Social Science Information Gateway (SOSIG), based at Bristol University. This accepts only worthwhile databases and sources and classifies them into subject areas. SOSIG is compiled voluntarily by a number of institutions and libraries: for example, the staff of the Fawcett Library edited the Women's Studies page. You can search the whole system by keyword, or just browse to see what is there. SOSIG also offers free on-line training to students, researchers and lecturers through the RDN Virtual Training Suite. These training sessions are designed to help you learn what the Internet can offer in your subject area.

> *Hint:* The web tends to run more slowly from about midday onwards (in the UK), which is when the USA begins to wake up. The evening is also a peak time for home users, benefiting from cheaper call rates. Early morning is, therefore, a good time to go on-line.

The adequacy of an Internet search – as when you are searching a library catalogue on a system such as OPAC – relates to the key words that you have entered. You need to take care that you refine your search appropriately. Most search engines use Boolean operators and syntax. This means that you can group words together, or exclude words, to ensure that your search is as precise as possible. For example, a search using the single word 'education' or 'business' will produce thousands of items of information. By refining the search to a specific area of education or business, using additional key words and one or more of the operators 'AND', 'OR', 'AND NOT' and ( ), you are more likely to find the sites that you are particularly interested in.

---

**Box 46: Boolean operators**

Most search engines support full Boolean operators and syntax. You can use the AND, OR, NOT and AND NOT operators, and parentheses ( ) for grouping. The expressions and symbols AND, OR, NOT, AND NOT and ( ) are known as Boolean operators.

The operator AND indicates that items must contain all the words joined by the AND operator. This is the equivalent of putting a plus sign (+) in front of each word.

The operator OR means that documents found must contain at least one of the words joined by OR.

The operator AND NOT means that documents cannot contain the word that follows the term AND NOT. This is the equivalent of putting a minus sign (–) in front of a word.

Finally, ( ) or parentheses are used to group portions of Boolean queries together. This allows for excluded and required words, and complex combinations of words.

*Source*: Adapted from McGuinness and Short (1998: 384–5).

---

If, for example, you key in 'adult AND education', this should list all those items or titles that contain both words. Or, if you key in 'business AND NOT small', the search should exclude all items referring to small business. Box 46 gives some guidance on the use of Boolean operators to help you to refine your searches. Box 47 reproduces the Economic and Social Research Council's advice on how to restrict and extend your search on their own database. You will see that this uses Boolean operators, but it also illustrates the usefulness of checking the 'help' tips on any system you are using to facilitate your search.

## ☐ Good enough reading

### How to 'read' a book in five minutes

If you are engaged in a research project, you will normally have to understand a great deal of published material of various kinds. If you attempt literally to read all of this it will take you ages. Most likely, you simply will not have the time to do so on top of all of your other plans and responsibilities. So you will have to be much more selective in your reading of most of it.

Can you read books, reports and articles quickly and effectively for research purposes? Can you get to the gist of the argument and pull out the material or details you want within minutes? If you are not sure, try Exercise 27.

If you were able to complete Exercise 27 to your satisfaction, you probably need read no further in this section. If you didn't find the exercise so straightforward, have a look at Box 48 for some hints and advice.

---

**Box 47: Too much or too little information?**

*Finding too many records?*

Try narrowing your search by:

• Using AND to combine terms, e.g. social AND exclusion.
• Use phrase searching, connect terms using underscore, e.g. social_exclusion.
• Use the advanced search option and restrict your search to a section of the record, e.g. title.
• Exclude words or phrases by using NOT.

N.b.: AND will automatically be used to connect terms unless you type in a connector, e.g. if you type social exclusion the search will be social AND exclusion, but if you type social NOT exclusion then AND will be overridden by NOT.

*Not finding enough records?*

Try broadening your search by:

• Using OR to combine terms, e.g. forest or woodland.
• Using truncation – type the stem of a word followed by an asterisk to find any other endings, e.g. econ* will retrieve economy, economics, economist etc. Be careful, however, as truncation can retrieve unwanted results: e.g. car* will find cars but will also retrieve carnation and carnage.

N.b.: If you switch on truncation by adding an asterisk in the search all the terms in that search will also be truncated. For example, econ* AND forest will retrieve economics, economist etc., but will also retrieve forestry, forester and so forth.

*Source:* http://www.regard.ac.uk/regard/help/tips/singletips/basic

---

**Exercise 27: Five minute reading**

Pick up a book of relevance to your research, one you have not read before. Give yourself five minutes, and then note down all the salient points you can about the book. Your aim should be to summarize the key message(s) of the book for your research. You might concentrate on the content, method or theory of the text, or try to do all three.

---

You should, with some practice, be able to get to the gist of a book, report or article in five minutes. In many cases, this will be quite enough, and you can move on to read or do something else. In other cases, however, your initial reading will allow you to identify which parts of the book or article need to be read more carefully. But you should rarely need to read more than 25 per cent of any book to get the best out of it for your own purposes.

Even this more detailed reading can be done selectively. You may find it particularly useful to scan relevant sections looking for passages which succinctly

---

**Box 48: Getting to the gist: some hints and tips**

- Note down the author(s), title, publisher and date of the book, report or article. Keep this record, and any notes on the content, safely.
- Look for an introduction, concluding chapter, abstract or executive summary. If there is one, read it quickly, scanning the contents. If the book or report has a cover, publishers' blurbs may also be useful.
- If it is a book or report, look for the contents page. Identify any chapters which you think may be of particular relevance and focus on them, again starting from the introduction and/or conclusion. You can find your way through a chapter or section by using the sub-headings.
- If it is a book or report, look for an index. If there are specific points you are interested in (people, institutions, events etc.), you should be able to locate from the index where they are discussed in the text.
- In the text itself, key points will often be highlighted, or in the first or last paragraphs. Similarly, the first and last sentences of paragraphs are often used to indicate and summarize their contents.

---

summarize or advance the argument. These sections are often worth noting down as potential quotations.

*Hint:* If can afford it, print off or take photocopies of key chapters or articles. You will then be able to mark these with highlighter pen, and make notes in the margins. Do this with books that you have purchased as well, or use Post-its.

Finally, in case you are worried that the approach suggested here is in some way inadequate, let us assure you of the contrary. All researchers use these techniques, or something similar. We couldn't pursue our work, let alone have time to do things other than research, if we didn't. Many suggested reading techniques – e.g. SQ3R and SQ4R (see Box 49) – are based on this kind of approach, and encourage you to interact with the text rather than repeat it uncritically or verbatim.

We must stress, however, that a superficial knowledge of the research literature relevant to your topic is not adequate. You will need to know enough about what has been written to criticize and summarize it intelligently. This means being able to give both a broad picture of the appropriate literature and a more focused account of those parts of the literature that are of particular significance.

## How to assess what you are reading critically

Reading academic material is not just about becoming an elegant reader who can grasp the overall sense of a piece, translate jargon in order to

---

**Box 49: SQ3R and SQ4R: strategies for reading**

*SQ3R*

SQ3R is a flexible strategy. You can apply it in different ways to different materials, to suit your own purposes. The basic stages, however, are these:

1 Try to get the general drift of the material you are looking at by carrying out a quick preview or *survey*.
2 While you are doing your survey, start asking yourself *questions* that you might expect to find answers to if you think the text worth reading more carefully.
3 *Read* the text carefully (if it seems worthwhile).
4 When you have finished reading, try to *recall* the main points.
5 Check how well you've recalled by going back to *review* the text.

(Rowntree 1991: 76–7)

*SQ4R*

1 Survey and question.
2 Read to answer questions.
3 Recite and write answers and summaries.
4 Review.

Advantages and disadvantages:

SQ4R is designed to help you focus on learning what is important to you . . . You learn to organise and structure your studying. You state your goals as questions, seek answers, achieve your goals and move on. You focus on grasping the key concepts.

It is difficult to change old study habits . . . It takes more energy to ask questions and develop summaries than it does to let your eyes passively read printed pages.

(Walter and Siebert 1993: 89–96)

---

extract facts from a text, while taking notes efficiently. Ideally, readers should learn to engage with a text in a way which enables them to assess its worth . . . being critical is learning to assess the logic and rationale of arguments and the quality of the substantiating data . . . it is being able to ask how important the flaws are, and so to weigh the worth of evidence. This means being able to ask questions of the text beyond what it means, what it is saying.

(Peelo 1994: 59)

Critical reasoning is centrally concerned with giving reasons for one's beliefs and actions, analysing and evaluating one's own and other people's reasoning, devising and constructing better reasoning. Common to these activities are certain distinct skills, for example, recognizing reasons and conclusions, recognizing unstated assumptions, drawing conclusions, appraising evidence and evaluating statements, judging whether conclusions are warranted; and underlying all of these skills is the ability to use language with clarity and discrimination.

(Thomson 1996: 2)

In everyday language, if someone is 'critical' we may be referring to a dressing down or personal attack. In research terms, however, critical reading, critical thinking and critical assessment refer to a considered, though not necessarily balanced, and justified examination of what others have written or said regarding the subject in question. An important skill at the heart of these processes is the ability to recognize, analyse and evaluate the reasoning and forms of argumenta-

---

**Box 50: Assessing an argument**

*Analysing*

1 Identify conclusion and reasons: look for 'conclusion indicators' (keywords to look for are 'therefore', 'so', 'hence', 'thus', 'should'); look for 'reason indicators' (keywords to look for are 'because', 'for', 'since'); *and/or*

- Ask 'What is the passage trying to get me to accept or believe?'
- Ask 'What reasons, evidence is it using in order to get me to believe this?'

2 Identify unstated assumptions:

- assumptions supporting basic reasons;
- assumptions functioning as additional reasons;
- assumptions functioning as intermediate conclusions;
- assumptions concerning the meaning of words;
- assumptions about analogous or comparable situations;
- assumptions concerning the appropriateness of a given explanation.

*Evaluating*

3 Evaluate truth of reasons/assumptions: how would you seek further information to help you do this?
4 Assess the reliability of any authorities on whom the reasoning depends.
5 Is there any additional evidence which strengthens or weakens the conclusion? Anything which may be true? Anything you know to be true?
6 Assess the plausibility of any explanation you have identified.
7 Assess the appropriateness of any comparisons you have identified.
8 Can you draw any conclusions from the passage? If so, do they suggest that the reasoning in the passage is faulty?
9 Is any of the reasoning in the passage parallel with reasoning which you know to be faulty?
10 Do any of the reasons or assumptions embody a general principle? If so, evaluate it.
11 Is the conclusion well supported by the reasoning? If not, can you state the way in which the move from the reasons to the conclusion is flawed? Use your answers to questions 5 to 10 to help you to do this.

*Source:* Thomson (1996: 99–100).

---

**Box 51: What is a critical reading?**

- One that goes beyond mere description by offering opinions, and making a personal response, to what has been written.
- One that relates different writings to each other, indicating their differences and contradictions, and highlighting what they are lacking.
- One that does not take what is written at face value.
- One that strives to be explicit about the values and theories which inform and colour reading and writing.
- One that views research writing as a contested terrain, within which alternative views and positions may be taken up.
- One that shows an awareness of the power relations involved in research, and of where writers are coming from.
- One that uses a particular language (authors assert, argue, state, conclude or contend), may be carefully qualified and may use an impersonal voice.

---

**Exercise 28: Practising critical reading**

Take a short article or part of an article. Using the information in Box 50, highlight 'conclusion indicators' and 'reason indicators'. If none are present, ask the two sub-questions indicated. Compile a bullet list of 'conclusions' and 'reasons for these conclusions'. Now use the questions under 'Evaluating' to make a judgement on the adequacy of the reasoning in your chosen article.

---

tion in the texts and articles that you will read. This skill is called critical reasoning. Developing a systematic approach to the analysis of the arguments of others is an essential research skill. Box 50 provides a summary of the key points involved in analysing and evaluating arguments, while Box 51 summarizes what is meant by a critical assessment of your reading.

Reading and writing critically can be difficult skills to learn. Exercise 28 encourages you to practise critical reasoning by applying the points in Box 50 to an article or short passage of your choosing.

*Hint:* Being critical does not mean rubbishing or rejecting someone else's work. As a researcher and thinker you should be able to entertain two or more contradictory ideas at one time.

The topic of writing critically is considered further in the section on **How to criticize** in Chapter 8.

## ☐ Reading about method as well as subject

### Why read about method?

We have already stressed a number of times the importance of understanding your research approaches and techniques, as well as the subject of your research. As the lists of further reading in this book indicate, there is a considerable published literature on research methods. As a researcher, you could gain a great deal from studying some of this literature. If you doubt this, consider Box 52, which identifies nine linked reasons for reading about method as well as subject.

### Where to read about method

There are a variety of sources in which you can read more about methods:

- *Methodological texts.* These may review a range of methods or focus in more detail on just one or two. The extensive bibliographies included in this book include many examples of such texts.
- *Methods journals.* These specialize in articles on the use and development of particular methods. Some examples are given in Box 53. Subject journals sometimes also have special issues which focus on methodological questions.
- *Confessional accounts.* These are articles or books which tell the story of what it actually felt like doing research, what problems were encountered and how they were dealt with. They help to undermine the idea of research as a clear, fault-free process, and you may find them very supportive when you encounter

---

**Box 52: Nine reasons for reading about method**

1 You are going to be using one or more research techniques or methods in your project work, so it is as well that you understand as much as possible about them and their use.

2 You may need to evaluate a number of possible alternative approaches and techniques before deciding which ones you are going to use.

3 If you are likely to engage in a series of research projects, you will need to develop your understanding of the broad range of research methods used in your disciplinary or subject area.

4 In doing so, you will be developing your knowledge of research practices, and will be better able to reflect upon your own practice.

5 It will help you to justify what you are doing, or proposing to do, and why.

6 It will allow you to see research for what it is, a social process with its own varying conventions and changing practices, rather than an artificial and object-ive set of procedures.

7 Your methods may be of more interest to you than the subject of the research.

8 You may need, or be expected to, write a methodological section or chapter in your research report or dissertation.

9 Simply to expand your knowledge.

---

**Box 53: Some examples of methods journals**

Behaviour Research Newsletter
Cognitive Psychology
Development Psychology
Education and Psychological Measurement
Evaluation and Methodology
Evaluation and the Health Professions
Evaluation Review
Historical Methods
International Journal of Qualitative Studies in Education
Journal of Applied Behavioural Science
Journal of Contemporary Ethnography
Journal of Philosophy, Psychology and Scientific Methods
Qualitative Health Research
Qualitative Inquiry
Sociological Methodology
Sociological Methods and Research
Studies in Qualitative Methodology

*Note*: This list is illustrative rather than comprehensive. It includes journals which specialize in discussing and analysing methods, those which have a methods section, those which regularly contain articles which focus on methods and those which report research using particular methods.

---

difficulties of your own. You will come across quotations and references to these throughout this book.

• *Reports on methodology in published research.* Any research paper will probably give some indication of the methods used to conduct the research described. This may be minimal or fulsome, and may include reflections on problems that occurred and suggestions for changed practice in the future.

The last of these suggestions is possibly the most problematic, as Exercise 29 may well reveal.

---

**Exercise 29: What methods do researchers use?**

Pick up a research report, paper or text of relevance to your field of study. If you can, choose a paper in a published journal, but, if not, any example will probably do.

See if you can detect what methods were used in carrying out the research reported. How fulsomely are these described? Is there any critical assessment? Are any suggestions made for future changes in practice? Have the authors indicated any other possible methods, and justified their choice and approach? Are details given of, for example, sample sizes and response rates? Are problems or difficulties mentioned?

---

Many published reports of social research contain relatively little discussion of the methods and techniques employed. Where methods are described, the tendency is to present them in a relatively unproblematic light, so that the research strategy is difficult to evaluate or question. However, in subject areas where methodology has not been a major preoccupation, such as in policy analysis, a growing emphasis can be detected towards making underlying concepts and processes more visible.

It would certainly be difficult to replicate most pieces of research using just the information contained in a journal paper. This is partly, of course, a function of the restricted length of most research articles, and of the pressures to focus on reporting and interpreting results in the available space. Yet it scarcely represents what might be called good practice.

It is usually necessary to study lengthier, and often unpublished, research reports, where these are available, in order to get a full understanding of the process of research. Even these may be inadequate, however, in which case a direct approach to the researcher(s) concerned is the only option.

## ☐ Recording your reading

Meticulousness, along with creativity, flexibility, persuasiveness and the ability to get funding, has to be one of the most prized qualities in the researcher. Being meticulous, from the beginning of your research project right through to its end and beyond, will save you time and trouble in the long run.

This is particularly important when it comes to recording your reading. You should resolve, right from the start, to note down full details of everything you read. These details should include:

* the author or authors;
* the title of the paper, report or book;
* the date of publication;
* if it is a book or report, the publisher and place of publication;
* if it is a chapter in an edited book, the title and editor of the book, and the page numbers of the chapter;
* if it is a paper in a journal, the title of the journal, volume and issue number, and pages;
* if it is a website, the date you accessed the information.

*Hint:* A number of guides to how to cite Internet sources are available on the Internet. See, for example, the following sites:

http://www.spaceless.com/WWWVL/
http://www.bedfordstmartins.com/online/
http://www.itcompany.com/inforetriever/

All the references listed at the end of the chapters in this book contain all this information. In addition, you should note the location and page number(s) of any material which you may quote.

There are a number of ways in which you might collect and store this information. Index cards are one obvious way, since they can then be kept in alphabetical or some other kind of order, as best suits your needs. Box 54 contains some examples of what your index cards might look like.

Alternatively, you could use a notebook. Or, if you have access to one, you could type your referencing details, together with a note of the contents and of possible quotations, directly on to a computer or wordprocessor. These usually have facilities for sorting your records, and for placing selected quotations directly in your text without the need for retyping.

---

See also the section in Chapter 5 on **Using wordprocessors and computers.**

---

It may seem tedious, but if you aren't meticulous in this way, you will give yourself much trouble and irritation later, when you are trying to locate and check details, particularly when you come to write up your research.

## ☐ The literature review

A literature review is a systematic, explicit, and reproducible method for identifying, evaluating, and interpeting the existing body of recorded work produced by researchers, scholars, and practitioners.

(Fink 1998: 3)

Initially we can say that a review of the literature is important because without it you will not acquire an understanding of your topic, of what has already been done on it, how it has been researched, and what the key issues are. In your written project you will be expected to show that you understand previous research on your topic. This amounts to showing that you have understood the main theories in the subject area and how they have been applied and developed, as well as the main criticisms that have been made of work on the topic. The review is therefore a part of your academic development – of becoming an expert in the field.

(Hart 1998: 1)

The ability to carry out a competent literature review is an important skill for the researcher. It helps to place your work in the context of what has already been done, allowing comparisons to be made and providing a framework for further research. While this is particularly important, and will be expected if you are carrying out your research in an academic context, it is probably a helpful exercise in any circumstances. Spending some time reading the literature relevant

---

**Box 54: What to put on your index cards**

---

Bryman, A.
*Research Methods and Organization Studies.*
London, Routledge, 1989.

The focus of this text is the application of research methods to the study of organizations. Designed for students in management and business, the contents include experimental, survey, qualitative, case study, action and archival research.

---

Kemmis, S.
Action research
pp. 42–49 in Keeves J (ed.), *Educational Research, Methodology and Measurement: an International Handbook.* Oxford, Pergamon, 1988.

A basic introduction to the nature and use of this research approach in education.

---

Francis, J.
Supervision and examination of higher degree students
*Bulletin of the University of London*, 1976, 31, pp. 3–6.

Includes discussion of the idea of originality in postgraduate research projects.

---

Winter, G.
A comparative discussion of the notion of 'validity' in qualitative and quantitative research.
*The Qualitative Report*, Volume 4, Numbers 3 and 4, March 2000 (Available: http://www.nova.edu/sss/QR/QR3–4/winter.html)

This article explores issues surrounding the use of validity in social research. It begins by exploring 'validity' in quantitative and qualitative approaches, and proceeds to examine the various claims to 'validity' made by researchers. The article concludes by suggesting that an understanding of the nature of 'truth' is central to the ways in which 'validity' is theorized.

---

to your research topic may prevent you from repeating previous errors or redoing work that has already been done, as well as giving you insights into aspects of your topic which might be worthy of detailed exploration. Box 55 provides an example of some of the questions a literature review can answer.

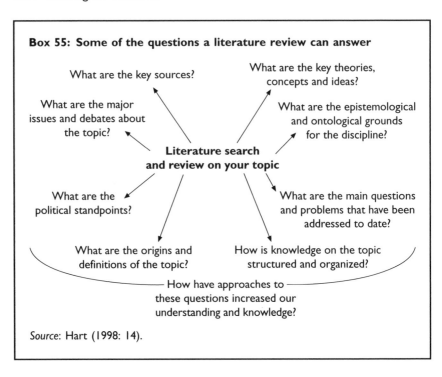

**Box 55: Some of the questions a literature review can answer**

What are the key sources?

What are the key theories, concepts and ideas?

What are the major issues and debates about the topic?

What are the epistemological and ontological grounds for the discipline?

**Literature search and review on your topic**

What are the political standpoints?

What are the main questions and problems that have been addressed to date?

What are the origins and definitions of the topic?

How is knowledge on the topic structured and organized?

How have approaches to these questions increased our understanding and knowledge?

*Source*: Hart (1998: 14).

Nevertheless, it is possible to approach your literature review in a variety of ways, and with a range of different purposes in mind. A number of these are summarized in Box 56.

A key point to note is that good literature reviews go beyond the stage of simply listing sources to offer an analytical study of the area, through which you can develop your own position, analysis and argument. A literature review is a critical summary and assessment of the range of existing materials dealing with knowledge and understanding in a given field. It may be restricted to books and papers in one discipline or sub-discipline, or may be wider ranging in approach. Generally, its purpose is to locate the research project, to form its context or background and to provide insights into previous work. A literature review may form part of an empirical study or it may be a study in itself.

In undertaking a literature review, you should find the general advice given in the rest of this chapter of some use. For more specific guidance, have a look at Box 57, which offers a number of suggestions designed to make your review more focused, relevant and enjoyable. In the past couple of years, there have been a small number of publications produced that have been specifically written

You will find guidance on writing up your literature review in Chapter 8, **Writing up**.

---

**Box 56: Literature review functions and typologies**

*Functions*

There are four main functions of a literature review. These are:

1 To give reasons why the topic is of sufficient importance for it to be researched . . .
2 To provide the reader with a brief up-to-date account and discussion of literature on the issues relevant to the topic . . .
3 To provide a conceptual and theoretical context in which the topic for research can be situated . . .
4 To discuss relevant research carried out on the same topic or similar topics.

(Stevens *et al.* 1993: 67)

*Typologies*

*as a list* . . . The primary focus is on the listing rather than on the knowledge contained within the literature represented . . .
*as a search* . . . Source materials act as an intermediary directing the researcher towards or providing an awareness of existing literature . . .
*as a survey* . . . the student's focus is on the literature, with his/her interest centred on the knowledge base of the discipline . . .
*as a vehicle for learning* . . . the student's focus is beyond the literature and on his or her personal development . . .
*as a research facilitator* . . . The impact of the literature moves beyond influencing the researcher to have an impact on the research project . . .
*as a report* . . . The report is not only a synthesis of literature relevant to the research, it is a final representation of interaction with the literature.

(Bruce 1994: 224–5)

---

to help students with literature reviews. Examples are listed at the end of the chapter.

## ☐ Issues in reading

As a novice researcher, you are quite likely to encounter some difficulties in reading for your research topic. The most common problems raised are:

• nothing has been written on my research topic;
• there is too much;
• it has all been done;
• how many references do I need?

These issues are complementary. Indeed, they may all be uttered by the same researchers at different points in the research process.

---

**Box 57: Doing a literature review**

- Ask your supervisor, manager, colleagues or fellow students for advice as to what is expected. If you are researching in an academic context, there may be quite precise expectations.
- Look at previous examples of literature reviews in your area of research. They may have been completed by former students or researchers in your institution, or published in books or journals. Many articles include at least a brief literature review. While you may take account of such previous reviews, try not to follow slavishly their structuring or argument. Read the sources referred to yourself wherever possible, rather than relying on others' interpretations.
- Make sure you include what are thought of as the key texts in your field, and that you locate this work within the broader traditions of your discipline, sub-discipline or subject area.
- If your work is going to be examined, and you are aware of the examiners' identities and/or their preferences, it is sensible to address these in your review. Examiners are human beings too. Refer to some of your examiners' work, demonstrate that you have read it and do not be unduly critical.
- Structure your review in sections to reflect different approaches, interpretations, schools of thought or areas of the subject.
- Your review should both summarize what others have done and thought in the subject area, and indicate your own response to their work and conclusions. Be critical – just because a work is published, even if by one of the key thinkers in your field, this does not mean that it is the last word – but not destructively so.

---

## Nothing has been written on my research topic

This is unlikely to be literally true, if only because it is difficult to be quite as original as this suggests.

It may be that you are defining your area of interest too narrowly. It is, after all, unlikely that anything will have been written on your particular issue or combination of issues, using your chosen methods and focusing on the particular cases or sample you have selected (if it has, consider changing your topic or approach slightly). But there is likely to be material on some or all of the issues of concern to you, perhaps in different contexts. And there will be books and papers on the method or methods you are using. And there may well be discussions of your cases or sample for other purposes. All of this material should be of some interest.

It may be that you cannot find relevant material and that you need further advice on how to get started.

Have another look at the section on **Basic reading strategies** earlier in this chapter.

If you are in this position, you might start again by focusing on the disciplinary debates which relate to your research topic, or by looking for relevant sections in basic textbooks by key authors.

If, however, it is really the case that you have stumbled upon a topic about which very little has been written which is accessible to you, you should probably consider changing your topic. Ploughing a little-known furrow as a novice researcher is going to be very difficult, and you may find it difficult to get much support or help.

## There is too much

> See also the section on **Coping with the research literature** earlier in this chapter.

It is normal to be overwhelmed by the volume and complexity of the available research literature, and much of this chapter is about how you respond and get to grips with this. The only answer is to start somewhere, eventually to begin to see patterns and linkages, and to get as much support and guidance as you can. Set yourself reasonable and limited targets, and remember that you cannot be expected to do everything.

If you still feel, after a period of time, that there is too much, you should consider refocusing and limiting your research topic, so that you just have to concentrate on one aspect of the broader literature you have discovered.

> *Hint:* If you carry out a search of the literature using a computer database, and this results in hundreds of references, do not download them all. Narrow your search further, perhaps by limiting it to works published after a certain date, or by adding to or changing your keywords. See Box 46 for advice on searching on the Internet.

## It has all been done

The worry that you will one day come across a piece of published research which effectively replicates what you are doing is a common research nightmare. It very rarely happens. It is highly unlikely that someone else will have made exactly the same research choices as you. There will be differences, however slight, in location, sample, size, instruments, context and/or issues considered. It is common, on the other hand, to come across material which closely relates to what you are doing, and which may suggest some changes in direction or focus. This is usually helpful.

> See also the section on **Panics** in Chapter 8.

### How many references do I need?

Even if you are carrying out a wholly library-based project, reading is only part of your research project. You need time to think about what you are reading, and to write. If you are doing fieldwork, you will also need lots of time to plan, carry out, evaluate and analyse this work, in addition to engaging in relevant reading.

Somehow, then, you need to be able to put boundaries on your reading. How and where? If you feel that you do not have much of an idea of the answer to these questions, try Exercise 30.

Exercise 30 should give you a rough guide as to what you might aim for in terms of references, but only a rough guide. Some authors over-reference, seeming to show off by cramming in as many references in a page as possible. Others under-reference, appearing to assume that all their readers have a good grounding in the field and are aware of the texts on which they are drawing, but perhaps giving the impression that they have read nothing. Some give bibliographies, but make little actual direct use of the works referred to in their text. Some never quote directly, while others produce texts which are little more than a series of linked quotations. There are also considerable differences in referencing styles between journals and publishers (see Box 58).

You should be aiming for a balanced approach between these extremes, but one which you are personally comfortable with, and which takes account of any regulations or expectations applying to your research. Box 59 makes some suggestions as to how you should, and should not, make use of references.

You cannot possibly read everything that might be of relevance to your research topic. So, as with other aspects of your research project, you have to reach a compromise between what you would ideally like to do and what is feasible, and do the best that you can within these constraints.

---

### Exercise 30: How many references?

Get hold of one or more reports or dissertations which have been produced successfully by other researchers in your organization or department. If possible, get advice on which are good examples or models.

If this is not possible, get hold of a research paper, report or book which you think, or you are advised, is a good example of writing in your field. This should preferably be an example of similar length and style to what you intend to write.

Work out how long the paper, report, book or dissertation is, in terms of pages and words, and note how many references there are.

---

---

**Box 58: Journal referencing practices**

Three issues of different academic journals in the social sciences were examined.

In one ethnographic journal, the number of references per article varied from 12 to 60.

In one social policy journal, the number of references per article varied from 10 to 140. The latter, a literature review, was an extreme case.

In one management journal, the number of references per article varied from 18 to 135. The latter, a research review, was again an extreme case.

While, in each case, the amount of literature cited was partly a function of the length of the article, this was clearly not the only factor.

---

**Box 59: Use and abuse of references**

You should use references to:

• justify and support your arguments;
• allow you to make comparisons with other research;
• express matters better than you could have done so;
• demonstrate your familiarity with your field of research.

You should not use references to:

• impress your readers with the scope of your reading;
• litter your writing with names and quotations;
• replace the need for you to express your own thoughts;
• misrepresent their authors.

---

It is common to spend too much time on reading, proportionate to other aspects of the research project. You should try to get a good understanding of the literature as early as you can in your research, aiming to appreciate the breadth of the literature and to understand in more depth the specific parts of it of most relevance to you. You should then move on to the actual research itself, but keep up with and return to reading to refresh, check and update yourself when you can.

## ☐ Summary

Having read this chapter, you should:

• understand the vital importance of reading as part of the research process;
• feel more confident about how to find relevant materials to read;

- realize that reading for research is a very selective process;
- appreciate the importance of meticulously recording what you have read;
- have a better idea of what is involved in producing a literature review.

## ☐ Further reading

In this section, we list a limited selection of books which are of particular relevance to the topics discussed in this chapter, together with an indication of their contents. While these focus on skill and technique, you should also be aware of debates with regard to 'reading' for the values and position of the author, and related to the conventional textual form as representation. Some relevant texts are indicated in the further reading for Chapter 9.

Brown, A. and Dowling, P. (1997) *Doing Research/Reading Research: A Mode of Interrogation for Education*. London: Routledge.
 Designed to help beginning researchers to organize and evaluate the research that they read, and implement small-scale research projects of their own.
Fairbairn, G. J. and Winch, C. (1996) *Reading, Writing and Reasoning: A Guide for Students*. Buckingham: Open University Press.
 This text comprises three parts: 'Reading, writing and talking'; 'Writing as a student'; and 'Developing coherent trains of thought'. Advice is given on drafting, developing argument and understanding the text.
Fink, A. (1998) *Conducting Research Literature Reviews: From Paper to the Internet*. Thousand Oaks, CA: Sage.
 A thorough guide using checklists, examples and exercises. Topics covered include refining questions to guide the review, identification of sub-headings and keywords, use of databases and the Internet, quality and reliability, and how to report the results.
Girden, E. R. (1996) *Evaluating Research Articles from Start to Finish*. Thousand Oaks, CA: Sage.
 Using examples of good as well as flawed articles, this book indicates how to read qualitative and quantitative research articles critically. Topics covered include case studies, narrative analysis, surveys, correlation and regression analysis, factor and discriminant analysis. Numerous questions are included to guide the reader.
Hart, C. (1998) *Doing a Literature Review: Releasing the Social Science Research Imagination*. London: Sage.
 Considers the role of the literature review, the processes of reviewing, classifying and reading, argumentation and organization, mapping and analysis, and writing the review. Lots of practical examples. Appendices cover, for example, how to cite and dos and don'ts.
Jones, S. (ed.) (1999) *Doing Internet Research: Critical Issues and Methods for Examining the Net*. Thousand Oaks, CA: Sage.
 Includes chapters on methodological considerations for online research, studying on-line social networks, survey research, measuring Internet audiences, naturalist discourse research and cybertalk.
McGuinness, K. and Short, T. (1998) *Research on the Net*. London: Old Bailey Press.
 Provides more than 4000 links to current sites for primary research information. Topics covered include accounting and finance, business, industry and labour, the humanities, health and science, law, national, international and general sources.

Mann, C., and Stewart, F. (2000) *Internet Communication and Qualitative Research: A Handbook for Researching Online.* London: Sage.
This book reviews on-line research practice and basic Internet technology, details the skills required by the on-line researcher, examines ethical, theoretical and legal issues, and considers power, gender and identity issues in a virtual world.

# 5

## MANAGING YOUR PROJECT

☐ **Introduction**

So, you've decided what topic to focus on in your research project. You've worked out your research approach, and settled on the techniques and methods you will use. You've located and begun to read some of the literature relevant to your topic. How do you actually manage and progress your plans so that you carry out and complete your project in the time and with the resources you have available? That is the subject of this chapter.

The chapter focuses on the various skills you will need to bring into play, or develop, in order to manage your research project effectively, and to cope with the problems that will arise as you proceed with your work.

The following issues are covered:

- **Managing time**. How to use your time for research.
- **Mapping your project**. Scheduling your research into the time you have available.
- **Piloting**. Testing your research plans before committing yourself.
- **Dealing with key figures and institutions**. The roles of supervisors, managers, employers and universities.
- **Sharing responsibility**. Using formal and informal relationships to support your research.
- **Using wordprocessors and computers**. Getting the available technology to work for you.
- **Managing not to get demoralized when things do not go as planned**. The ups and downs of the research process.

## ☐ Managing time

Before I started my course, an established mature student advised me to do a forty-hour week. This I seldom quite achieved but the self-imposed pressure kept me feeling that I ought to be working! Work meant anything directly related to my undergraduate studies, so included all the necessary reading and writing, and any discussions with fellow students that I can honestly say contributed to my learning. I tried to keep the forty hours away from the weekend, and definitely away from Sunday. I work much better after a break, and family relationships need nurturing.

(Hoyte 1992: 26)

People think about, describe and manage their time in a wide variety of different ways. How do you think about time? Try Exercise 31.

Now compare your answer with the options outlined in Box 60. Do you recognize yourself in any of these statements?

You should find it of help to you in carrying out your research project to have an appreciation of your own attitudes towards, and usage of, time. You need to understand your own ways of managing your time in relation to your energy levels and coping strategies, and to the demands made upon you. You also need

---

**Exercise 31: Thinking about time**

Write a sentence describing your attitude towards, and use of, time. Try to encapsulate within it how you think of time.

---

**Box 60: Attitudes to time**

I'm a night owl.
I'm an early bird.
I juggle lots of tasks.
I schedule everything in my diary.
I over-schedule!
I compartmentalize (e.g. I keep Sundays for the family).
I slot things in when I can.
There are too few hours in the day.
I sleep fast.
I don't have time even to go to the loo.
I cook the children's dinner and write my essays on the corner of the table.
I have to know I will be uninterrupted.
The less time I've got, the more I get done.
Time, for me, is really more about energy and motivation.

to think about the rhythms of your day, week, month and year. For example, some people cannot work in the school holidays because of the demands of childcare, while others see holiday time as a space which is sacrosanct and separate from work (and research). Some people like to keep Sunday free for 'family' activities, while others see it as an ideal time to study.

Think about the demands on your time and your own preferences in relation to how others think about it. In our rushaway world, time is perhaps the most precious commodity. No one ever has enough of it. However, as people living in an industrialized society, we do have a particular view of time. Whereas agricultural societies viewed time as essentially cyclic, bounded by the pattern of seasons and days, industrial societies view it as linear and finite. Yet we may still have glimpses of eternity (see Box 61).

---

### Box 61: Speaking of time

To sense time, to speak about time you have to sense that something has changed. And you have to sense that within or behind this change there is also something that was present before. The perception of time is the inexplicable union in the consciousness of both change and constancy.

In peoples' lives, in your's and mine, there are linear time sequences, with and without beginnings and endings, conditions and epochs that appear with or without warning, only to pass and never come round again.

And there are repetitions, cycles: ups and downs, hope and despair, love and rejection, rearing up and dying away and returning again and again.

And there are blackouts, time-lags. And spurts of time. And sudden delays.

There is an overwhelmingly powerful tendency, when people are gathered together, to create a common time.

And in between all of these, every conceivable combination, hybrid and intermediate state is to be found.

And, just glimpsed, incidences of eternity.

(Hoeg 1995: 233)

Part of the confusion about whether different activities are competitive or mutually enhancing has to do with the fact that we all necessarily live in two different economies, one an economy of finite resources, the other an economy of flexible and expanding resources . . . It is not possible to "have it all" because of the finite economy. There are only so many hours in the day, and no one can be in two places at once. But the potential value of any hour is variable. Sometimes, having more – or giving more – means there is more there . . . Fatigue may sometimes be an energy problem, related to biochemical depletion of various kinds; but much fatigue is really a vitality problem . . . When women argue that going back to school or taking a job outside the home will not detract from their capacity to be homemakers, they are often proved right by infusions of vitality.

(Bateson 1990: 168–71)

---

**Box 62: Using time for research**

*Delegation*
Can you delegate certain aspects of your research? For example, making appointments, carrying out interviews, tape transcription, inputing data to the computer, statistical analysis, typing of drafts.

*Reading effectively*
Train yourself to get through the literature, and to get at the nub of the arguments within it, more quickly.

> You will find that Chapter 4, **Reading for research**, contains much useful advice.

*Chunking*
You may be able to divide some of your research tasks up into small chunks which can be tackled whenever you have a little spare time. For example, if you take photocopies of materials you need to read, you could bring these out (e.g. during a train journey) as and when you have time.

*Relaxing with a purpose*
Make sure all your down-time activities have a clear purpose. You might, for example, be idly looking through a book to gain a sense of what it is about. Or you might use time spent walking the dog or having a bath to give you time to think. Don't think of such time as wasted: one of the keys to doing worthwhile, effective research is to allow yourself plenty of space in which to mull over what you are doing.

> You might commit such thoughts to your research diary. See the section on **Keeping your research diary** in Chapter 2.

---

We may set against the broader, almost spiritual, view of time enunciated in Box 61 a series of pragmatic, time management principles. These should be of use to you in managing your research, almost regardless of your attitude towards time and the amount of it you have available. Box 62 contains a series of such hints and tips.

## ☐ Mapping your project

Once you are clear about your own preferences and attitudes towards the usage of time, you should be able to draw up a draft schedule for your research. This will relate the time you have available in which to carry out the research – a

---

**Exercise 32: Seven questions to help you to use time effectively**

1 What are the most important things you have to do? Make a list.
2 How do the things you have to do depend on each other? What order must you do them in? Structure your list to see what can be done simultaneously and what the necessary order is.
3 What are the deadlines? Make a visual display.
4 How long can you afford to take? Work out how long you have available once everything you are required to do (e.g. attending lectures, taking the children to school) has been accounted for.
5 How can you estimate how long things will take? Time yourself in set tasks such as reading and making notes on an article, or conducting an interview.
6 What do you do if an essential activity is going to take more time than you can afford? Ask if there are alternative ways of doing it that would save time, or see if you can cut out some other activity. Can you speed up your performance through learning to touch-type or by taking a study skills course?
7 Whom else do you depend on for meeting deadlines? Remember other people's priorities are different to yours. You need to plan ahead and make your arrangements in good time.

Adapted from Orna with Stevens 1995: 75–82

---

given number of hours, days, weeks or perhaps years – to your other responsibilities and commitments, and slot in the various research activities you will need to engage in at times when you expect to be both free and in the mood to work on your research. Exercise 32 sets out a number of questions to help you to use time effectively for your research.

Just because you have drawn up a schedule, this doesn't mean that you have to keep strictly to it. It is difficult, even with experience, to estimate precisely the time that different research activities will take in advance. Some will take longer than expected, while others may need less time. Some will be abandoned, while other unanticipated activities will demand attention. So it is a good idea to allow for some spare time or flexibility in your scheduling. You should also revisit your schedule from time to time, and make revisions, to allow for such changes and to keep yourself on track.

There are a number of ways of scheduling your research time. Two are illustrated in Boxes 63 and 64. Each of these project maps has the disadvantage that it suggests a simplified view of research. The table, in particular, presents a rather linear view. The grid, by comparison, more adequately conveys the overlap or concurrence between the tasks to be carried out. Both are, however, real examples, as developed and used by small-scale researchers. While both were held to, broadly speaking, by the researchers involved, there were numerous minor changes in their plans.

When you have examined the two examples, see if you can draw up your own research schedule, if you have not already done so. Try Exercise 33.

## Box 63: Scheduling research using a grid

| MONTH | 1 | 2 | 3 | 4 | 5 | 6 | 7 | 8 | 9 | 10 | 11 | 12 | 13 | 14 | 15 | 16 | 17 | 18 | 19 | 20 | 21 | 22 | 23 | 24 |
|---|---|---|---|---|---|---|---|---|---|---|---|---|---|---|---|---|---|---|---|---|---|---|---|---|
| LITERATURE REVIEW | X | X | X | | | | | | | | | | | | | | | | | | | | | |
| FEASIBILITY STUDY: DATABASE QUESTIONNAIRE TO EUROPEAN PROVIDERS (INC UK) | | | | X | | | | | | | | X | | | | | | X | | | | | | |
| ANALYSIS OF FEASIBILITY DATA | | | | | | | X | X | | | | | | X | X | | | | | X | X | | | |
| CASE STUDIES UNSTRUCTURED INTERVIEWS PARTICIPANTS OBSERVATION: MOTHERS EDUCATORS | | | | | | X | X | X | | | X | X | X | | X | X | X | | X | X | X | | | |
| | | | | | | X | X | X | | | X | X | X | | X | X | X | | X | X | X | | | |
| ANALYSIS OF CASE STUDY DATA | | | | | | | X | X | | | | X | X | | | | X | X | | | X | X | | |
| WRITING DISSEMINATION | | | | X | | | | X | | | | | X | | | | | X | | | | X | X | X |

## ☐ Piloting

Piloting, or reassessment without tears, is the process whereby you try out the research techniques and methods which you have in mind, see how well they work in practice and, if necessary, modify your plans accordingly.

> The idea of 'informal piloting' was discussed in the section on **Focusing** in Chapter 2.

---

### Exercise 33: Scheduling your research

Draw up a grid, table or some other kind of schedule of your research plans. Break down the time you have available into units – of days, weeks, months or whatever. Identify the different and separate tasks you will have to carry out in order to complete your research. Allocate these tasks to appropriate time periods.

You may find it useful to include your intellectual development as well as the practical tasks involved in getting the research done in your schedule. This might include starting a research journal to record your thoughts, your general reading and your ideas for further research.

You should also allow some time for unanticipated tasks.

When you have finished, critically examine your schedule and ask yourself whether it is realistic. If you don't think it is achievable, you should seek advice, and you may need to revise your plans to something rather less ambitious.

---

**Box 64: Scheduling research using a table**

**Timetable**

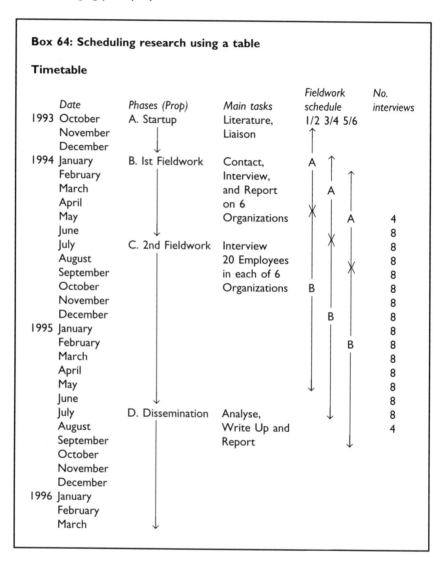

| Date | Phases (Prop) | Main tasks | Fieldwork schedule 1/2 3/4 5/6 | No. interviews |
|---|---|---|---|---|
| 1993 October | A. Startup | Literature, | | |
| November | | Liaison | | |
| December | | | | |
| 1994 January | B. 1st Fieldwork | Contact, | A | |
| February | | Interview, | | |
| March | | and Report | A | |
| April | | on 6 | | |
| May | | Organizations | A | 4 |
| June | | | | 8 |
| July | C. 2nd Fieldwork | Interview | | 8 |
| August | | 20 Employees | | 8 |
| September | | in each of 6 | | 8 |
| October | | Organizations | B | 8 |
| November | | | | 8 |
| December | | | B | 8 |
| 1995 January | | | | 8 |
| February | | | B | 8 |
| March | | | | 8 |
| April | | | | 8 |
| May | | | | 8 |
| June | | | | 8 |
| July | D. Dissemination | Analyse, | | 8 |
| August | | Write Up and | | 4 |
| September | | Report | | |
| October | | | | |
| November | | | | |
| December | | | | |
| 1996 January | | | | |
| February | | | | |
| March | | | | |

You may think that you know well enough what you are doing, but the value of pilot research cannot be overestimated. Things never work quite the way you envisage, even if you have done them many times before, and they have a nasty habit of turning out very differently from how you expected on occasion. So try a pilot exercise. If you don't, you will probably find that your initial period of data collection turns into a pilot in any case. In a sense, of course, all social research is a pilot exercise.

If you would like to pilot your research, and are not sure of the processes involved, try Exercise 34.

**Exercise 34: Piloting your research**

You have a fairly clear vision of your research topic and questions, of the techniques and methods you are going to use to study them, and of how you are going to schedule your research project into the time and resources you have available.

This exercise focuses on the process of collecting and analysing data. You may be using interviews or questionnaires, making observations or studying documents, or using any combination of these and other techniques. Do two or three practice interviews, or observations, or whatever else it was you had planned. It doesn't matter if the questions or structures you use are not fully developed.

Once you have finished your pilot collection of data, try to analyse the material you have collected.

Note how long these processes take you. Will you have enough time to collect and analyse all the data you had envisaged? Will it matter significantly if you do not? Should you reduce the scope of what you had planned to do?

Note also how well your data collection and analysis techniques work. How might you need to change them to improve their effectiveness for your purposes? Have you the time and expertise you need to do this?

## ☐ Dealing with key figures and institutions

There are a variety of key figures and institutions with which most researchers have to deal at some time or another. In this section, we consider the issues involved in dealing with the most common of these:

- at the individual level, your supervisor, tutor, mentor or manager;
- at the institutional level, your university, employer or sponsor.

Just how significant these individuals and organizations are will, of course, vary depending on your research project and circumstances. Here we focus on those that are likely to be of most relevance to you in agreeing, progressing, reviewing and assessing your research.

> The issues involved in dealing with informants and case study institutions are covered in the section on **Access and ethical issues** in Chapter 6.

### Key figures

The two individual figures which we have identified as being likely to be of most importance to you as a researcher are your supervisor and/or manager. A rough definition of these two roles would be:

- a supervisor has an academic responsibility for guiding and advising you on your research project;
- a manager has a responsibility for directing and overseeing your work in a more general sense.

In your case, you may have either, neither or both of these as key figures in your research project. The two roles may even be combined in the same person, though in most circumstances this is probably not advisable.

If you are doing research for academic credit, you will almost certainly have a supervisor (or supervisors), though his or her importance to you may be relatively major or minor, depending on your topic, level of study, institutional practices and individual predilections. If you are doing research within your employing or work organization – and you may be doing this for academic credit as well – your manager may be of significance. Their importance will, similarly, vary depending upon a range of factors, including whether you are sponsored by your employer, and whether your employer or manager has determined your research topic.

> The question of what you might expect from your supervisor is considered in the section on **Finding and choosing your supervisor** in Chapter 2.

I don't want to convey the impression that I needed to be guided by my supervisor throughout. In fact, it was just the opposite. It was more that I needed to talk to other people and to listen. It was not that I needed a supervisor telling me what to do, because if they had done that it would have had the opposite effect.

(Hampson 1994: 41, quoting an MA student)

You may in practice have a splendid relationship with your supervisor and/or manager, and receive good advice and sufficient support throughout your research work. If so, consider yourself fortunate, and be thankful. Other researchers have to make do with uninterested or overworked supervisors, mentors or managers. One point to remember is that your supervisor or manager is probably a member of an organization which will have its own expectations regarding both this role and other duties. You may want to discuss these with them.

Where your relationship gets off to a good start, it may change to your disadvantage during the course of your research (or vice versa). Or your supervisor or manager may move on, and you will be passed on to someone else. Box 65 details some general lessons about dealing with your supervisor and/or manager.

How, then, can you, as a relatively inexperienced researcher, go about developing more authority in these relationships and greater responsibility for your own learning needs? If possible, and if you have not already done so, draw up and agree a contract with your supervisor and/or manager. This should set out the tasks involved in managing and progressing your research project, and detail the specific roles and responsibilities of the individuals concerned.

---

**Box 65: Handling your supervisor or manager**

- Investing too much authority or responsibility in key figures in your research life is likely to lead to disappointment. It is as important to develop your own sense of authority and responsibility.
- In supervisor/researcher and manager/researcher relationships, responsibility is two-way. Just as you may rightly have expectations of your supervisor and/or manager, in terms of support and advice, so may they rightly have expectations of you. These may cover aspects such as scheduling, regularity of work and reporting back.
- Where you are carrying out a research project as part of a group, the situation is inevitably rather more complicated. A whole web of relationships and attendant responsibilities will exist between you, the other members of your group and your joint supervisor(s) or manager(s). Because of this complexity, it is important to be as clear as possible about the nature of the relationships involved.
- You should ideally aim to be in a position of sharing responsibility for, and authority over, your research. After all, it is you who are doing, and to a large extent managing, the research.
- If you ask for assistance or advice from your manager or supervisor, be prepared to have it refused, and still be able to move forward with your research.

---

Although such contracts are by no means foolproof, they should give you rather more leverage to influence matters if something goes wrong, and they help to clarify roles and expectations for all involved. Having some kind of contractual agreement, with your research colleagues as well as your supervisor and/or manager, is doubly important if you are carrying out a group research project. Box 66 gives some examples of the things a research contract might include.

You might like to try to draft a contract for your own research work, on your own, with your research colleagues or directly with your manager or supervisor. Try Exercise 35.

---

**Exercise 35: Drawing up a research contract**

Try to draft a contract for your research work. This should specify the duties and responsibilities of all the key individuals involved in the research project. This will include yourself, plus any co-researchers, and your supervisors or managers. You might want to include others, such as your partner or colleagues, in the contract as well.

Take into account any existing expectations and regulations of which you are aware. Try to anticipate the different stages or processes involved in your research, and how the duties and responsibilities you have identified may change over time.

Do not take more than one hour over the initial drafting process.

Discuss this draft contract with your supervisor and/or manager.

---

**Box 66: What a research contract might include**

*Responsibilities at university level*
- Defining university-level policy on admission of candidates for research degrees and monitoring the implementation of this policy by departments.
- Ensuring that students have access to appropriate information technology and library facilities, careers advice and, where necessary, English language tuition and welfare guidance.
- Ensuring that training and staff development are provided for research student supervisors . . .

*Responsibilities at departmental level*
- Providing an induction and research training programme which covers research methodology, the use of equipment and computer software, health and safety, ethical issues, intellectual property rights and transferable skills as appropriate to the discipline.
- Establishing and operating clearly documented monitoring procedures for research student progress, including feedback to students on their progress.
- Ensuring that departmental monitoring procedures are adhered to and that students are given every encouragement to complete their research to the required standard within their period of full registration . . .

*Responsibilities of supervisors*
- To give detailed advice on the necessary completion dates of successive stages of the work, agreeing objectives for each stage so that the thesis may be submitted within the scheduled time.
- To maintain contact with students through regular supervisory meetings and other types of structured communication as appropriate, to ensure that meetings are largely uninterrupted and of adequate length.
- To encourage the student to approach other workers in the field and appropriate academic bodies and societies . . .

*Responsibilities of research students*
- To seek advice from their supervisor(s) in an active manner, recognizing that it is the students' responsibility to have their own topics to raise with the supervisor(s).
- To provide an annual report on their progress to the graduate school.
- To accept a commitment to complete their project and submit their thesis in good time . . .

*Source:* University of Warwick (1999).

---

Research contracts can, of course, have disadvantages as well as advantages. These are summarized in Box 67. You may be able to think of additional advantages and disadvantages of drawing up a research contract with the key figures involved in your research. If your supervisor or manager, or your research colleagues, are unwilling to agree a research contract with you, you should at least be able to talk about your aims, needs and constraints, and how you will work together, with them.

---

**Box 67: Advantages and disadvantages of research contracts**

*Advantages*
1 They can help to specify your respective roles and responsibilities.
2 They can indicate the expectations held by both sides of the relationship, in terms, for example, of meetings or outputs.
3 They can help you to establish an initial working relationship, or to change an existing relationship.

*Disadvantages*
1 They may become rigid if not reviewed or revisited at intervals.
2 They may commit you to certain things you would rather avoid or keep fluid.

---

The key message here is to ask yourself what you want from your relationship with your supervisor and/or manager, and do what you can to get it. Open discussions about these issues during your initial meetings. Renegotiate or revisit these discussions, and your contract, as necessary throughout the life of your research project. Keep a record of these discussions, and of your contract, in the file you have opened on the regulations and expectations governing your project.

*Health warning:* In seeking to negotiate a contract with your supervisor, manager or mentor, be aware of the power relationships and institutional constraints involved.

## Key institutions

The institutions which we have identified as being likely to be of key importance to you in your research are your university or college, if you are carrying out your research project for academic credit, and your employer or sponsor. It may be the case, of course, that only one, or perhaps neither, of these institutions is of significance for you.

If you are researching, at least in part, for academic credit, you will, as we have stressed already, need to know as much as possible about the rules, facilities and practices of the university or college involved. You will need this information at an early stage, preferably before you even register and start your research project, if you are to manage your research effectively. Similar advice applies in the case of your employer and/or sponsor (who may also have a supervisory role). You should inform yourself as fully as possible about any expectations or conditions which they may set. Box 68 contains details of the kinds of issues you will need information on.

You should adjust your schedule to take account of all the points covered in Box 68, and try to build them into your research contract. Don't forget to add all

**Box 68: What you need to know from your institution**

*From your university or college*

In terms of facilities, you should know:

- what resources are available (e.g. libraries, computers, language laboratories, rooms), and when they are available;
- what research services are offered (e.g. questionnaire design, data input, tape transcription, statistical advice, writing workshops, language teaching);
- what library services are offered (e.g. databases, Internet, inter-library loans, photocopying), and on what basis;
- how these facilities are organized at university or departmental level.

You will also need to be aware of both your university's and department's written regulations and their unwritten, informal practices. These might include, for example:

- expectations of supervisors and/or tutors;
- rules about the roles of external supervisors and examiners;
- regulations about the time allowed to complete research, and regarding possible suspension or extension of registration;
- rules about the use of other's materials (e.g. plagiarism);
- pre-publication rules associated with the submission of your thesis.

*From your employer or sponsor*

- If you are being given some time out or work release, find out if you are getting cover or will be expected to do five days' work in four.
- Will your manager accept that every Thursday you are not at work, or will you have to forgo your study day when a contract has to be completed or a colleague is off sick?
- Will your employer or sponsor help to buy your books or give you an allowance?
- Will you get access to computing facilities at work for research purposes? If so, find out what is available.
- In what format will they require you to report back (e.g. verbal and/or written presentation)?
- Will you be required to pay back fees and funding if you fail, the research is deemed unsatisfactory or you leave within a certain period?

this information to the file you have opened on the regulations and expectations governing your project.

## □ Sharing responsibility

In the previous section, we encouraged you to take responsibility for your research project by recognizing the roles of key figures and organizations, and establishing your independence from them. It is also important, however, to develop interdependence with fellow researchers and colleagues. These relationships can greatly strengthen your support network and the value of your research. They may be formal, required or implicit to your project, as in the case of group research, or where you are under the direction of someone else. Or they may be informal, and developed in part by you, as in the case of personal links with other researchers or colleagues.

### Group research

The advantages and disadvantages of group, as opposed to individual, research have already been discussed in Chapter 2.

> You may like to have a look at the section on **Individual and group research** in Chapter 2.

In practice, of course, you may have little choice about engaging in group research: it might be a requirement of your work or your degree. You may, in such cases, be given guidance by your supervisor or manager on how to manage the group's dynamics. Nevertheless, there is no doubt that you will need, both individually and as a group, to work out early on your respective roles and tasks.

Researchers on groups dynamics have identified a series of group roles which need to be filled if a group is to work effectively. One such formulation, focused on reaching consensus, is given in Box 69.

To help you to think about the working of your group, you may like to try Exercise 36.

### Informal relationships

Even if you are not doing research as part of a group, or are not required to do so, you may like to set up a variety of informal relationships with others to help

---

**Exercise 36: Managing group research**

List all the members of your group.

Identify through discussion each individual's skills, motivations and working preferences. Do you wish to work as one team, as a set of groups or as individuals? Can you also identify group members who fill the roles identified in Box 69?

Using this information, and bearing in mind the nature of your research project, and the time and resources which you have available, negotiate how you are collectively going to undertake the work. Who will have responsibility for which elements? What arrangements will you make for sharing and progressing your work?

---

---

**Box 69: Consensus meetings**

*Roles in a consensus meeting*

The *facilitator(s)* aids the group in defining decisions that need to be made, helps it through the stages of reaching an agreement, keeps the meeting moving, focuses discussion to the point at hand, makes sure everyone has the opportunity to participate, and formulates and tests to see if consensus has been reached . . .

A *mood-watcher* is someone besides the facilitator who watches and comments on individual and group feelings and patterns of participation . . .

A *recorder* can take notes on the meeting, especially of decisions made and means of implementation, and a *time-keeper* keeps things going on schedule so that each agenda item can be covered in the time allotted for it . . .

*Attitudes and behaviour which help a group to reach consensus*

*Responsibility:* Participants are responsible for voicing their opinions, participating in the discussion, and actively implementing the agreement.

*Self-discipline:* Blocking consensus should be done only for principled objections. Object clearly, to the point, and without putdowns or speeches. Participate in finding an alternative solution.

*Respect:* Respect others and trust them to make responsible input.

*Cooperation:* Look for areas of agreement and common ground, and build on them. Avoid competition, right/wrong, win/lose thinking.

*Struggle:* Use clear means of disagreement – no putdowns. Use disagreements and arguments to learn, grow and change. Work hard to build unity in the group, but not at the expense of the individuals who are its members.

(Jones 1983: 138–9)

---

you in developing and progressing your work. Indeed, your employer or university may encourage you to do so, and may have a system of buddies, mentors or peer tutors in place already. Or it may be the case that some of your colleagues, or other researchers, are interested in the work you are doing, and get in touch with you.

How can you establish and make the best use of such informal research relationships? Box 70 contains some pertinent suggestions.

The most general advice we would give about developing and using research relationships, of whatever kind, is much the same as that given for managing relations with key individuals or institutions. That is, view the relationship as a bargain which requires the active participation of the parties concerned, a shared understanding of what is going on and a good deal of give and take.

---

**Box 70: Managing informal relationships**

- Find out what seminars, meetings and conferences you can attend, at your own institution and elsewhere. Attend a range of these, making contributions where possible. These will help you network, keep up to date, share anxieties and successes.
- Your university or employer may run a mentoring or 'buddy' system, which will pair you, or put you in touch with a student or colleague who has more experience and can show you the ropes.
- Get in touch with relevant research or professional organizations in the area in which you are working. These will have their own sets of meetings, will probably be interested in the research you are undertaking and could provide useful contacts as well as a sounding board for your ideas.
- Talk about your research with interested relatives, neighbours, colleagues and others in your 'communities'. You may be surprised at how useful some of them can be, particularly as research is partly about communicating your ideas and findings.

---

**Exercise 37: Your view of technology**

How do you feel about using technology in your research? Is it relevant to your topic? Would it be useful? Are you competent in its use? If not, are you prepared to make yourself competent?

---

☐ **Using wordprocessors and computers**

**Attitudes to technology**

Before you read this section, answer the questions in Exercise 37.

There is a wide range of responses to the idea of using wordprocessors or computers in research. Some people are highly competent in the use of information technologies. Others are scared stiff and have long devised personal strategies to avoid their usage. Most people probably lie somewhere in between these extremes, having some familiarity with new, and ever changing, technologies through running simple programs and playing computer games.

Information technologies are now an essential tool for the management of information. We would suggest that having an understanding, and some facility in the use, of computers and wordprocessors is a key skill for all researchers in the social sciences. There are three aspects of particular importance:

---

**Exercise 38: Computer skills and resources check**

Note all the computing and wordprocessing facilities which you have access to: at home, at work, at university or college, or elsewhere. What packages, programs and facilities do they support? How useful might these be in your research, and which of them do you plan to make use of?

Thinking beyond these available facilities, what other facilities exist which are of relevance to your research project and subject area? Should you, and could you, make use of any of them? You should include everything from basic typing through databases to advanced programming.

If you do not know how to use these facilities, and you wish to develop your skills in these areas, how would you go about it? Is it adequate to teach yourself, making use of such manuals as are available? Are there colleagues or friends you could turn to for help? Is tuition available locally?

Draw up a list of the skills you would like to develop, and how you propose to do so, and include this in your research planning.

---

- You should be able to type reasonably competently. You may be going to get your research report or dissertation typed out by someone else, but you might have to type letters, notes and corrections yourself. It is probably also a good discipline to type up your own research: you are, after all, the person who knows most about it, and you can make changes and amendments as you go along.
- You should know of, and be able to access and use, the Internet and the various computer databases of relevance to your field of research. You may also wish to make use of electronic means of communication.
- You should be aware in general terms of the kinds of packages and programs available for analysing and presenting research data in your subject area. This awareness should extend to knowing how they work, what their requirements are, and what their advantages and disadvantages may be.

You may already be well versed in all these areas: if so, well done, and please share your knowledge with someone else! If not, however, you could see your research as giving you an opportunity to develop new skills in this area, skills which are likely to have a wide future application. Alternatively, you may want to do the minimum in this respect, and avoid areas which heighten your insecurities. Whatever your perspective, however, you should find it useful to do a skills and resources check (see Exercise 38). The purpose of this is to get you to think about where you want to get to with your research, and how you might use computers and wordprocessors as tools to help you to get there.

### Commonly available facilities

The kinds of technological facilities you are likely to have available, or be able to get access to, can be divided into three groups:

- *Typing and wordprocessing*: beyond basic typing, you may find a wide range of facilities available on your typewriter, wordprocessor or computer, many of which are likely to be of some use to you in carrying out, and particularly in writing up, your research (see Box 71).
- *Databases and communications*: an increasing variety of information databases and communications networks are available in libraries, educational and other institutions, and over the web.
- *Analytical packages and programmes*: many package programmes are available which can be invaluable to the social science researcher in storing, recording and analysing their data.

---

**Box 71: Useful facilities available on wordprocessors**

- *Layout*
  You should be able to use a variety of page layouts, typefaces and type sizes to emphasize or get over complex information in an engaging fashion.
- *Spellcheck*
  Most wordprocessing packages will check your spelling for you and suggest possible corrections. Note, however, that many are based on American spellings.
- *Word count*
  They will also count the number of words you have written, useful if you are working to a limit.
- *Thesaurus*
  This will suggest alternative or synonymous terms, to stop you using the same words all of the time.
- *Grammar check*
  This will check that your sentences obey the basic rules of grammar.
- *Searching*
  Wordprocessors can search through your text to find particular words or passages. They can do this with other texts as well once they have been input.
- *Tabulation*
  Wordprocessors often have special facilities for laying out tables and charts. Most have the ability to box or shade areas of text.
- *Graphs and maps*
  Your wordprocessor may have programmes to produce graphs or maps from your input data. If not, there are special packages available.
- *Contents*
  Your wordprocessor should be able to draft and lay out a contents page for you.
- *Indexing*
  If you enter certain labels as, or after, you type, your wordprocessor will index your work for you.

> See the section in Chapter 4 on **Using the Internet** for examples of databases and search engines.

> See the sections in Chapter 6 on **Interviews** and **Questionnaires** for discussion of the use of the Internet and email in the collection of data.

> See the section in Chapter 7 on **Managing your data** for examples of packages and programs.

**If you do not intend to use a computer or wordprocessor yourself**

You may have decided, for very good reasons, that you do not have the time, resources or desire to develop your own information technology skills. It is possible, though not very likely, that they have no great relevance to your research topic. Yet you are still likely to need to make use of some facilities, even if only in getting your research report or dissertation typed up.

Here are some points to bear in mind if you are in this position: .

- Do you need to ask someone to input data? If so, when will they be available?
- Do you need a typist? If so, you might think about identifying one and booking them now.
- Is your wordprocessor compatible with the printer you intend to use? It will be less stressful to sort this out earlier on in your research.
- Will you need to provide equipment, or upgrade existing equipment? Check out the possibilities and costs now.
- If you are not doing the work yourself, remember to allow sufficient time for checking the work of others, and for making necessary revisions.

> *Health warning:* You don't want your information technology skills to control the practice or outcomes of your research in unforeseen ways because you can't get the technology to work for you. Think ahead!

☐ **Managing not to get demoralized when things do not go as planned**

Even in the most carefully managed research project, things do not always go quite as planned. Most changes are likely to be fairly trivial in nature, and are

---

**Box 72: Twenty things that can go wrong**

1 You run out of time.
2 Access is refused by a key institution or individual.
3 A key contact in an organization you are studying leaves.
4 You discover that someone has already done your research.
5 You lose your job.
6 Your response rate is very low.
7 Your manager or supervisor interferes with your plans.
8 You fall ill.
9 You change your job, making access to the site of your research difficult.
10 You split up with your partner.
11 You lose the citation for a key reference.
12 You find that you have too much data to analyse, or too little.
13 Your tape recorder doesn't work, or runs out of batteries.
14 You run out of money.
15 You cannot find key references in your library.
16 You are absolutely fed up with your project.
17 The dog eats your draft.
18 You have written too much, or too little.
19 Your computer crashes.
20 The margins on your text are not the right size for binding.

---

not recognized as such. Yet when they are recognized, the things that went wrong can seem to mount up and assume an unwarranted importance. They can be very disheartening and demotivating. It would be difficult to find an honest researcher who had not made significant mistakes. You are going to make mistakes. Box 72 offers, for your amusement and enlightenment, a list of 20 things that can go wrong.

How can you overcome such difficulties and get beyond them? Perhaps the golden rule is to remember that research is a process of learning. Just as we learn by our mistakes, at least in part, so changes in plans are an essential part of research. It might even be said that research without such mistakes or changes is not real research, and is unlikely to tell us much that we do not already know. Research is really about getting misdirected, recognizing this as such, understanding why it happened, then revising our strategy and moving on.

If you think you have been particularly unfortunate in your research experience, or are feeling lucky, try Exercise 39.

---

**Exercise 39: Making mistakes**

Look at the list of 'twenty things that can go wrong' in Box 72.

How would you respond to each of these dilemmas?

---

---

**Box 73: Reponses to adversity**

- Remind yourself that the purpose of carrying out a research project, particularly as a novice researcher, may be as much about developing your understanding of the research process and/or the use of particular research methods as about exploring substantive issues.
- Remember that it may be just as valid, and possibly a lot more helpful to other researchers, to write up your research in terms of, for example, the problems of gaining access to a particular group, or of getting an adequate response from that group once access has been gained.
- Make it part of your business in writing up to reflect upon your research strategy, explore what went wrong and why, and include recommendations for doing it better 'next time'.
- View research as being about the skills you have learnt and developed on the way. As we have said already, few research projects are truly ground-breaking, or shocking in their conclusions. Part of doing research is about appreciating what is involved, and where it may be leading you.
- If you have time and resources you may, of course, choose to redirect your research strategy when you are stymied in one direction. This is very common, not an admission of failure.
- Welcome to the club! All is not lost.

---

In Box 73 you will find some possible, more positive responses to the kinds of dilemmas you may face in managing your research project. Box 74 then gives some real-life examples of how social science researchers coped with problems or changes in their plans.

## ☐ Summary

Having read this chapter, you should:

- be better equipped to manage your time to carry out the activities necessary for your research project;
- understand how you might go about ordering your relationships with the key figures and institutions for your research;
- be more aware of how you might use wordprocessors and computers more effectively for your research;
- be more confident that you can make changes to, or mistakes in, your research plans, without being a bad researcher.

---

**Box 74: Researchers coping with problems and changes**

Tofi, an MA student trying to complete a case study of industrial training during the early summer, found that access was agreed just as the factory's holiday fortnight began. He had to redesign his strategy to lay less emphasis on original data, while focusing more on the methodological issues. Having done so, he then received an invitation to talk to a shop stewards' meeting, just three days before his thesis was due for submission. He decided to go to the meeting to learn more about his subject, but not to write up his thesis on the assumption that he could use data from that meeting.

> I found it impossible to complete my evaluation because of unresolved doubts and reservations about how to analyse and present the differences I uncovered . . . With the benefit of hindsight and more experience as an applied social researcher, I can now see a number of courses of action I could have taken. I could have facilitated communication between the SSD [social services department] and the Project about the differences . . . Neither had I then enough confidence to conduct research which prioritised real-life situations rather than textbook methods and solutions.
>
> (Poland 1990: 81, 86)

Jim finished writing his report on a laptop computer that he was able to borrow to take on holiday with him. He finished it in time to experiment with the layout and make each page look professional. He returned with two days left to print and bind the report, only to find that his printer was not set up to print from the package he had used. He did not want to panic, so decided to spend some money. He contacted an office business which had experience of solving such problems. And they did!

> [O]ne problem that I encountered when doing interviews for my project on mass production in the inter-war period in the London area was to keep the people I was interviewing off the subject of the Second World War. Once they started talking about this it was disastrous because I could rarely get them back to describing their working life before the war . . . Often then I gave up on what I had actually come for.
>
> (Glucksmann 1994: 154, 162)

---

# ☐ Further reading

In this section, we list a selection of books which are of particular relevance to the topics discussed in this chapter, together with an indication of their contents.

Arksey, H., Marchant, I. and Simmill, C. (eds) (1994) *Juggling for a Degree: Mature Students' Experience of University Life*. Lancaster: Unit for Innovation in Higher Education, Lancaster University.
Personal experiences of being a mature student provide the framework for this text. Issues considered include: being a mature student with children; having fun; living on a shoestring; health, ill-health and disability; and team work.

Delamont, S., Atkinson, P. and Parry, O. (1997) *Supervising the PhD: A Guide to Success.* Buckingham: Open University Press.
A practical guide for novice and experienced supervisors.

Delamont, S., Atkinson, P. and Parry, O. (2000) *The Doctoral Experience: Success and Failure in Graduate School.* London: Falmer Press.
An empirical study of the experiences of research students and their supervisors in a range of disciplines. Discusses how students cope with uncertainty and frustration, how research groups can act as socializing environments and how supervisors handle the tensions between student autonomy and their academic responsibilities.

Hampson, L. (1994) *How's Your Dissertation Going? Students Share the Rough Reality of Dissertation and Project Work.* Lancaster: Unit for Innovation in Higher Education, Lancaster University.
First-hand student accounts of the process of writing a dissertation. The chapters include discussions of selecting a topic, choosing a supervisor, pitfalls and assessment.

Hector-Taylor, M. and Bonsall, M. (eds) (1993) *Successful Study: A Practical Way to Get a Good Degree.* Sheffield: Hallamshire Press.
Written for students in higher education, this text includes chapters on writing, group work, problem-solving and presenting your material.

Kornhauser, A. W. (1993) *How to Study: Suggestions for High School and College Students*, 3rd edn. Chicago: Chicago University Press.
This text includes advice on creating favourable conditions for study, increasing concentration, reading effectively, listening and note-taking, cramming and examinations.

Lee, R. (ed.) (1995) *Information Technology for the Social Scientist.* London: UCL Press.
Designed to help social researchers to make the most of information technology for research design, management and data analysis. Topics covered include desktop tools, on-line services, computer-assisted interviewing, statistical software packages, simulations, expert systems and geographical computing.

Orna, E., with Stevens, G. (1995) *Managing Information for Research.* Buckingham: Open University Press.
Written for first-time researchers, this text looks at issues such as managing time and information, producing the written text and dealing with the emotions associated with research.

Phillips, E. M. and Pugh, D. S. (2000) *How to Get a PhD: A Handbook for Students and Their Supervisors*, 3rd edn. Buckingham: Open University Press.
Described as a 'survival manual for PhD students', this text discusses the nature of doctoral research, supervision, procedures and, for supervisors, how to supervise.

Stephenson, J. and Laycock, M. (eds) (1993) *Using Learning Contracts in Higher Education.* London: Kogan Page.
This text presents a number of case studies in the use of learning contracts. The contents discuss negotiation and developing skills, student–supervisor and employer–employee relationships.

Walter, T. L. and Siebert, A. (1993) *Student Success: How to Succeed in College and Still Have Time for Your Friends.* Fort Worth, TX: Harcourt Brace Jovanovich.
This is a guide designed to give strategies on managing the learning experience effectively. The contents include how to succeed, time management – self management, how to improve the instruction you receive and developing the support networks you need.

# 6

# COLLECTING DATA

## ☐ Introduction

All research involves the collection and analysis of data, whether through reading, observation, measurement, asking questions or a combination of these or other strategies. The data collected during and for research may, however, vary considerably in their characteristics. For example:

- data may be numerical, or may consist of words, or may be a combination of the two;
- data may be 'original', in the sense that you have collected information never before collected, or may be 'secondary', already put together by someone else, but reused, perhaps in a different way, by you;
- data may consist of responses to a questionnaire or interview transcriptions, notes or other records of observations or experiments, documents and materials, or all of these things.

The purpose of this chapter is to acquaint you with, and guide you through, the processes involved in data collection. The chapter is organized around the following themes and issues:

- **Access and ethical issues**. Gaining the cooperation of your research subjects or institutions, and dealing with the illegal, unethical and unprofessional.
- **Sampling and selection**. Choosing the subjects of your research.
- **Applying techniques to data collection**. The different methods you may use for your research.

- **Documents**. Using written materials as a basis for your research.
- **Interviews**. Questioning or discussing issues with your sample.
- **Observations**. Collecting data through watching or engaging in activities.
- **Questionnaires**. Gathering information through written questions.
- **Recording your progress**. Keeping a close check on your data collection.
- **The ups and downs of data collection**. Enjoyment, loneliness and obsession.

## ☐ Access and ethical issues

Two key issues are likely to confront you as a researcher as soon as you begin to consider collecting data for your project: access and ethics. These issues are also likely to be, and perhaps should be, a continuing concern throughout the process of data collection, and possibly also afterwards. They have to do with what information you are able to collect, how you get it and how you use it.

### Access

My first interview with Valerie Bragg occurred in March 1988 . . . It was made clear that I was far from the first person to ask for help. From the time of her appointment onwards, she had received a stream of people wanting to interview her, film her, conduct research in the college, and so on. Local and national press, television and radio reporters jostled with educational researchers of varying descriptions . . . She could not grant all requests from researchers. Why should she help me rather than anyone else? And, more importantly, how could she ensure that her pupils and the college were not disrupted?

(Walford 1991: 84)

You should already have given some consideration to the issues raised by access in choosing and focusing your research topic.

See the section on **Choosing a topic** in Chapter 2.

Your research topic may necessitate your gaining, and maintaining, access to any or all of the following:

- documents, held in libraries or by institutions;
- people, in their homes, places of work, the wider community or over the Internet;
- institutions, such as private companies, schools or government departments.

The kinds of questions you should consider before seeking such access are the subject of Exercise 40.

As part of the process of planning and managing your project, you may already have approached the key individuals or gatekeepers involved in enabling you to

**Exercise 40: Issues to consider before seeking access**

Can you give answers to the following questions?

1 Who or what do you want to research?
2 Who are the key individuals, or gatekeepers, that you need to get permission from?
3 How much commitment will you require for your research from your subjects in terms of hours, days, weeks or months?
4 Is this reasonable?
5 Can you identify any potential problems with regard to access?

access the documents, people and/or institutions you need for your research. The progress of your project, in the way you envisage it, and your ability to collect the kind of data you want, may be critically dependent on their cooperation. If they say 'yes', you are in and under way (but read on, for it is not usually as simple as that!); but if they say 'no', you may have to look elsewhere or revise your plans.

How, then, can you increase your chances of getting access? Box 75 contains some suggestions.

If you adopt a reasoned, planned and modest strategy, you are more likely to get the access you need. If, however, despite all your skills of negotiation, you are rebuffed, you may need to consider other strategies. Some of these are outlined in Box 76.

---

**Box 75: How to increase your chances of gaining access**

- Begin by asking for advice on how it would be most appropriate to negotiate access.
- Be modest in your requests: limit their scope to what you can handle, and don't start by asking for everything.
- Make effective use of your existing contacts, and those of your supervisor, manager and colleagues.
- Base your research (and perhaps register yourself as a student) within the institutions to which you need access; for example, if they have specialist library facilities or staff with particular expertise, or if they are institutions you wish to study.
- Offer something back to your research subjects: perhaps a report or a workshop. Ask their advice on what might be useful to them. If your research is of potential interest and use to them, they will be more likely to allow you access.
- Ask at the right time. Some institutions need to plan ahead, while others like to act immediately. Busy periods and holidays are not good times.
- Be as clear as possible about what you are asking for: which documents and people, and how long it will all take.
- Explain the reasons for doing your research, why it will be of value, and what the outcomes might be (don't claim too much!).

---

---

**Box 76: Strategies to consider if access is refused**

- Approaching other individuals. For example, if one person refuses to be inter-viewed or to answer your questionnaire, you might approach another person in a similar position or with similar characteristics.
- Approaching other institutions. If the institution you had chosen for a case study, as part of your sample or because of its library facilities is uncooperative, you may be able to get access to another institution of a similar kind.
- Approaching another individual within the same institution. This is a more risky strategy, because of their possible communication, but there is usually more than one person who can grant you access, even if this is more limited.
- Try again later, when it may be less busy, attitudes may have changed, people may have moved on and you may have more to show to demonstrate the value of your research. This is also a risky strategy, since it involves you in going further down a chosen path which may still turn out to be blocked.
- Change your research strategy. This is something you should probably be prepared to do, and plan for, throughout the research process. It may involve using other, perhaps less sensitive, methods for collecting data, or focusing on a slightly different set of issues, or studying alternative groups or organisations.
- Focusing your analysis and writing up on the process of undertaking research, why you were unable to gain the access you wanted and the possible implica-tions of this for your topic.

---

Relatively few researchers end up studying precisely what they set out to study originally. In many cases, of course, this is because their ideas and interpretations change during the research, but the unpredictability of access negotiations is also a major influence.

Gaining access to the people, institutions or documents you wish to study for your research is not just a one-off exercise, which you conduct immediately before beginning your data collection. Rather, it is a continuous and potentially very demanding process. If you doubt this, consider the questions posed in Exercise 41.

Franks maintained I request his permission to observe his class directly before each print session. This caused four problems. The first was, as I explained, my concern to avoid a reactive effect on either himself or class

---

**Exercise 41: Continually negotiating access**

1 In what ways do key variables such as race, class and gender influence access?
2 What is the role of your initial contact, or gatekeeper, in ensuring your continuing access?
3 What is the relationship between access and data collection?
4 Is access no more than a mixture of serendipity and pragmatism?

---

members. The second problem was in locating Franks before lectures, which proved to be extremely difficult. The newsroom has two doors and in order to see him before teaching I had to hover between the two entrances at least five minutes before class. On several occasions I suspected he was operating a policy of positive avoidance. The third problem was that once located his usual reaction was to say no. Although on most occasions he would give way, the uncertainty of not knowing had a detrimental effect on my confidence as a competent researcher. The final problem was that I became wary of upsetting relationships between Franks and Parker who taught these classes jointly.

(Parry 1992: 70)

Just because your initial contact within an organization has given the go ahead to your research plans, this does not mean that the data collection process will be smooth and trouble free. This will be the case even if your contact is in charge of the organization you are studying. Every time you meet another individual, or meet the same people again, within that organization, you will need to engage, whether explicitly or implicitly, in a renegotiation of access.

Simply because one person has said 'yes' does not mean that their colleagues cannot say 'no'. Indeed, in some circumstances, of which you may initially be blissfully unaware, it may increase the chances of them doing so. You may be unable to call upon your initial contact for help in these conditions: doing so may even exacerbate the problem. Similarly, while an individual may have happily undergone one interview, filled in one questionnaire or responded helpfully and promptly to your requests for documentation, this does not mean that they will react as favourably to subsequent or repeated requests.

Ultimately, therefore, research comes down to focusing on what is practically accessible. Research is the art of the feasible.

## Ethics

It is worth standing back for a moment and considering what effect your actions might have on others as the result can be quite damaging to yourself. While the researcher feels excitement at finding key facts and pride in producing a full report, the readers of that report might be shocked at just how much intimate detail is included. Even if the information is all publicly available, many people do not realise how much can be found. There is also a difference between it being available in some obscure locations where it might be hoped that few people would trouble to look, and seeing it written out in a single, comprehensive report which is readily available at a moment's notice.

(Hack 1997: 37)

While electronic communication is in transit . . . the researcher has no control over it. The networks it will pass through are owned by other people who may employ unscrupulous system administrators to maintain them. These administrators have the power to access anything they want. When service provider Prodigy faced protests for raising its charges, it intercepted, read and destroyed messages from dissenting clients and dismissed some members. The latter had no legal recourse and no way to picket the provider. If online discussion relates to criminal activity, law organizations may 'tap' the line and researchers might lay themselves open to being subpoenaed to disclose participants' identities . . . Apart from 'listening in', other users can copy and distribute messages to unintended recipients without the knowledge of the writers. The content of messages can also be changed with great ease . . . although researchers can promise confidentiality in the way that they use the data, they cannot promise that electronic communication will not be accessed and used by others.

(Mann and Stewart 2000: 42–3)

The conduct of ethically informed social research should be a goal of all social researchers. Most commonly, ethical issues are thought to arise predominantly with research designs that use qualitative methods of data collection. This is because of the closer relationships between the researcher and researched. Nevertheless, all social research (whether using surveys, documents, interviews or computer-mediated communication) gives rise to a range of ethical issues around privacy, informed consent, anonymity, secrecy, being truthful and the desirability of the research. It is important, therefore, that you are aware of these issues and how you might respond to them. You owe a duty to yourself as a researcher, as well as to other researchers and to the subjects of and audiences for your research, to exercise responsibility in the processes of data collection, analysis and dissemination. If you doubt this, think about some of the ethical problems posed in Exercise 42.

You might think that some of the problems outlined in Exercise 42 are rather extreme, and of the sort which are unlikely to be encountered in most research projects, but these are all real dilemmas which were faced and dealt with by real researchers. These researchers include the authors of this book, and some of the students they have supervised, as well as some examples of dilemmas reported in the research literature.

Research ethics are about being clear about the nature of the agreement you have entered into with your research subjects or contacts. This is why contracts can be a useful device. Ethical research involves getting the informed consent of those you are going to interview, question, observe or take materials from. It involves reaching agreements about the uses of these data, and how the analysis will be reported and disseminated. And it is about keeping to such agreements when they have been reached.

The use of research contracts is discussed in the section on **Dealing with key figures and institutions** in Chapter 5.

The common problems listed in Box 77 may be among the ethical issues you will have to face in your research project.

**Exercise 42: Dealing with ethical problems**

Consider how you would deal with the following situations:

1 You are researching the parenting behaviours of the parents of hospitalized children. You believe that when they are left alone some parents harm their children. You have a video camera. Do you set it up and use it?

2 You have been granted access to an archive of rare documents of crucial importance to your research. It would save you a lot of time if you could take some of the documents home, and security is very lax. Do you 'borrow' some of the documents?

3 You have finally found just the textbook that you need for your research, but it is in the reference section of the library and you cannot take it home to read at your leisure. You take it to the photocopier and notice the copyright rules that limit how much you can copy. You need more than the stated amount. Do you keep to the limit or photocopy as much of the text as you need?

4 You are part of a team researching issues of sexuality and you are using email to conduct interviews. You realize that the male members of the team have greater access to men and female members of the team have greater access to women. To help with validity your team decides that female researchers should interview male respondents and vice versa. You log on and your new respondents refuse to discuss issues with a member of the opposite sex. You are worried that this will look bad for you and damage your chances of promotion. Do you try again but this time change your name and pretend you are the same sex as the respondents to ensure access?

5 Your research has highlighted unethical practices in your organization about the use of expenses claims. Do you publish it?

6 You find a newsgroup on the web that is discussing issues central to your research. Do you 'lurk' (listen in without participating)?

7 You have been offered £1,000,000 to conduct research into GM foods. The funder is a multinational chemical company with interests in GM crops. Do you accept the funding?

8 You have been offered £100 to conduct research into GM foods. The funder is a local direct action group opposed to the development of GM crops. Do you accept the funding?

9 You find a document on the web that has done much of the background work on your topic. The deadline for completion of your work has passed and this document is really useful. Do you include the relevant detail in your dissertation but omit the reference?

10 Your research involves interviews with children under 5 years old. How do you ensure they are able to give 'informed consent'?

All the problems and examples which we have quoted concern conflicts of interest. These may be between the demands of confidentiality or anonymity, and those of legality or professionalism. Or, more generally, they may be between your desire, as a researcher, to collect as much good data as you can, and the wishes or demands of your subjects to restrict your collection or use of data.

---

**Box 77: Common ethical issues**

*Confidentiality*
It can be extremely tempting, in cases where confidentiality has been agreed or demanded, to use material collected in this way. You may think it is unimportant, or will never be detected, but its use could threaten your sources and undermine your whole research project.

*Anonymity*
This is often linked to the issue of confidentiality. Where you have assured individuals or organizations that they will not be identifiable in your report or thesis, careful consideration may need to be given to how you disguise them. For example, to refer to a university in a 'northern town of 150,000' rather gives the identity away. If you are quoting from interviews with people in a named organization, disguising people's identities as 'woman, 30s, manager' may also be inadequate.

*Legality*
If you are a police officer, it is your duty to report any illegal activities of which you become aware in the course of your research. The same applies, though to a lesser extent, to certain other categories of employees, such as social workers or fire officers. More generally, it could also be seen as an obligation shared by all citizens. In some circumstances, where the infringement is minor or occurred long ago, you may be happy to overlook it, but this may not always be the case.

*Professionalism*
If you are a member of a professional group, as many researchers are, this imposes or assumes certain standards of conduct in your professional life. These may overlap into your research work, particularly if you are conducting research among fellow professionals. You may need to think, therefore, about what you do if you discover what you believe to be unprofessional conduct during the course of your research.

---

The research process is in part about negotiating a viable route between these interests. The 'pursuit of truth', and the 'public's right to know' are not held as absolute values by everyone.

This point is evident in ethical concerns that are arising from the increased use of the Internet and associated communication technologies. For example, there can be no certainty about the confidentiality of materials sent by email, as they can be easily forwarded and copied. It is not unusual to hear about cases of 'hackers' who gain access to the customer databases of public or private organizations. Particular kinds of ethical issues also arise when computer-mediated communication is used as a data collection instrument. The lack of non-verbal and social cues makes it more difficult for the researcher to monitor how interviewees are responding to questions about sensitive issues. When computer-mediated communication is used for group activities and research, ethical questions are raised about how, when and if those who remain silent (often referred to as 'lurkers') should be 'made' to take part, and what effects 'lurking' has on those who are more fully taking part.

Many professional associations and employers working in the social sciences have drawn up their own ethical guidelines or codes of conduct for researchers. You should try to get hold of a copy of those that are relevant to your subject area. Giving consideration to ethical issues is also a requirement for those seeking funding, whether as students or academic researchers, from funding bodies. For example, in the UK the Economic and Social Research Council asks proposers to detail the ethical implications of their project. In addition, it may be a requirement (e.g. in health care or social work) that you submit your proposal to an ethics committee. The function of the committee is to consider whether your proposed research conforms to ethical guidelines set out by the relevant professional body and/or employer, and that it does not infringe applicable laws.

Ethical issues do not solely relate to protecting the rights and privacy of individuals. They can also relate to the methodological principles underpinning the research design. For example, those with social justice concerns will include the very topic of the research as part of their ethical framework, by asking whether it raises socially responsible questions or has the potential to create a more just world. Box 78 gives two examples of such research, and indicates how there is no easy resolution of the dilemmas that are raised. It also shows that ethical issues arise at all points in the research process, including analysis and interpretation. As such, the researcher's values, position and notions of truth are integral to ethical concerns. Researchers need to recognize the complexity and the many facets of ethical issues.

The discussion in this sub-section suggests three general conclusions about research ethics:

- that a consideration of possible or actual ethical issues is an essential part of any research project;
- that such a consideration is likely to need to take place throughout the research project, from initial planning through data collection to writing up and dissemination;
- that in many cases there will be no easy answers to the ethical questions which you may have to face.

## ☐ Sampling and selection

While most people would associate the words 'sampling' and 'selection' with survey approaches, there will be elements of these involved, whatever approach you are taking to your research project. If your research involves observation, you will not be able to observe everyone of interest all the time. If you are carrying out a case study, you will need to select the case or cases which you are going to focus on. Whatever your approach, you should, therefore, give some consideration to the related issues of sampling and selection.

This may seem unnecessary if your research topic and strategy have been largely determined for you, or if you have a particular case study or action research project in mind. In such circumstances, however, you may still need to

---

**Box 78: Ethical dilemmas for social justice research**

Ethics have methodological implications in research on/for/with human beings, especially where that research is explicitly intended to improve social justice. An example is the use of control groups. These are, methodologically, extremely useful if repetition is not possible. Thus, they are widely used in botanical experiments, in order to test the influence of a single factor on a population (of flowers, say, or beans). Agency and interpretation can be taken into account by the use of 'double blind' tests, where neither the experimenter nor the subject know which is the control group or treatment. For instance, much medical research depends on the double blind use of placebo treatments. The ethical problem for education (as for medicine, but not for botany) is that the method depends on putting some subjects into a 'control' group and deliberately giving treatment thought to be inferior so that better treatments can be tested . . . For anyone wanting to do educational research for social justice, resolutions to these ethical issues of deception depend on judgements about 'on/for/with'.

(Griffiths 1998: 39–40)

As the writer, I had the ultimate power of production but my interpretations were not produced without consultation and discussion. Rather than change my analysis to fit the analysis of the women of the research, which has been suggested by some feminist researchers, I want to make a claim for using the interpretations produced through dialogue, but over which I have ultimate responsibility and which are generated in relation to the research questions I investigated. I discussed my ideas and interpretations with them [the subjects of the research] and they would challenge, contradict, confirm, etc. This would enable me to reassess my speculations and frameworks, sometimes leading to modification, abandonment, but also to reassertion. Questions of epistemic responsibility and the ethics of this interpretative process were most obvious in relation to social class. The women did not want their actions interpreted as class responses for this reproduced the position they wanted to disassociate from. However, their rejection of class did not lead me to abandon it. In fact, it did the opposite. It heightened my sensitivity to its ubiquity and made me construct theories to explain their responses.

(Skeggs 1997: 30)

---

justify your choice and relate it to other examples. If you have not yet determined the subjects or objects of your research project, however, you should certainly think about how you are going to choose them.

There are a wide variety of sampling strategies available for use. The main options are summarised in Box 79, and illustrated diagrammatically in Box 80. They are divided into two main groups, *probability* and *non-probability sampling*.

The most widely understood probability sampling approach is probably random sampling, where every individual or object in the population of interest (e.g.

---

**Box 79: Sampling strategies**

*Probability sampling*

- *Simple random sampling*: selection at random.
- *Systematic sampling*: selecting every *n*th case.
- *Stratified sampling*: sampling within groups of the population.
- *Cluster sampling*: surveying whole clusters of the population sampled at random.
- *Stage sampling*: sampling clusters sampled at random.

*Non-probability sampling*

- *Convenience sampling*: sampling those most convenient.
- *Voluntary sampling*: the sample is self-selected.
- *Quota sampling*: convenience sampling within groups of the population.
- *Purposive sampling*: handpicking supposedly typical or interesting cases.
- *Dimensional sampling*: multidimensional quota sampling.
- *Snowball sampling*: building up a sample through informants.

*Other kinds of sampling*

- *Event sampling*: using routine or special events as the basis for sampling.
- *Time sampling*: recognizing that different parts of the day, week or year may be significant.

---

MPs, dog owners, course members, pages, archival texts) has an equal chance of being chosen for study. For some readers, this may accord with their understanding of what sampling is. But both more complex approaches, such as systematic and stratified sampling, and more focused approaches, such as cluster and stage sampling, are possible within a probabilistic framework.

Which approach is used will depend in part on your knowledge of the population in question, and the resources at your disposal. Thus, a small-scale researcher wishing to survey public attitudes may not be in a position to sample from the whole country, but will instead restrict the sampling to a local cluster. Or, if you do not have access to random number tables, you might choose to sample from a list of subjects by taking every twentieth person.

Non-probability sampling approaches are used when the researcher lacks a sampling frame for the population in question, or where a probabilistic approach is not judged to be necessary. For example, if you are carrying out a series of in-depth interviews with adults about their working experiences, you may be content to restrict yourself to suitable friends or colleagues. Or you may be studying an issue which is relatively sensitive, such as sexual orientation in the armed forces, and have to build up a sample confidentially and through known and trusted contacts. Market researchers commonly use a quota sampling approach, with targets for the numbers they have to interview with different socio-demographic characteristics.

Box 80: Sampling strategies illustrated

Box 81 summarizes some real examples of the sampling strategies that were adopted for actual research projects.

Exercise 43 asks you to consider what sampling approaches might be most appropriate in particular circumstances, and to justify your choice.

## ☐ Applying techniques to data collection

### Approaches and techniques

In Chapter 3, we identified a series of research approaches and techniques. The four approaches – action research, case studies, experiments and surveys – provide

---

**Box 81: Examples of research sampling strategies**

A   A study of 48 highly successful women, where it was judged important to have a range of occupations represented. The sample was contacted through the chairpersons of women's business networks across the country. While a nationwide sample had been hoped for, there was a predominance of respondents from London, the South East, Bristol and the North West. Once the names of potential respondents had been provided to the researchers, they were contacted by letter with an outline of the purposes of the research. Each participant was interviewed for an hour, and subsequently asked to complete a set of questionnaires.

(White et al. 1992)

B   The research was concerned to test the hypothesis that, unlike European governments, Latin American governments 'do not dominate the policy making process'. An analytical methodology is outlined which would enable this hypothesis to be tested. To assess the level of influence of government parties in terms of context and time would ideally require the researcher to monitor the ways in which the political parties behaved across *all* policies. Given the impossibility of this, a random sampling strategy is suggested. This would start 'with a conventional classification of public policies (social, economic and institutional)', and select for each type 'one or two outstanding issues in the specific national contexts'.

(Cansino 1995, quotes from pp. 169 and 174)

C   I recall one use of opportunistic sampling during my first ethnographic trip to West Pakistan. The abundant visitors who voluntarily came to my home served as respondents for innumerable questions. I sought to plumb their motivations and other personality characteristics, and in some cases begged them to take the Rorschach test. Occasionally I solicited my guests with my interview schedule (that had been prepared for a random sample) to learn if they had attended the motion picture showings, and if so, what they had seen and heard. Responses from such opportunistically selected subjects were kept separate from those of randomly selected subjects.

(Honigman 1982: 81)

---

alternative, though not necessarily mutually exclusive, frameworks for thinking about and planning research projects. They were separately considered in Chapter 3. In this chapter, we focus on the four main techniques, or methods for producing data, which were identified: documents, interviews, observation and questionnaires.

---

You might like to take another look at Chapter 3 at this point, particularly the section on **Families, approaches and techniques**, and Box 25.

---

**Exercise 43: Which sampling strategy and why?**

Refer to the range of sampling strategies summarized and illustrated in Boxes 79 and 80.

Which of these strategies would you use if you were researching the following topics? Justify your choice in each case.

1 You wish to study the care arrangements of terminally ill AIDS patients.
2 You have been commissioned to find out the opinions of workers in a factory on changed working arrangements.
3 You want to investigate whether people's use of local sporting facilities varies with their age and sex.
4 You want to study changing attitudes to immigration over the past 500 years, as evidenced in the holdings of a large library.

---

### In the field or at the desk?

> Housing is of vital importance in fieldwork, and choices about which part of the village to stay in, whether to stay with a family or not, all have to be taken before anything is known about the community. I was told there was a widow who rented rooms in St Llorenc de Cerdans and who was great fun and would be ideal for me to stay with. I sensed that there was a consensus among the people who had taken me under their wing that she would be an appropriate guardian for me. It was almost as if she was appointed as the representative of the community. I visited the widow, who turned out to have the builders in for a six-month stint. Since otherwise the situation was perfect – a small street right in the middle of the village and a nice, friendly woman was to have been my protector – my disappointment was great. However, the large damp house opposite was empty, and available for rent. Comments were passed about the unsuitability of my living alone, and in such a cold and damp place, but the proximity of the neighbour-protector meant that I felt it was not impossible, and I moved in.
>
> (O'Brien 1993: 235)

For many social science researchers, particularly perhaps in anthropology, geography and sociology, the collection of data involves fieldwork. Having refined their research projects, developed their questions and methods, the researchers then 'go into the field' to collect data directly through observation and/or questioning. For such researchers and disciplines, fieldwork has a considerable mystique and associated traditions.

In other cases, and commonly in disciplines such as economics and psychology, fieldwork as such may be unusual. Much research in these subjects is done using pre-existing data, or data which can be collected, perhaps experimentally, within one's employing institution.

---

**Exercise 44: Going into the field**

When you engage in the collection of data for your research, will you:

• Wear different clothes from those you normally wear?
• Go away from your workplace or university to some other place?
• Engage in forms of behaviour you would not normally engage in elsewhere?

---

If you are not sure whether your research project involves fieldwork or not, try Exercise 44. If your answer to any or all of the questions posed is 'yes', then you may consider yourself as involved in fieldwork. You will probably have, or will develop, all kinds of rituals and behaviours associated with your fieldwork.

If your answer to all the questions posed is 'no', then your research does not involve fieldwork in this sense. This does not mean, of course, that your research is not valid or worthwhile. You don't have to do fieldwork to be a researcher. You may choose to, if you enjoy it, if your research topic demands it, or if it is expected of you. Or you may, for equally valid reasons, choose not to do fieldwork, but to base your research within the library, office or laboratory. Whether the collection of data for your research project involves fieldwork or not, the processes you go through may be seen as broadly analogous.

## ☐ Documents

All research projects involve, to a greater or lesser extent, the use and analysis of documents. Researchers are expected to read, understand and analyse critically the writings of others, whether fellow researchers, practitioners or policy-makers. Considerable attention has, therefore, already been given to the techniques of reading for research.

---

See Chapter 4, particularly the section on **Good enough reading**, and Chapter 8, especially the section on **How to criticize.**

---

For some research projects, however, the focus of data collection is wholly, or almost entirely, on documents of various kinds. They might, for example:

• be library-based, aimed at producing a critical synopsis of an existing area of research writing;
• be computer-based, consisting largely of the analysis of previously collected data sets;
• have a policy focus, examining materials relevant to a particular set of policy decisions;
• have a historical orientation, making use of available archival and other surviving documentary evidence.

---

**Box 82: Examples of the use of documents in research**

- Mason (1999) interviewed families about their *wills* as part of a research project into family networks and relationships. Questions about who is and who is not listed as a beneficiary can shed light on how stepfamilies view family ties.
- Nixon (2000) examined the *web pages* and *newspaper* reports of a small group of Australian schoolchildren who had been noted for their advanced information technology skills. Her analysis illustrated how their learning was conducted outside of formal school environments, and how this was related to issues of national identity and the commodification of these children's lives.
- Tight (2000) analysed a year's worth of the *Times Higher Education Supplement* to discover what images of the higher education world it presented. He found varied images of the sector, ranging from one in crisis to one where employment opportunities were plentiful.
- Walkerdine and Lucey (1989) obtained the *archived data* of a classic psychological study of the home lives of young children. Their re-analysis illustrated the ways in which middle-class values impacted on the findings of the original research.
- Arber and Ginn (1995) used *General Household Survey* data to explore the relationship between informal care and paid work. They found that it is the norm to be in paid work and also be providing informal care.

---

Using documents can be a relatively unobtrusive form of research, one which does not necessarily require you to approach respondents first hand. Rather, you can trace their steps through the documents that they have left behind. While unobtrusive methods do not solely rely on documents – they can also involve searching dustbins (garbology), looking at gravestones or monuments, and examining graffiti (Lee 2000) – there is no doubt that documents are an invaluable methodological tool. Some examples of research projects which have made considerable use of documents are summarized in Box 82, while Box 83 lists some documentary sources for social research in the United Kingdom.

Researchers who base their studies on documents may make considerable use of secondary data; that is, data which have already been collected, and possibly also analysed, by someone else. The most common forms of secondary data are official statistics collected by governments and government agencies. However, the potential for secondary analysis of qualitative data is increasingly being realised.

For further examples of secondary data sets available online, see the section in Chapter 4 on **Using the Internet**, in particular Box 45.

As the term suggests, secondary data analysis is the analysis of an existing data set. This may, for example, involve the re-analysis of a government survey

---

**Box 83: UK documentary sources for research**

1 *Government surveys*

A full listing of these can be found at the UK National Office for Statistics at http://www.statistics.gov.uk/

The StatBase currently contains 1470 data sets. Examples are:

- Census of Employment.
- Census of Population.
- Labour Force Survey.
- General Household Survey.
- Family Expenditure Survey.

2 *Government legislation*

Government white papers and legislative documents are important sources for policy research. The websites of key government departments offer search facilities and information on the latest policy initiatives. As well as the individual departments listed, try http://www.psr.keele.ac.uk for links to many legislative and government bodies.

- Department of Trade and Industry: http://www.dti.gov.uk/
- Department of Health: http://www.doh.gov.uk/
- Department of Social Security: http://www.dss.gov.uk/
- Department of Environment, Transport and the Regions: http://www.detr.gov.uk/
- Department for Education and Employment: http://www.dfee.gov.uk/
- Department for Culture, Media and Sport: http://www.culture.gov.uk/
- Lord Chancellor's Department: http://www.open.gov.uk/lcd/lcdhom.htm/

3 *Historical records*

Research into all aspects of social history (including political and business history) relies on archives.

- The Historical Manuscripts Commission (HMC) has published 239 volumes of reports and holds 42,500 unpublished reports in the National Register of Archives (http://www.hmc.gov.uk/nra/).
- ARCHON is the principal information gateway for UK archivists and users of manuscript sources for British history (http://www.hmc.gov.uk/archon/).

4 *Media documents*

Newspapers, magazines, television and radio all have websites that can provide interesting sources of data and useful material for research analysis. Websites of newspapers internationally can be found at http://library.uncg.edu/news/ These documents are useful for analysis of job and other advertisements, the letters pages, personal columns, obituaries and wedding announcements as well as the news pages.

5 *Personal documents*

Internet home pages of individuals have been used very creatively for research (see Nixon 2000). More generally, however, researchers will have to rely on paper-based sources. These include diaries, letters, wills and photographs.

6 *International organizations*

Comparative information on other countries, and on international policies and programmes, may be found on the websites of international organizations, such as the World Bank, World Health Organization, International Labor Office and Organization for Economic Cooperation and Development. For example:
http://www.worldbank.org/
http://www.oecd.org/

or of the interview transcripts from more qualitative forms of research. As some of the examples in Box 82 indicate, secondary analysis can give fresh insights into data, and ready-made data sets or archives do provide extremely valuable and cost-efficient resources for researchers. However, there are several cautions that have to be born in mind.

The questions you need to ask of any existing document are:

- What were the conditions of its production? For example, why, and when, was the document produced/written and for whom?
- If you are using statistical data sets, have the variables changed over time? For example, 'ethnicity' was not recorded in the British Census until 1991. This means that you cannot undertake some forms of analysis.
- If you are using statistical data sets, have the indicators used to measure variables changed? For example, the measurement of unemployment has undergone many changes in the past two decades. This impacts on any comparative or historical analyses that you might seek to make.

*Health warning:* Statistics don't fall out of the skies. Like words – of which they are of course an extension – they are constructed by human beings influenced by culture and the predispositions and governing ideas of the organisations and groups within which people work. Statistical methodologies are not timeless creations. They are the current expression of society's attempts to interpret, represent and analyse information about economic and social (and other) conditions. As the years pass they change – not just because there may be technical *advances* but also because professional, cultural, political *and* technical conventions change in terms of *retreat* as well as advance . . . Every student of social science . . . needs to be grounded in how information about social conditions is acquired. Statistics form a substantial part of such information. Acquiring information is much more than looking up handbooks of statistics. We have to become self-conscious about the process of selection.                                    (Townsend 1996: 26)

Exercise 45 invites you to consider the reasons for using secondary data. Try it, whether the use of documents forms a major part of your research project or not.

## Exercise 45: Why use secondary data?

What reasons can you identify for collecting and using secondary data, whether in the form of statistics or documents, for your research? Note down as many different reasons as you can.

1

2

3

4

---

**Box 84: Reasons for using secondary data**

1 Because collecting primary data is difficult, time consuming and expensive.
2 Because you can never have enough data.
3 Because it makes sense to use them if the data you want already exist in some form.
4 Because they may shed light on, or complement, the primary data you have collected.
5 Because they may confirm, modify or contradict your findings.
6 Because they allow you to focus your attention on analysis and interpretation.
7 Because you cannot conduct a research study in isolation from what has already been done.
8 Because more data are collected than are ever used.

---

How many reasons could you think of? You may like to compare your own suggestions with those given in Box 84. You may conclude from this both that you cannot really avoid the use of secondary data to some extent, and that it is legitimate and interesting to base your research project entirely upon such data.

## ☐ Interviews

The unstructured interview has been variously described as naturalistic, autobiographical, in-depth, narrative or non-directive. Whatever the label used, the informal interview is modelled on the conversation and, like the conversation, is a social event with, in this instance, two participants. As a social event it has its own set of interactional rules which may be more or less explicit, more or less recognized by the participants. In addition to its generally social character, there are several ways in which the interview constitutes a learning process. At the level of this process, participants can discover, uncover or generate the rules by which they are playing this particular game. The interviewer can become more adept at interviewing, in general, in terms of the strategies which are appropriate for eliciting responses, and in particular, in our case, in enabling people to talk about the sensitive topic of sexuality, and thus to disclose more about themselves.

(Holland and Ramazanoglu 1994: 135)

The interview method involves questioning or discussing issues with people. It can be a very useful technique for collecting data which would probably not be accessible using techniques such as observation or questionnaires. Many variations on the interview method are possible: some of the main options are summarized in Box 85. Of particular note is the growth of the Internet and focus group interviews. For example, through email, the Internet offers a relatively cheap way of conducting interviews at a distance. Focus groups offer the opportunity to interview a number of people at the same time, and to use the interaction within a group as a source of insight. Of course, Internet systems allow for both individual and group interviews to be conducted as, through asynchronous conferencing, you can arrange for several people to be on-line simultaneously.

---

**Box 85: Alternative interview techniques**

- Interviews may take place face-to-face, or at a distance, e.g. over the telephone or by email.
- They may take place at the interviewee's or interviewer's home or place of work, in the street or on some other 'neutral' ground.
- At one extreme, the interview may be tightly structured, with a set of questions requiring specific answers (cf. questionnaires), or it may be very open-ended, taking the form of a discussion. In the latter case (see the quotation from Holland and Ramazanoglu), the purpose of the interviewer may be simply to facilitate the subject talking at length. Semi-structured interviews lie between these two positions.
- Different forms of questioning may be practised during the interview. In addition to survey questioning, Dillon identified classroom, courtroom and clinical questioning, as well as the domains of personnel interviewing, criminal interrogation and journalistic interviewing (Dillon 1990).
- Prompts, such as photographs, can be useful for stimulating discussion.
- Interviews may involve just two individuals, the researcher and the interviewee, or they may be group events involving more than one subject and/or more than one interviewer.
- The interviewee may, or may not, be given advanced warning of the topics or issues to be discussed. This briefing might be very detailed to allow the subject to gather together any necessary detailed information.
- The interview may be recorded in a variety of ways. It may be taped, and possibly later transcribed by an audio-typist. The interviewer may take notes, during or after the interview, or, where there is more than one interviewer, one might take notes while the other conducts the interview.
- Interviews may be followed up in a variety of ways. A transcript could be sent to the subject for comment. Further questions might be subsequently sent to the subject in writing. A whole series of interviews could be held over a period of time, building upon each other or exploring changing views and experiences.

**Exercise 46: Developing interview skills**

- You are researching reasons for non-participation in adult learning classes. Some of the people you are interviewing are very uncomfortable about talking to a researcher. What tools or techniques would you use to facilitate the interview?
- The person you are interviewing expresses some extreme racist views. What do you say in response?
- You are facilitating a focus group discussion. How do you deal with the following?

    (a) Two members of the group begin an argument.
    (b) One member of the group dominates the conversation.
    (c) Several members of the group get up to help themselves to refreshments and begin a conversation in the corner of the room.
    (d) One member of the group never speaks.

- You have set up a series of email interviews. After three weeks the responses from your interviewees are becoming shorter and less reflexive. What do you think are the reasons for this? How can you respond?
- The transcripts from your interviews indicate that you are talking more than your interviewees. What kind of training would be of benefit to you?

Some contrasting examples of the use of the interview method for research are given in Box 86. Exercise 46 suggests some issues which you might like to consider in developing your interview skills.

If you have decided to carry out a number of interviews for your research project, one of the basic decisions you will have to take is whether to tape the interview or to take notes. In practice, of course, you may not have much choice, if, for example, you cannot afford or get access to a tape recorder. Even if you do decide to tape, you may find that some of your interviewees refuse you permission to do so, so you should practise note-taking, whatever your plans.

Each of these strategies has associated advantages and disadvantages:

- Using a tape recorder means that you need only concentrate on the process of the interview. You can focus your attention on the interviewee, give appropriate eye contact and non-verbal communication. You will have a verbatim record of the whole interview.
- Tape recording may, however, make respondents anxious, and less likely to reveal confidential information. Tapes also take a long time to transcribe and analyse.
- Note-taking gives you an instant record of the key points of an interview. You do not need to acquire a tape recorder, and do not need to worry about initial sorting, categorizing and analysis of the data collected.
- However, note-taking can also be distracting. Putting pen to paper may lead interviewees to think that they have said something significant. Conversely, when you don't make a note, they may think that you find their comments unimportant. Concentrating on asking questions, listening to the responses *and* taking notes is a complex process, and you will not get a complete verbatim record.

## Box 86: Examples of using interviews in research

For his MA dissertation, Shu-Ming wanted to interview his ex-colleagues working in Taiwan about their experiences of mentoring. He drew up a sample and, using email, sent each of them a brief outline of his topic, its purposes and some details of how he planned to conduct the research, including the amount of time it would require of respondents and the broader time-scale within which he was operating. His colleagues responded very positively, but there was an immediate problem. They were unfamiliar with the concept of mentoring, and so Shu-Ming's early work with them was to explain what he had understood about mentoring from studying in England. These initial interviews developed more into on-line tutorials than an exchange between peers, but the data that were produced were extremely useful in highlighting the culturally specific meanings of mentoring. Using these data, Shu-Ming's dissertation was refocused so that it explored the implications of on-line learning and research in the context of these culturally specific meanings. As a result, later interviews were conducted with his interviewees about their changing understandings and knowledge of mentoring.

Hollway and Jefferson (2000) used interviews to explore fear of crime with those they describe as 'defended subjects'. These are people who will protect themselves against any anxieties arising from the information provided in a research context. For example, defended subjects may not hear the questions in the same ways as other interviewees, and they may not know why they experience or feel things in the ways they do. They may invest in particular discourses to protect vulnerable aspects of themselves, and unconscious motivations may disguise the meanings of some of their feelings and actions. Hollway and Jefferson illustrate how early interview approaches were disappointing, but they argue that the problem 'went deeper than a few mistakes, which all interviewers make – through tiredness, lapses of concentration, a clumsily worded question or tapping into unknown (and unknowable) sensitivities' (p. 30). In consequence, they argue that a biographical-interpretive method was more appropriate than traditional interview approaches. This method has four principles: use open questions, elicit stories, avoid 'why' questions and follow respondents' ordering and phrasing. In addition, Hollway and Johnson argue that in their research the use of free association was an important adaptation of the biographical-interpretive method.

Field and Spence (2000) used focus group and individual interviews to explore aspects of informal learning in Northern Ireland. They undertook ten focus group interviews and 25 semi-structured interviews.

Both focus groups and individual interviews involved people with formal responsibilities for human resource issues; for some, training or education constituted their continued professional role, and for others it was one among many responsibilities. The aim of both focus groups and interviews was to consider a number of aspects of the relationship between initial and continuing education, and to explore the reasons for participation patterns among adults. (p. 36)

If you do decide to record your interviews, bear in mind that the most expensive recorder is not necessarily the best. A solid, second-hand and relatively cheap tape recorder may be a sound investment. The key qualities are that it is not too large or heavy, that it can work off batteries as well as the mains and that it can record quiet talkers when there is a lot of background noise. The availability of a transcribing machine may also be an issue for you.

*Health warning:* Interview tapes take a great deal of time to transcribe and analyse. Tizard and Hughes (1991) made recordings of children at school and at home to study how they learnt. Each hour of the home tapes, which included a lot of talk, took 12 hours to transcribe and a further five hours to check and add context. The transcripts of the home tapes averaged 60 typed A4 pages.

Another key issue in carrying out interviews, as well as other forms of questioning like questionnaires, is how best to ask potentially sensitive questions. These may include, for example, the age of your respondents, and their ethnic group, marital status, income, social class and educational level. Exercise 47 invites you to consider this problem.

Some possible answers to this problem are given in Box 87. Compare them with your suggestions, and try them out in practice to see how well they work.

*Hint:* Instead of asking all of your questions directly and verbally, you could make some use of prompt cards, particularly for sensitive questions, and ask your interviewee to point to the answer.

---

### Exercise 47: Asking sensitive questions

In face-to-face interviews, how would you ask strangers about:

* their age;
* their ethnic group;
* their marital status;
* their sexuality;
* their income;
* their social class;
* their educational level?

---

---

**Box 87: Different ways of asking sensitive questions**

**About age**

• Ask for year of birth.
• Or the year when they left school.
• Or how old their first child is.
• Or when they are due to retire.

**About ethnic group**

• Ask them to select from a range of options.
• Or to write it down for you.
• Or ask them how they would like you to describe their ethnic group.
• Or make an assessment yourself.

**About income**

• Ask them if they could afford to buy a new car or house.
• Or whether they would regard their income as above average, average or below average.
• Or which of a number of income bands they come in.

---

## ☐ Observations

A standard approach to participant observation treats the options available to the researcher as lying between complete participation – with associated difficulties of observation – and total concentration on observation with hardly any participation . . . No doubt the *practice* of participant observation has taken many forms and doubtless, the range of *practices* can be ranged on a scale from participation to observation and overt to covert, but the most fruitful way of looking at this range of practices is, I suggest, as a range of compromises where the ideal solutions are not open to the fieldworker. The ideal solutions lie at either end of the continuum. What is more, the continuum turns out to be not a continuum at all, for the ideals aim at quite different sorts of results, and they grow out of two quite different philosophical and methodological traditions . . . Thus I divide participant observation into 'unobtrusive observation' and 'participant comprehension'.
(Collins 1984: 55–6)

Structured observation, as used to monitor classroom events, requires an observer to assign such events into previously defined categories. These events may either be recorded by mechanical means such as film, audiotape or videotape and subsequently coded, or the observer can record and code the events simultaneously while present in the classroom. The three stages of the process therefore involve (a) the recording of events in a systematic manner as they happen, (b) the coding of these events into prespecified categories, and (c) subsequent analysis of the events to give descriptions of teacher–pupil interaction.

(Galton 1988: 474)

I find that nurses are the worst people to do participant observation because they cannot sit in the corner and 'do nothing'. They have to go and tuck in the bed, take the bedpan, get the water, and before you can turn around, they are working.

(Morse 1991: 72)

---

**Box 88: Examples of the use of observation in research**

1 *Purpose of study*: to observe how many motorists broke the speed limit on a stretch of the M40 . . . This study took place on Saturday 5th January 1994 between 9.45 and 10.30 am.
*Information to be recorded*: number of vehicles breaking the 70 mph speed limit, type of car, year of car, male/female driver.
*Method*: I drove at a steady 70 mph in the slow lane, except when I had to overtake five vehicles travelling at less than 70 mph. Using a tape recorder I logged the above information for every vehicle that overtook me.
*Results*: 167 cars broke the speed limit of 70 mph. The majority of the drivers were male. I was unable to record all makes of car because I was unfamiliar with some manufacturers' logos. Age of car did not appear to have any effect.

2 I had decided to visit the local leisure centre and observe the kind of people who were using the swimming pools on a Saturday morning. I had some idea about fathers and children being together on Saturdays. However, I didn't observe what I intended to! I arrived at the pool at 9.30 am, and the children's pool and adjacent cafe area were empty, so I went to the main spectator gallery overlooking the 'adult' pool. There were several different activities going on – swimming classes, adult recreational swimming and disabled swimming. I found that I could only concentrate on one of these areas, so decided to observe the interactions between the disabled and the volunteer helpers . . . The spectators ignored the disabled swimmers, with one exception, when a severely cerebral palsied man came to get into the pool, and he attracted a lot of attention. The volunteer helpers were all older, and predominantly males. There was one man in his 30s, but the rest were 50, even 60, or older. The lack of women helpers was very noticeable, as even the female disabled had to be helped into the pool by a man. This made me very aware of their situation.

*Source*: Material generated by Margaret Collins and Sandra Millar, Research Methods course, Department of Continuing Education, University of Warwick, 1994.

---

**Box 89: Issues in observation**

1 Are the times at which you carry out your observations relevant?
2 Do you need to devise an observational schedule or determine precoded categories? If so, you might like to test these out in a pilot observation before they are finalized?
3 If the answer to the last question was negative, how are you going to organize your data recording?
4 Is it important to you to try and record 'everything', or will you be much more selective?
5 Are your age, sex, ethnicity, dress or other characteristics likely to affect your observations?
6 How artificial is the setting? How visible are you as the observer? Does this matter?
7 Is observation enough, or will you need to participate and/or use other means of data collection?
8 Are there any situations to which you cannot get access but where observation may be important? How can you get 'off the road' or 'backstage'?
9 If you are going to participate more directly in the events you will be observing, how are you going to balance the demands of participation and observation? Again, you should find some practice beneficial here.

---

The observation method involves the researcher in watching, recording and analysing events of interest. Two examples of its use by postgraduate students are given in Box 88.

As the quotations and examples given indicate, a range of different approaches are possible in observation studies:

- the events may be recorded, either at the time or subsequently, by the researcher, or they may be recorded mechanically;
- the observation may be structured in terms of a predetermined framework, or may be relatively open;
- the observer may also be a participant in the events being studied, or may act solely as a 'disinterested' observer.

These differences are analogous to those already noted for interviews. There are, of course, many other details which need to be considered before you begin your observations. Box 89 outlines some of the key questions.

Using observation as a method of collecting data – whether you also act as a participant in the events you are observing or not – is, like interviewing, potentially very time consuming. The time absorbed occurs not just during the observation, but afterwards as well, when you come to interpret and analyse what you have recorded. Pre-categorizing and structuring your observations can reduce the time commitment dramatically, though at the risk of losing both detail and flexibility.

At one extreme, where the researcher's focus is on a limited number of specific events, and with noting or measuring participants' responses to certain stimuli, the observational technique shades into the experimental approach. At another, where the observer is a key and active participant in the events being studied, it shades into action research.

## ☐ Questionnaires

Questionnaires are one of the most widely used social research techniques. The idea of formulating precise written questions, for those whose opinions or experience you are interested in, seems such an obvious strategy for finding the answers to the issues that interest you. But, as anyone who has tried to put a questionnaire together – and then tried again to interpret the responses – will tell you, it is not as simple as it might seem.

Box 90 summarizes two examples of the use of questionnaires in social research, and, in doing so, begins to suggest some of the potential difficulties in devising and using questionnaires.

There are a number of different ways in which questionnaires can be administered. They can be sent by post to the intended respondents, who are then expected to complete and return them themselves (preferably, if you want them to respond, using a reply-paid envelope). They can be administered over the telephone or face-to-face, in the latter case becoming much like a highly structured interview. They can be sent over the Internet.

Each of these methods has advantages and disadvantages. Face-to-face surveys may get a better response rate, but are more time consuming for the researcher. Postal and email surveys are likely to have lower response rates, and possibly poorer answers because the respondent has no one available to answer any queries; but they may allow a larger number of people to be surveyed.

Just as questionnaires can be administered by different means, so there are a variety of ways in which questions can be asked. Box 91 illustrates seven basic question types: quantity or information, category, list or multiple choice, scale, ranking, complex grid or table, and open-ended. These types may be combined in various ways to give questions of increasing complexity.

As the examples given so far may have suggested, there are a number of issues to be considered when wording questions for survey purposes. Exercise 48 invites you to consider these.

Of course, there is no such thing as the ideal questionnaire, but some basic guidelines regarding question wording may be useful. See if those given in Box 92 accord with your answers to Exercise 48. Box 93 adds to these with some suggestions as to how questionnaires might best be laid out and presented.

If you follow these guidelines, you should be able to produce a competent questionnaire, though you are unlikely to produce a foolproof one. There will always be at least one question which proves to be inadequate, or which brings an indignant response. You would be well advised, as with the use of any research technique, to pilot your questionnaire before you carry out the full survey, and to modify your questions in the light of the responses you receive.

---

**Box 90: Examples of the use of questionnaires in research**

To answer our specific research questions on the use of GAs [graphic accents], we developed a three-condition survey study that we planned to conduct via the Internet. To that end, we drew on traditional methods of questionnaire design ... Our survey instrument contained extensive formatting to maximise clarity in the electronic environment. Each questionnaire element included (a) response scales with each item so that it would not be necessary for end users to scroll up and down if they wished to refer to the scales, (b) response boxes aligned on the left margin to minimize keystrokes, and (c) graphic rules and white space for maximum readability. We then set about pretesting the questionnaire with friends and acquaintances. To our surprise, even though these particular respondents knew us and supported our project, they were either unwilling or unable to complete the questionnaire and return it. It was clear that data collection through email potentially could stall our project ... We therefore suspected that the low response to our preliminary questionnaire might be, at least in part, the result of its length. Our instrument consisted of 42 stimulus items, which were constituted of 12,860 characters and formatted to 384 lines. This translated to 19 screens on a desktop computer.

(Witmer *et al.* 1999: 145–8)

At the point of collating the data from the questionnaire, a pack containing 35 replies was accidentally misplaced. The results of the 'first' set of data were not substantially changed by the insertion of the 'second' set. Whilst the total number of respondents, 89 out of a possible 360 was disappointing, it is to be contended that these figures are representative ... It is possible that a disproportionate number of replies might have been received from Language tutors, because of the amount of training I undertake throughout the County for Modern Languages. There may, therefore, be an element of repaying favours in the returns ... It is possible that this could bias the results of the questionnaire. However, as the subject being taught was not asked for in the questionnaire there is no way in which this can be thoroughly checked.

(Corder 1992: 31–2)

---

## Exercise 48: Wording questions

You have been given a number of examples of survey questions, and will probably have seen and answered a variety of questionnaires in recent years. You may have laughed or reacted indignantly to some of the questions which surveyors have asked you.

What suggestions would you make, in the light of this experience, regarding the wording of research questions, particularly in questionnaires?

**Box 91: Types of survey questions**

I Quantity or information

1. In which year did you enrol on the part-time degree? _____

2 Category

17. Have you ever been, or are you now, involved almost full-time in domestic duties (i.e. as a housewife/househusband)?

Yes (currently) ☐    Yes (in the past) ☐    Never ☐

3 List or multiple choice

39. Do you view the money spent on your higher education as any of the following?

a luxury ☐          an investment ☐       a necessity ☐

a gamble ☐          a burden ☐            a right ☐

none of these ☐

4 Scale

5. How would you describe your parents attitude to higher education at that time? Please tick one of the options below:

| very positive | positive | mixed/ neutral | negative | very negative | not sure |
|---|---|---|---|---|---|
| ☐ | ☐ | ☐ | ☐ | ☐ | ☐ |

5 Ranking

32. What do you see as the main purpose(s) of your degree study? Please rank all those relevant in order from 1 downwards:

personal development ☐      career advancement ☐

subject interest ☐          recreation ☐

fulfil ambition ☐           keeping stimulated ☐

other (please write) _____

6 Complex grid or table

11. How would you rank the benefits of your degree study for each of the following? Please rank each item:

| for: | very positive | positive | neutral | negative | very negative | not sure |
|---|---|---|---|---|---|---|
| you | | | | | | |
| your family | | | | | | |
| your employer | | | | | | |
| the country | | | | | | |
| your community | | | | | | |
| your friends | | | | | | |

7 Open-ended

41. We would like to hear from you if you have any further comments.

_____

_____

_____

---

**Box 92: Hints on wording questions**

- Try to avoid questions which are ambiguous or imprecise, or which assume specialist knowledge on the part of the respondent.
- Remember that questions which ask respondents to recall events or feelings that occurred long ago may be answered with a lesser degree of accuracy.
- Two or three simple questions are usually better than one very complex one.
- Try not to draft questions which presume a particular answer, or lead the respondent on, but allow for all possible responses.
- Avoid too many questions which are couched in negative terms, though in some cases, such as when you are asking a series of attitude questions, it can be useful to mix positive and negative questions.
- Remember that hypothetical questions, beyond the experience of the respondent, are likely to attract a less accurate response.
- Avoid questions which may be offensive, and couch sensitive questions in a way and in a place (e.g. at the end of the questionnaire) such that are not likely to affect your overall response rate.
- Do not ask too many open-ended questions: they take too much time to answer properly, and too much time to analyse.

---

## ☐ Recording your progress

As we noted in Chapter 4, meticulousness is an important skill for the researcher to develop. This is as true during the data collection phase of your research as it is when you are reading. There are two key aspects to recording the process of data collection: keeping notes on the progress of your project, and chasing up.

See also the section on **Recording your reading** in Chapter 4.

### Keeping notes

To record, and reflect upon, your progress during this phase, you will need to keep notes in some form. These may deal with your plans, how they change in practice, your reactions, what you read, what you think, significant things that people say to you and what you discover.

You have considerable flexibility about how you keep records of the progress of your research project. Here are some alternatives:

- *Research diaries*: an ideal way of noting down what you are doing, experiencing and thinking throughout the research project as it happens.

---

**Box 93: Hints on questionnaire layout and presentation**

- Questionnaires should be typed or printed, clearly and attractively laid out, using a typesize which is legible.
- If you are administering your questionnaires by post or email, you should enclose a covering letter identifying yourself and describing the purposes of your survey, and providing a contact address or telephone number.
- If you are administering your questionnaires face-to-face, or over the telephone, you should introduce yourself first, give a contact address or telephone number if requested and be prepared to answer questions about your survey.
- If the questions you are asking are at all sensitive, and this will be the case for almost any questionnaire, you should start by assuring your respondents of the confidentiality of their individual replies.
- Make sure any instructions you give on how the respondent is expected to answer the questions are clear.
- It is usually better to keep the kind of response expected – ticking, circling or writing in – constant.
- It is desirable that the length of the questionnaire is kept within reasonable limits, but at the same time it is better to space questions well so that the questionnaire does not appear cramped.
- If the questionnaire is lengthy or complicated, and you are expecting a substantial number of replies, you should think about coding the answers in advance on the questionnaire to speed up data input.
- Remember to thank your respondents at the end of the questionnaire, and to invite their further comments and questions.

---

See the section in Chapter 2 on **Keeping your research diary**.

- *Boxes or files*: keep all the material you are collecting in a number of boxes, one for each subject or chapter.
- *Coloured paper and sticky notes*: some people find these a helpful, and fun, way of organizing their records.
- *Computers*: you may input your thoughts, records and references directly on to a computer. Software is available to help to extract, arrange and index materials. Remember to keep a back-up copy, and to print out an up-to-date version every so often.

See the section in Chapter 5 on **Using wordprocessors and computers**.

- *Card indexes*: these can be particularly useful for keeping details of references, organized by author or subject.

---

**Box 94: Keeping research records**

1 William decided that he would keep all his material according to its relevance to particular chapters of his thesis. He made this decision after a few months of his research, when he was feeling overwhelmed and directionless. Putting material into chapter files helped him to gain a sense of progress and control, although he recognized that he would subsequently move material between files.

2 Jane decided that she would not use cards as the basis of her bibliographic index, as they would not be easily transportable. Instead, she bought a note-book with alphabetic sections and used this to record her growing literature. It provided her with a manageable resource which she subsequently typed on to her wordprocessor.

3 Mary wanted to store the different types of material she was collecting according to type. She therefore used A4 box files, which were categorized in terms of literature reviews, interview transcripts, respondents' completed diaries and tape recordings.

---

Some examples of the alternative strategies developed by actual small-scale social science researchers for keeping research records are included in Box 94.

*Hint:* However you decide to keep a record of your research in progress, it is very sensible to keep two copies of your records, each in a different place. Spare yourself the heartache of lost and irreplaceable files.

## Chasing up

The other aspect to being meticulous is chasing up your own progress, and the responses that you are expecting from others. Your research plans may look fine on paper, and you may have allowed plenty of time for collecting data, but you cannot expect other people to be as enthusiastic about, and committed to, your research as you are yourself. You may not be able readily to access all the documents that interest you. Not everyone will readily grant your requests for interviews. You may be denied access to some of the events or settings which you wish to observe. The response rate to your questionnaire survey may be disappointing.

What can you do about this? There are two kinds of responses, which can be used in conjunction. On the one hand, you may need to be realistic and flexible about your expectations for collecting data. You don't need a 100 per cent response rate; you don't need to read every last word written on your subject area; perhaps it doesn't matter if you don't interview every member of the management team or observe every meeting. You can get a great deal of information without experiencing everything, and even then you will probably never have time to analyse it all.

On the other hand, you can increase your response rate significantly by keeping tabs on your progress and assiduously following up your respondents. Possible strategies here might include:

- sending reminder letters to potential survey respondents who have not replied by your initial deadline;
- telephoning unwilling interviewees on a number of occasions;
- making yourself amenable to the librarian or custodian of the documents which you wish to get access to;
- maintaining regular contacts with the key people, or gatekeepers, for your research.

## ☐ The ups and downs of data collection

The process of collecting data may be quite a lengthy and demanding part of your research project. It may be a part which you particularly enjoy, or you may dislike it intensely. Either way, however, you are likely to encounter ups and downs during the process. There may be days when you really enjoy yourself, when you discover something interesting, or when someone says something which casts your whole project in a new and exciting light. There will also be days when you can barely force yourself to do the necessary work, when you just go through the motions or when you begin to doubt where it is all leading. Things will go wrong, and you will have to find ways of coping.

This section identifies two of the most common 'downs' encountered when collecting data – loneliness and obsessiveness – and suggests how you might counter them. It then offers some positive thoughts about how you might ensure that you get more enjoyment out of data collection. Finally, the issue of when to stop collecting data is discussed.

### Loneliness

All researchers, even those who are involved in group research, have to learn how to cope with working alone. For some it may be enjoyable, but for others it can be stressful. It is, however, an essential part of research, since it is you who has to decide at the end about the meaning of what you are doing. It will affect you even if you are working on a project close to your heart and with people you can relate to comfortably.

Loneliness is, therefore, inevitable, and is particularly prevalent during the process of data collection. Alan Sillitoe wrote a book entitled *The Loneliness of the Long Distance Runner*, but there is little to compare with the feelings of the lone researcher, particularly if they are conducting a lengthy piece of research.

A special form of isolation is common if you are carrying out fieldwork. In such cases, you will commonly be both an insider, having been accepted by the individuals, groups or institutions you are researching, and an outsider. However well you are accepted, you will still not be one of them. You may become a member of the group for a time, but you will simultaneously be operating as an external observer and analyst of the group's activities. The dual roles of stranger and colleague, of insider and outsider, can be difficult to manage and sustain psychologically.

Your loneliness will be magnified if you have no one sympathetic with whom you can discuss your progress and problems. This will be particularly so if your supervisor, manager or colleagues are unhelpful, or if you are conducting an obscure, sensitive or challenging piece of research. This is why it is so important to spend time, when beginning your research, on developing your support networks.

> You may like to refer back to the section on **Sharing responsibility** in Chapter 5.

The other way to combat loneliness is to compartmentalize your research, to give it a certain time and space in your life, but no more, making sure that you leave opportunities for you to maintain and engage in some of your other interests.

## Obsessiveness

The problem of obsessiveness may be closely related to that of feeling alone, particularly if you are carrying out your research project on your own. Research may be both an intensely stimulating and a very demanding experience. Whether you are conducting it on a part-time or full-time basis, it can take over your life, so beware! It may come to take up every spare moment that you have. You may want to talk about nothing else. You may be unable to wait to get back into the library, or for your next interview, observation or experiment. Research can get into your dreams!

This is likely, however, to cause you problems with your family, friends and colleagues, even with those who have been most ardent and reliable in supporting your research work. It can also be damaging to your research, as you can lose your understanding of the broader context for your work. The phrase 'going native' is used to describe a particularly severe form of research obsessiveness. It originated in an anthropological context, but has a more general application as well. Researchers who have gone native have become so immersed in the subject of their research that they are unable to separate their interest from those of their research subjects. They have lost the distance, strangeness or disassociation which is usually so important for the researcher.

Most researchers probably get obsessive about their research at one time or another. This may actually be useful or essential; for example, if you are under pressure towards the end of the project to get it written up and finished on time. More generally, though, obsessiveness is to be guarded against. Three basic strategies might help you:

- Planning and scheduling your research from the start, and revising your plans regularly throughout the project so as to keep the work required feasible. This should make it less likely that you will need to devote a disproportionate amount of your time to the research at any one point, and hence reduce the likelihood of your becoming obsessive.

> You may find it useful to look again at the sections on **Managing time** and **Mapping your project** in Chapter 5.

- Instructing a friend, relative or colleague to take on the responsibility for identifying when you become obsessive, telling you so and distracting you from your research. This will need to be someone you both trust and respect, and who is capable of putting up with your possibly terse reaction.
- Developing and using a network of fellow researchers, so that you can share your progress and concerns, take an interest in the work of others and get support in this way.

> The section in Chapter 5 on **Sharing responsibility** suggests how you might go about networking and seeking support.

### How to enjoy data collection

As the previous discussion indicates, doing research can become fascinating and all-absorbing. The process of collecting data has its attractions as well as its drawbacks. So how might you enable yourself to enjoy data collection more? Some suggestions have already been made earlier in this book.

One obvious strategy is to focus on a topic, a methodology or a group of research subjects which you find of particular interest.

> The section in Chapter 2 on **Choosing a topic** suggests how you might go about this.

There will probably be times, however, when the attraction of your project, and in particular the data collection involved, pales a little, regardless of how interesting it is or how well motivated you are.

Another strategy is deliberately to combine the process of collecting data with other activities which give you pleasure. These might include visiting friends, tea shops (our favourite!), football grounds, bookshops or other places of interest.

Take pleasure in your progress and achievements, and try not to be too down-hearted when you experience setbacks. Allow yourself little rewards along the way. You'll miss it when it's over!

## When to stop collecting data

You may find great pleasure in data collection, particularly if it takes you away from your everyday world into an arena which you find interesting or attractive. You may doubt that you have collected sufficient data for the purposes of your research, and continue to search for further information to confirm, complement or deny your understanding. You may wish to delay beginning the analysis and writing up of your research findings.

However, unless you have an open-ended schedule and as many resources as you need for your research, it is critically important that you stop collecting data at a certain point. You should have drawn up a schedule or timetable, and will have allocated only so much time to the data collection process. Even allowing for some leeway, this period cannot be indefinitely extended if you are to complete within a reasonable time.

There is another issue here, however. In small-scale research, you cannot expect to collect all the data you might like. No social research project, in a more general sense, is ever going to provide the last, definitive word on any topic. The purpose of small-scale research is likely to be a mixture of practical application, illumination, self-directed learning and/or research training. You should not, therefore, place yourself under enormous pressure to produce the 'perfect' piece of work. So:

- keep to your schedule as much as possible;
- collect only sufficient data, allowing particularly for the time and facilities which you will have available for analysis;
- move on to analysing your data as soon as you have collected sufficient.

## ☐ Summary

Having read this chapter, you should:

- have an appreciation of the complex access and ethical issues involved in doing social research;
- be aware of how you might go about sampling and selecting cases to research;
- better understand the different ways in which the use of documents, interviews, observations and questionnaires could contribute to your research project;
- be aware of the advantages and disadvantages of these different techniques for collecting data;
- be better prepared to cope with the ups and downs of the data collection experience.

## ☐ Further reading

In this section, we list a limited selection of books which are of particular relevance to the topics discussed in this chapter, together with an indication of their contents.

Abbott, P. and Sapsford, R. (eds) (1992) *Research into Practice: A Reader for Nurses and the Caring Professions*. Buckingham: Open University Press.
The chapters in this edited collection are concerned with nursing, the study of health and community care. They describe the processes involved in undertaking small-scale research within a range of approaches. The book is in three sections: observing and participating; talking to people and asking questions; controlled trials and comparisons.

Arksey, H. and Knight, P. (1999) *Interviewing for Social Scientists: An Introductory Resource with Examples*. London: Sage.
Intended as an 'interviewer's bible', this text covers the whole process of interview-based research from design through practice to transcription, analysis and reporting. Different approaches to interviewing, specialized contexts and ethical issues are also given attention.

Buckeldee, J. and McMahon, R. (eds) (1994) *The Research Experience in Nursing*. London: Chapman and Hall.
A set of first-hand accounts of research experiences in nursing. Written to illuminate the frustrations and pressures of research, particularly for first-time researchers. The contents include discussions of triangulation, analysis, piloting, conducting experiments, defining a research question, sampling, choosing a methodology, measurement and the politics of nursing research.

Czaya, R. and Blair, J. (1995) *Designing Surveys: A Guide to Decisions and Procedures*. London: Pine Forge.
Written for first-time researchers, this book is a guide to undertaking a survey. It includes sections on data collection, designing a questionnaire and sampling.

Dillon, J. T. (1990) *The Practice of Questioning*. London: Routledge.
Using transcripts of examples from each setting, this text explores the variety of purposes and forms in which 'questioning' can take place. The contexts include classrooms, courtrooms, psychotherapy, medical clinics, personnel interviews, journalism and surveys. Discussion includes advice on improving the art of questioning and techniques for situations where asking questions may not work well.

Eichler, M. (1991) *Non-sexist Research Methods: A Practical Guide*. New York: Routledge.
Using examples of sexism in existing research, this book provides guidelines for the recognition and avoidance of sexism in future research. Includes, in an appendix, a non-sexist research checklist.

Hall, D. and Hall, I. (1996) *Practical Social Research: Project Work in the Community*. Basingstoke: Macmillan.
Discusses issues such as negotiation of projects with local voluntary organizations, gaining access and the philosophy of collaborative research. The use of surveys, interviews, oral and life histories, observation and documents is covered, with abundant examples from actual projects used as illustrations.

Hobbs, D. and May, T. (eds) (1993) *Interpreting the Field: Accounts of Ethnography*. Oxford: Oxford University Press.
An edited collection based on first-hand accounts of conducting ethnographic studies. The contexts of study include the miners' strike 1984–5, football hooliganism, entrepreneurial crime, Greenham Common, drug dealing, 'race' and sexuality. The issues discussed include ethics, publication and fieldwork.

Holstein, J. A. and Gubrium, J. F. (1995) *The Active Interview*. London: Sage.
Guidelines are provided for those new to interviewing in this text which is located in terms of the interviewee and interviewer being 'equal' partners. The text includes guidance on sampling and analysis.

Homan, R. (1991) *The Ethics of Social Research*. Harlow: Longman.

Designed for undergraduate social science students, and those researching in education, sociology and psychology, this text explores a range of ethical issues associated with social research. Privacy, informed consent, covert methods, writing and publishing are all discussed.

Keats, D. M. (2000) *Interviewing: A Practical Guide for Students and Professionals.* Buckingham: Open University Press.

Considers the structure and process of interviews, their use in research and other settings, and the particular issues involved in interviewing children, adolescents, the aged, people with disabilities and people from different cultural backgrounds.

Lee, R. M. (1993) *Doing Research on Sensitive Topics.* London: Sage.

Through addressing questions such as sensitivity in the access process and the handling of data, sampling, surveying and interviewing, this text explores issues which can make research contentious. Indicative chapters are sampling rare or deviant populations, asking sensitive questions on surveys and in interviews, covert, adversarial and collaborative research.

Maynard, M. and Purvis, J. (eds) (1994) *Researching Women's Lives from a Feminist Perspective.* London: Taylor & Francis.

This collection of papers by well known feminist researchers indicates the practical issues involved in feminist research. The variables of 'race', age and sexuality are discussed in the context of issues such as employment, motherhood and violence.

Renzetti, C. M. and Lee, R. M. (eds) (1993) *Researching Sensitive Topics.* London: Sage.

This edited collection draws on work from psychology, sociology, nursing, public health, public policy, anthropology and economics. The five parts cover: what is sensitive research?, designing research on sensitive topics, sensitivity in field research, the use of feminist methodologies in researching sensitive topics, disseminating sensitive research findings.

Riessman, C. K. (ed.) (1994) *Qualitative Studies in Social Work.* Thousand Oaks, CA: Sage.

This collection of papers is written by social work practitioners and lecturers and emphasizes a range of qualitative approaches to issues of practice. The text includes discussion of observation, organizational documentary sources and interviews and is divided into three parts. These cover: grounded theory and health, narrative approaches to trauma, subjectivity matters, and the positioned investigator. The issues researched include pregnancy, sexual abuse, homelessness and child welfare.

Rosnow, R. L. and Rosenthal, R. (1997) *People Studying People: Artifacts and Ethics in Behavioral Research.* New York: W. H. Freeman.

With examples from actual experiments, considers how things can go wrong in research when people are involved, and what to do about it. The final chapter focuses on ethical and methodological issues.

Sapsford, R. and Jupp, V. (eds) (1996) *Data Collection and Analysis.* London: Sage.

Contains 13 chapters providing an overview of issues in research design, data collection and analysis for both quantitative and qualitative approaches. The most common methods are covered, including observation, questioning, databases and documents, along with statistical and multivariate analysis, and documentary and textual analysis.

Schratz, M. and Walker, R. (1995) *Research as Social Change: New Opportunities for Qualitative Research.* London: Routledge.

This text has a focus on the workplace as a site for research and a concern for the integration of research with professional practice. Using varied textual formats the book explores memory work, theorizing and the emotional work of undertaking research.

Seale, C. (1999) *The Quality of Qualitative Research*. London: Sage.
    Discusses the evaluation of qualitative research, and provides guidance on the collection of good quality data and its thoughtful analysis. Chapters examine issues such as contradiction, generalization, reliability and reflexivity.
Shakespeare, P., Atkinson, D. and French, S. (eds) in collaboration with Bornat, J., Brechin, A., Peace, S. *et al.* (1993) *Reflecting on Research Practice: Issues in Health and Social Welfare*. Buckingham: Open University Press.
    These reflective accounts are based on the personal experiences of research undertaken by the authors. They are written from a range of disciplines in the social sciences and humanities and seek to place 'self' at the centre of the analysis. The chapters focus on thinking, negotiating, explaining, observing, relating, sharing, presenting, performing, interpreting and telling.
Walford, G. (ed.) (1991) *Doing Educational Research*. London: Routledge.
    This text is composed of semi-autobiographical accounts of educational research. The issues discussed include obtaining funding, access, analysis, writing and dissemination.
Walford, G. (ed.) (1994) *Researching the Powerful in Education*. London: UCL Press.
    This edited collection focuses on the issues arising from studying the powerful. Four sections examine researching central government policy-makers, interpreting interviews, feminist perspectives and historical perspectives. The papers discuss access, use of dual interviewers, encouraging interviewees to be forthcoming, interpreting responses and ethical and political problems.
Wolf, D. L. (ed.) (1996) *Feminist Dilemmas in Fieldwork*. Boulder, CO: Westview Press.
    Eleven chapters reflect on the experiences of feminists in a variety of research settings. Discussion focuses on the contradictions stemming from the researchers' multiple positions as insiders, outsiders or both, and on attempts to overcome the power relationships that exist between researchers and researched.

# 7

## ANALYSING DATA

### ☐ Introduction

We hope that you are reading this chapter well before you have finished collecting your research data. You are likely, after all, to begin analysing your data before you have collected them all, possibly starting as soon as you have some data to work on. Analysis is an ongoing process which may occur throughout your research, with earlier analysis informing later data collection. Research is, as we have said at a number of places in this book, a messy process, and the stages and processes involved do not simply follow one after the other.

> You might like to refer back at this point to the section on **What is research?** in Chapter 1, particularly the discussion of representations of the research process.

You would probably be best advised to look through this chapter before you finally decide how you are going to focus your study, and what kinds of approaches and techniques you will apply. It makes sense to have some understanding of the kinds of data analysis you might engage in, and how the kinds of data you collect will affect and limit this, before you commit yourself to a particular project.

The purpose of this chapter, then, is to help you to get your data into shape, and to suggest how you might go about analysing and interpreting them. We start from those unsure, initial feelings, which are so common to both novice and more experienced researchers, of having an overwhelming or chaotic collection of research data. By the time you have finished this chapter, however, we aim to have taken you to a position where you can begin to write up your results and conclusions.

The chapter is organized in terms of the following themes:

- **The shape of your data**. The condition which your research data are in, and the facilities you have available for analysis.
- **The nature of data**. What research data are, the meaning of numbers and words.
- **Managing your data**. Coding, reducing and summarizing your raw data.
- **Computer-based analysis**. Using software packages with quantitative and qualitative data.
- **The process of analysis**. Thinking about and planning your analysis.
- **Analysing documents**. How to make sense of your notes.
- **Analysing interviews**. How to make sense of your transcripts.
- **Analysing observations**. How to make sense of your records.
- **Analysing questionnaires**. How to make sense of your replies.
- **Interpretation**. How to understand and contextualize the results of your analyses.

---

*Hint:* If you feel traumatized or terrorized by the  process of analysing the data you have collected, you might like to think of it as analogous to cooking. What and how you cook depends on your taste, skills and the resources you have available. You may like your food simple and freshly prepared, or carefully blended over a long period, or fast and processed. You may mix the ingredients together using a recipe, or based on previous experience, or you may buy a packet already prepared. You may use a range of tools in your cooking, from a simple knife or spoon through to an expensive food processor. You may be preparing food just for yourself or for a banquet. See if you can find further parallels as you cook your data!

---

## ☐ The shape of your data

Two basic issues affecting your whole approach to data analysis are considered in this section:

- the condition which the data you have collected are in;
- where, and with what facilities, you are able to analyse them.

### Order or chaos?

You will probably spend a considerable amount of time collecting your research data, and – unless you are relying entirely on secondary data sources with which

---

**Box 95: Ordered or chaotic data?**

| Appearance of order | Appearance of chaos |
|---|---|
| Neat notebooks | Odd notes |
| Card indexes | Scraps of paper |
| Piles of questionnaires | Baskets of cuttings |
| Colour-coded folders | Bulging or empty files |
| Labelled, transcribed tapes | Jotted down quotes |
| Highlighted photocopies | Half-remembered quotes |
| Clear plan and schedule | Old envelopes |
| Computer database | Illegible handwriting |

---

you are already familiar – the shape of the data collection you end up with will almost certainly be rather different from the way you had envisaged it when you started. While your plans for data collection may have seemed very methodical, the data you have actually collected may initially appear to be anything but. They may seem more chaotic than ordered (see Box 95).

Whether your data appear ordered or chaotic depends in part on your preferences, and in part upon your perceptions: one person's chaos may be another's order. The real issue is what works well for you. As long as you know where to find what you want or need to find, that is OK. If you are new to the process of research, of course, you may be finding this out as you go along. There is no single 'right' strategy for carrying out research, or for ordering and analysing data. Much of what is said in this book can be taken to indicate a preference for planning, structure and order, but these qualities may be conceived of very differently in practice.

The condition your data are in will undoubtedly, though, change during the process of analysis. However poor, ill-organized or inadequate you may think they are at the beginning, you are likely to find strengths as you proceed. Similarly, even if you start from the position that you have all the data you need, you are likely to recognize deficiencies as you get into the depths of analysis.

Data analysis is about moving from chaos to order, and from order to chaos, often simultaneously. Data which seem under control are likely to become somewhat more disorganized, at least for a while; while some semblance of order will be found, or imposed upon, even the most chaotic collection. The process may be uncomfortable at times. Which way do you need or want to move in analysing your data (see Box 96)?

Your data may, at any time during the process of analysis, appear to be both messy and structured. By the end of the process, however, you should at least be able to recognize both. Areas where you think that your data add to an understanding of the topic you are researching may be seen as ordered, while areas in which your work has raised more questions than answers (the normal pattern) may appear as more chaotic.

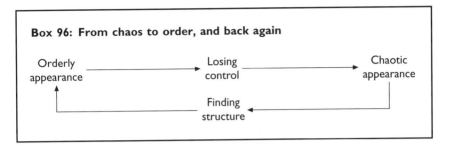

Box 96: From chaos to order, and back again

Orderly appearance → Losing control → Chaotic appearance → Finding structure → (back to Orderly appearance)

## Where to analyse, and with what

The resources you have available for your research, and how you might tailor your research plans to them, have already been considered elsewhere in this book.

You might like to have another look at the section on **Choosing a topic** in Chapter 2, and at the section on **Using wordprocessors and computers** in Chapter 5.

Obviously, you are restricted in how, where and when you carry out your data analysis by the available resources. There are, however, practical issues concerned with the place, space and time in which you do your analysis which are worth further consideration. These are the subject of Exercise 49.

Clearly, your answers to these and related questions will help to determine how you go about analysing your data. You will need to reconcile your preferences with what is feasible, and with the nature of the data you have collected.

---

**Exercise 49: Place, space and time for analysis**

Consider the following questions.

1 Do you prefer working at a desk or in an armchair?
2 Will you want to spread your work over the floor or a wall?
3 Do you like to work with paper and pen (or pencil) or straight on to the computer screen?
4 Does your analysis require large periods of time, or can it be done in smaller chunks, or are there elements of both?
5 Can you do your analysis in one place, or will it require visits to a number of separate facilities?

---

## ☐ The nature of data

The data you have collected are likely to be in a number of forms, though it is perfectly possible to carry out interesting and valid research with just one form of data. Take some time to remind yourself about the nature of your data, the amount you have, where they have come from and how they have been produced. Try Exercise 50.

Boxes 97 and 98 include a variety of examples of different sorts of data to remind you of some of the possibilities.

### The qualitative/quantitative divide

Among these different kinds of data we may recognize a basic distinction between the quantitative (i.e. numbers) and the qualitative (i.e. words). This distinction has a major influence on how data may be analysed, and also reflects the varied 'traditions', philosophies and practices of different social science disciplines or sub-disciplines. You are almost certain to have examples of both types among your data, though either the qualitative or the quantitative may predominate.

> You may wish to refer back to the sections on **Which method is best?** and **Families, approaches and techniques** in Chapter 3.

---

**Exercise 50: Thinking about your data**

What forms of data have you collected:

- questionnaires;
- computer-based databases;
- interview notes, recordings or transcripts;
- copies of documents;
- Internet materials;
- notes of readings;
- notes or videotapes of observations;
- measurements of behaviour;
- charts, maps, tables or diagrams;
- photographs;
- the notes in your research diary;
- other forms of data?

Make a note of the different forms of data you have collected, and roughly calculate the amount of each sort of data you have.

Think about where your different sorts of data have come from, how they have been collected or produced and how reliable they might be. Think also about by how much you will need to reduce the volume of your data in order to present, analyse and discuss them within the space you will have available.

---

## Box 97: Examples of quantitative data

| Subject | Providing institution | | | Totals (%) | |
|---|---|---|---|---|---|
| | University | Polytechnic | College | | |
| Architecture, building and surveying | 1 | 20 | 2 | 23 | (3.7) |
| Civil engineering | 1 | 7 | 2 | 10 | (1.6) |
| Electrical/electronic engineering | — | 9 | 3 | 12 | (2.0) |
| Materials studies | — | 7.5 | 1.5 | 9 | (1.5) |
| Mechanical/production engineering | — | 14 | 2 | 16 | (2.6) |
| Other engineering | — | 5 | — | 5 | (0.8) |
| Combined engineering | 1 | 5 | 1 | 7 | (1.1) |
| ENGINEERING | 3 | 67.5 | 11.5 | 82 | (13.3) |
| Biological sciences | 4 | 11 | 3 | 18 | (2.9) |
| Chemistry | 2 | 13 | 2 | 17 | (2.8) |
| Computer studies | — | 9 | | 10 | (1.6) |
| Environmental science | 4 | 2 | | 6 | (1.0) |
| Mathematical sciences | 2 | | | 17 | (2.8) |
| Physics | 2 | | | 11 | (1.8) |
| Combined science | | | | 13 | (2.1) |

| Region | Popn (m.) | FT stud/m resident | | | | PT stud/m resident | | | |
|---|---|---|---|---|---|---|---|---|---|
| | | U | P | C | O | U | P | C | O |
| 1. Greater London | 6.6 | 6994 | 5709 | 2635 | 666 | 1540 | 3132 | 1835 | 1605 |
| 2. South East | 5.3 | 3388 | 2239 | 1242 | 473 | 370 | 288 | 1506 | 1007 |
| 3. North Thames | 4.7 | 4363 | 1768 | 1813 | 251 | 549 | 564 | 2495 | 807 |
| 4. South West | 4.3 | 3659 | 2382 | 0 | 610 | 355 | 988 | 968 | 1043 |
| 5. East Anglia | 2.4 | 6580 | 4264 | 796 | 502 | 589 | 0 | 1332 | 748 |
| 6. East Midlands | 3.2 | 5163 | 3734 | 956 | 220 | 1495 | 877 | 506 | |
| 7. West Midlands | 5.1 | 3986 | 3642 | 613 | 358 | 599 | 1899 | 309 | 1142 |
| 8. Yorks & Humberside | 4.8 | 6370 | 3180 | 1732 | 157 | 448 | 1844 | 1001 | 702 |
| 9. North West | 6.4 | 4790 | 4491 | 1693 | 257 | 634 | 1506 | 1346 | 990 |
| 10. North | 3.1 | 4087 | | 302 | 332 | 514 | 1949 | 433 | 889 |
| England | 45.8 | 4947 | 3328 | 1485 | 389 | 273 | 1486 | 1270 | 1000 |
| | | | | | | 633 | | | |

Students/million residents
1  0–4999
2  5000–9999
3  10000–14999
4  15000–19999
5  20000+
Mean = 10149
Scale = 50 miles

| Variable | Factor 1 | Factor 2 |
|---|---|---|
| Canada | 1.98 | −.27 |
| United States | 2.15 | .18 |
| Japan | 1.06 | −.06 |
| Austria | −.98 | .20 |
| Belgium | −.28 | .04 |
| France | −.13 | .19 |
| | −.61 | .50 |
| | .05 | −2.43 |
| | −.59 | −.94 |
| | −.32 | .64 |
| ;dom | −.32 | .15 |
| | −1.31 | .00 |
| | −.66 | −1.53 |
| | −.69 | .71 |
| | .82 | .55 |
| | −.19 | 2.06 |

## Box 98: Examples of qualitative data

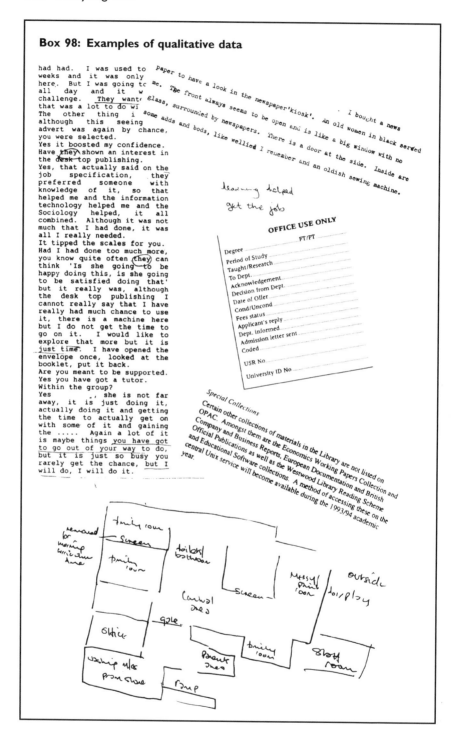

had had. I was used to weeks and it was only here. But I was going to all day and it w challenge. They want that was a lot to do wi The other thing i although this seeing advert was again by chance, you were selected.
Yes it boosted my confidence. Have they shown an interest in the desk top publishing.
Yes, that actually said on the job specification, they preferred someone with knowledge of it, so that helped me and the information technology helped me and the Sociology helped, it all combined. Although it was not much that I had done, it was all I really needed.
It tipped the scales for you. Had I had done too much more, you know quite often they can think 'Is she going to be happy doing this, is she going to be satisfied doing that' but it really was, although the desk top publishing I cannot really say that I have really had much chance to use it, there is a machine here but I do not get the time to go on it. I would like to explore that more but it is just time. I have opened the envelope once, looked at the booklet, put it back.
Are you meant to be supported.
Yes you have got a tutor.
Within the group?
Yes ., she is not far away, it is just doing it, actually doing it and getting the time to actually get on with some of it and gaining the ..... Again a lot of it is maybe things you have got to go out of your way to do, but it is just so busy you rarely get the chance, but I will do, I will do it.

Paper to have a look in the newspaper 'kiosk'. The front always seems to be open and is like a big window with no glass, surrounded by newspapers. There is a door at the side. Inside are some adds and bods, like wellied I remember and an oldish sewing machine.

. I bought a news me. . An old women in black served

learning helped
get the job

OFFICE USE ONLY
FT/PT
Degree
Period of Study
Taught/Research
To Dept.
Acknowledgement.
Decision from Dept.
Date of Offer
Cond/Uncond
Fees status
Applicant's reply
Dept. informed
Admission letter sent
Coded
USR No.
University ID No

Special Collections
Certain other collections of materials in the Library are not listed on OPAC. Amongst them are the Economics Working Papers Collection and Company and Business Reports, European Documentation and British Official Publications as well as the Westwood Library Reading Scheme and Educational Software collections. A method of accessing these on the central Unix service will become available during the 1993/94 academic year.

However, the distinction between words and numbers is not as precise as it might appear to be at first sight. Both offer representations of what we as individuals perceive of as our 'reality'. It may be that qualitative data offer more detail about the subject under consideration, while quantitative data appear to provide more precision, but both give only a partial description. Neither are 'facts' in anything but a very subjective sense. The accuracy of the representation is also likely to be reduced further during the research process, as we attempt to summarize or draw out key points from the vastness of the data available.

The quantitative and qualitative also have a tendency to shade into each other, such that it is very rare to find reports of research which do not include both numbers and words. Qualitative data may be quantified, and quantitative data qualified. For example, it is common practice in analysing surveys to assign, sometimes arbitrarily, numerical values to qualitative data, such as 'successful' (1), 'unsuccessful' (2).

Researchers who adopt an explicitly qualitative stance can find themselves giving prominence to numbers, and vice versa. Thus, if you conduct your research entirely through interviews, and analyse the results by searching for similarities and differences in the interview records, you are quite likely to end up using numbers or their written equivalents in your writing: 'all the interviewees', 'most of the respondents', 'half the women I spoke to' etc. Or, if you base your study wholly on numerical data, you will still introduce qualitative factors in your analysis, as in discussing the relative worth of different data sources, and in interpreting what your results mean for practice.

The next two sub-sections aim to make these points clearer. You may want to skip one or other of them if you are already familiar with quantitative or qualitative approaches.

## What do numbers mean?

Exercise 51 asks you to re-examine the examples of quantitative data included in Box 97.

Box 97 does not, of course, include examples of all the different kinds or uses of numbers which you might come across in the course of your research, but it

---

### Exercise 51: The meanings of numbers

Box 97 contains four examples of quantitative data: part of a table, a list of measurements from a survey, a map with areas shaded according to a scale and a list of factor scores.

Think about the following questions:

• What kinds of numbers are contained in these examples?
• How were these numbers collected or produced?
• What might you do with or say about these numbers?

---

does contain some of the most common. If you have carried out a survey or experiment as part of your research, you are quite likely to have produced figures not unlike those in the second example. These may include:

- direct measurements, or what might be called 'raw' or 'real' numbers;
- categories, where responses have been coded or assigned a numerical value;
- percentages, a measure of proportion;
- averages, which summarize a series of measurements.

The map in Box 97 is a particularly interesting example of quantitative data, since each area is coded according to its average score in terms of the scale given. Thus, we know within what range this score falls for each area, but do not know exactly what that score is. And, as with many reported averages, we do not know how variable the individual measurements from which it has been constructed were. In looking at the factor scores, many of you will probably have switched off, for, unless you know something of the multivariate technique known as factor analysis, you will have little idea of their possible meaning.

This last example highlights the relevance of the second question posed in Exercise 51. For these are undoubtedly quantitative data, and they might tell you a lot if you only knew how they were arrived at, and how to interpret them. This is a general issue, equally applicable to all the examples given. Every data source needs to be interrogated in terms of its representativeness, reliability and accuracy. Researchers ideally need to know by whom they were produced, for what purpose and in what ways. Numbers, by their very seeming precision, can hide their manufacture, imprecision and subjectivity. These issues are considered further in the section later in this chapter on *Interpretation*.

The third question posed in the exercise indicates that, once you are presented with a set of quantitative data, you can usually start to do other, quantitative or qualitative things, with it. You may have found yourself calculating averages, or thinking that one item was bigger or smaller than another, or of the same value. If you have sufficient information, you can calculate percentages from raw data, or produce the raw data from the percentages reported.

The quantitative data presented, whether you have produced them yourself or obtained them from a secondary source, are usually only the starting point of the analysis. In carrying out an analysis, the researcher inevitably gets further and further away from the original or 'real' data, and produces more and more highly manufactured abstractions. You need to be able to trace the routes taken in this process, whether they are your own or another researcher's.

### What do words mean?

Exercise 52, in a way analogous to the previous one, asks you to re-examine the examples of qualitative data included in Box 98.

As in the case of Box 97, Box 98 does not include examples of all possible forms or types of words. It is, obviously, restricted to English language sources for a start. Nevertheless, we can recognize from the examples given some of the most common forms of written data, including:

---

**Exercise 52: The meanings of words**

Box 98 contains four examples of qualitative data: part of an interview transcript, part of an official document, part of an unpublished circular, notes of an observation.

Think about the following questions:

• What kinds of words are contained in these examples?
• How were these words collected or produced?
• What might you do with or say about these words?

---

• directly written words, and spoken words which have been transcribed either directly or in the form in which they were reported;
• written notes, put together during, soon after or long after the events which they purport to describe;
• carefully considered written words, intended for publication and broad circulation, and those not published and meant for a smaller and more ephemeral distribution.

Within these examples, we can recognize different levels of abstraction. Notes clearly only offer a partial summary of events, focusing on those aspects which the person making the notes felt to be most significant at the time for their own purposes. Documents are usually only released after a process of drafting and redrafting, and may be as interesting for what they don't say as for what they do say, as well as for how they say it.

Even direct speech is selective, however, spoken only after the speaker has thought, for a lesser or greater period, about what to say; and determined in part by what the speaker thinks the listener might want to hear. It also, when compared with written English, betrays the effects of improvisation in its punctuation, stumblings, repetitions and pauses. Again, as with quantitative data, there is a need to interrogate the sources and ask where the speakers or writers are coming from and why.

This brief discussion suggests that some analysis has already occurred in all the examples given. Anything which you, as a researcher, may do to data such as these in the course of your analysis will further refine and select from the words given. Thus, you may choose (as we have) particular quotes or phrases as significant or illustrative, and will almost certainly in the end ignore the great bulk of the written texts available.

As you will probably have noted by now, the past two sub-sections, on the meanings of numbers and words, have been very similar in format and approach. We have taken this approach for two main reasons:

• the processes involved in analysing these forms of data are broadly analogous;
• neither form of data is intrinsically better, more accurate or actual – each has to be assessed, analysed and used on its own merits.

Having assembled your data for analysis, the next stage is normally a managerial one. This typically involves sorting, coding, reducing or summarizing the data from their original form, and getting them into a shape more suitable for analysis and reportage. These techniques are the subject of the next section.

## ☐ Managing your data

You might well find yourself, 6 months before the end of your study, with an alpine collection of information that might require a week just to read over carefully. A chronic problem of qualitative research is that it is done chiefly with words, not with numbers. Words are fatter than numbers and usually have multiple meanings . . . Numbers are usually less ambiguous and can be processed more economically. Small wonder, then, that many researchers prefer working with numbers alone or getting the words they collected translated into numbers as quickly as possible. We argue that although words may be more unwieldy than numbers, they can render more meaning than numbers alone and should be hung onto throughout data analysis.

(Miles and Huberman 1994: 56)

In answering the questions posed in Exercise 50, you should have realized, if you had not done so already, that you have collected a vast amount of data for the purposes of your research project. But your data in their raw state do not constitute the results of your research. You would be unlikely, for example, simply to bind together transcripts of all the interviews you have undertaken, or of all the questionnaires you have had returned, or of all the notes you have taken, and present that as your report or dissertation. That would be too long and too demanding for your readers, and it would lack insight and significance. The business of analysing the data you have collected, therefore, really involves two closely related processes:

*   managing your data, by reducing their size and scope, so that you can report upon them adequately and usefully;
*   analysing your managed set of data, by abstracting from it and drawing attention to what you feel is of particular importance or significance.

The first of these processes is considered in this section, the second in the remainder of the chapter. Each process is essential to research. The next section discusses the issues involved in deciding whether to use computer-based analysis or not.

*Hint:* Some of the tasks involved in analysing data are very basic and repetitive. Save these for when you are unable to do, or do not feel like doing, anything more demanding.

You may choose to manage your data in a whole series of related ways. Some of these you will already be familiar with, whether you realize it or not. Thus, the techniques described in Chapter 4, **Reading for research**, are all about management, and are used by many social science researchers. Those described in Box 99 are analogous, and also overlap to a considerable extent. You will probably use all of them in your own analysis.

All the techniques outlined in Box 99 may be applied to a range of types of data, both qualitative and quantitative. All of them also result, though perhaps not initially, in a reduction in the quantity of the data which you have available for analysis. This is essential if you are going to be able to carry out a manageable analysis. All are subjective to a greater or lesser degree, and all involve the loss of some information. Given the same data set, different researchers would proceed with its management in somewhat different ways, leading to different forms of analysis and different results. That is why, if you are involved in a group research project, it can be relatively easy for each of you to submit a different report.

## ☐ Computer-based analysis

It may be that your research project is sufficiently small-scale for you not to need to use sophisticated, computer-based software packages to analyse your data. Or you may have made a conscious choice not to do so: much analysis can, after all, be done manually, and you may prefer to do yours in this way. However, even if you have collected a relatively modest amount of data – say, a few dozen questionnaires, half a dozen interviews or the records of 20 observations – there is still much to be said for computer-based analysis. Once your data have been read into the computer, computer-based analysis is much quicker and more accurate than anything you might do manually.

If, then, you are considering using a software package to help you to manage and analyse your data, you will find it worthwhile to explore the various possibilities before committing yourself. The sooner you start doing this, the better.

> *Hint:* Doing a research project provides you with a splendid opportunity to learn about what some of these software packages can do. It is much more difficult to learn about them in the abstract, without any real data or any real purpose for analysing them.

Software packages designed to carry out quantitative analysis are much better established than those for qualitative analysis. The most widely available quantitative package in social science departments in universities is probably SPSS (the Statistical Package for Social Sciences). There are, however, other common quantitative data analysis packages, such as MINITAB; many spreadsheet and database packages also support the simpler forms of quantitative analysis.

**Box 99: Techniques for managing data**

*Coding*
The process by which items or groups of data are assigned codes. These may be used to simplify and standardize the data for analytical purposes, as when characteristics like sex, marital status or occupation are replaced by numbers (e.g. replacing 'male' by '1', 'female' by '2'). Or the process may involve some reduction in the quantity of the data, as when ages, locations or attitudes are categorized into a limited number of groups, with each group then assigned its own numerical identity (e.g. categorizing ages as 'under 21', '21–64' and '65 and over', and then replacing these by '1', '2' and '3' respectively).

*Annotating*
The process by which written (or perhaps audio or visual) material is altered by the addition of notes or comments. In books or papers, these may take the forms of marginal notes, or of underlining or highlighting of the text itself. The process may draw attention to what you consider to be the more significant sections, perhaps for later abstraction and quotation. Or it may serve as part of your continuing debate with your texts, a means to refine and progress your ideas further.

*Labelling*
Where you have an analytical scheme in mind, or are developing one, you may go through materials such as interviews or policy documents and label passages or statements with significant words (e.g. 'mother', 'conservative', 'career break', 'introvert'). These labels can then serve to direct your further analysis. A fine distinction might be drawn between the related processes of labelling and annotation, in that labelling smacks of stereotyping, of having your ideas or prejudices worked out in advance, whereas annotating seems more open or flexible.

*Selection*
A key process in the management of data, through which interesting, significant, unusual or representative items are chosen to illustrate your arguments. This may take the form, for example, of one member of a group, one institution, one answer to a survey, one particular quotation, one text or a number of such selections. The point is that you are choosing, for a variety of reasons, which examples of your data collection to emphasize and discuss. There is always a good deal of subjectivity involved in such a process.

*Summary*
The process where, rather than choose one or more examples from a larger body of data, you opt to produce a reduced version, precis or synopsis of the whole data set. This would probably aim to retain something of the variability of the original data collected, while saying something about the generality and/or typical cases.

*Note*: All these techniques may be carried out for qualitative or quantitative data, using available software as well as manually (see Box 100). The names given here to the techniques are often used in interchangeable ways.

SPSS enables you to input raw data, to modify and reorganize them once they have been inputted, and to carry out a wide range of simple, statistical and multi-variate analyses. These range from listing the frequencies of different responses and calculating means, through cross-tabulation, correlation and regression analyses, analyses of variance and covariance, to cluster and factor analysis. In the UK, the Economic and Social Research Council (ESRC) has funded a Teaching Resources and Materials for Social Scientists website (http://tramss.data-archive.ac.uk), which offers online training for those interested in statistical data analysis.

See also the section later in this chapter on **Analysing questionnaires**.

If your data are primarily qualitative, the choice of a software package to manage and analyse them may not seem as straightforward. Box 100 outlines some of the questions to bear in mind.

The Ethnograph, QSR NUD*IST and ATLAS.ti are probably the most familiar examples of data management packages for qualitative research. Another ESRC project, CAQDAS (http://caqdas.soc.surrey.ac.uk), provides a key site for information and knowledge about the software that is being developed to facilitate qualitative data analysis, with hot links to software developers and demonstrations. CAQDAS also provides transcription guidelines. SCOLARI, a division of the publishers Sage, produces many of the qualitative software packages, and offers free demonstration versions on its website (http://www.scolari.com).

## ☐ The process of analysis

Analysis can be a fearful word for the novice small-scale researcher. You will probably have started your research project with some preconceptions of what you would find. You have now collected a large data set on your topic, and have got it into a shape for analysis. But how do you get from the vast array of words and numbers that you have collected or produced to a seemingly neat set of conclusions or recommendations? What is this process called analysis? Exercise 53 asks you to think about the nature and meaning of analysis and some related words.

The five words listed in Exercise 53 – analysis, concept, explanation, theory and understanding – together with synonymous and related terms, are at the heart of the process of analysis. Put simply:

- *concepts* are abstract or general ideas, which are important to how we think about particular subjects or issues;
- *theories* are suppositions which explain, or seek to explain, something;
- *explanations* are statements which make something intelligible, about why things are the way they are;
- *understanding* is our perception of the meaning of something, in this case the subject area, the issues and/or the research questions under consideration.

---

**Box 100: Issues to consider when choosing data management packages for qualitative research**

1 Your primary concern should be your familiarity with computers. If you are new to this technology your safest choice is the wordprocessing package on your PC. Learn your computer's operating system, get used to moving text around and revising it. Find the *search* or *find* facility and learn how it works.

2 What kind of database and project is it? The issues to bear in mind include:

  - Whether you have single or multiple sources of data. If the latter, being able to make links between data sources will be important.
  - Whether you have single or multiple cases. If the latter, being able to select different groups of cases for analysis will be important.
  - Whether your records are fixed (e.g. official documents) or may be revised (e.g. interview transcripts). If the latter, facilities allowing you to revise your records (e.g. adding notes or codes) will be important.
  - Whether your data are strictly organized or free form. Some programs handle the former more efficiently.
  - Whether your data are uniform (e.g. all interviews) or diverse (e.g. interviews, documents, fieldwork notes). If the latter, linking facilities will again be important.
  - The size of your database.

3 What kind of analysis is anticipated? For example:

  - Exploratory or confirmatory? If the former, go for fast search and retrieval facilities; if the latter, theory-building features.
  - Is your coding scheme firm or evolving? If the latter, on-screen or automatic coding facilities will be useful.
  - Multiple or single coding?
  - Iterative or single analysis of data? The former need more flexible programs.
  - Fineness of analysis. Flexibility is again important.
  - Interest in the context of the data. Do you just want to look at particular words or phrases, or their context as well?
  - Display facilities. Program facilities vary a good deal.
  - Qualitative analysis only, or numbers as well?

4 Consider whether you should choose the best program for *this* project or the one that best covers the kinds of projects you may be doing over the next few years.

(Miles and Weitzman 1994: 313–15; see also Weitzman and Miles 1995)

---

Analysis is about the search for explanation and understanding, in the course of which concepts and theories will probably be advanced, considered and developed. You will find a great deal, and much more detailed, discussion of these and related ideas in some of the books listed in the **Further reading** section at the end of this chapter.

The next four sections pick up the discussion from Chapter 6, **Collecting data**, by focusing on the analysis of the four main techniques for data collection identified:

---

**Exercise 53: Some fearful words**

What do you understand the following words to mean?
- analysis
- concept
- explanation
- theory
- understanding

Try to write a brief definition in your own words. You probably won't find it very helpful to turn to a dictionary, as these tend to give sets of brief definitions, may well define some of the words given in terms of each other and do not have a research focus.

See also Exercise 10 in Chapter 2.

---

- documents;
- interviews;
- observations;
- questionnaires.

The examples and strategies discussed in these sections may seem to suggest that certain of these techniques are either predominantly qualitative or predominantly quantitative. It should be stressed, however, that each of these techniques may be applied to deal with either quantitative or qualitative data, or with both.

> *Remember:* Analysis is meant to be a rigorous process, using data that have been carefully produced and managed. In the end, however, what you produce from them is your own 'document', an attempt to persuade your readers of your own interpretation.

☐ **Analysing documents**

Documents . . . do not simply reflect, but also construct social reality and versions of events. The search for documents' 'meaning' continues, but with researchers also exercising 'suspicion'. It is not then assumed that documents are neutral artifacts which independently report social reality, or that analysis must be rooted in that nebulous concept practical reasoning. Documents are now viewed as mediums through which social power is expressed. They are approached in terms of the cultural context in which they were written and may be viewed 'as attempts at persuasion'.

(May 1993: 138–9)

The revisions to the unemployment count have implications for the comparability of unemployment data over time. Indeed, the Government Statistical Service has developed the seasonally adjusted unemployment consistent with current coverage (SAUCC) series which updates a back series of the claimant count to the current definition. However, the SAUCC series is not available at the local scale. Despite a series of analyses attempting to model these national changes at the local scale, most of the effects proved unquantifiable.

(Green *et al.* 1994: 144)

As we have already indicated, documentary analysis is akin to the processes gone through in reading for research purposes. These are discussed at some length elsewhere in this book.

---

See Chapter 4, especially the section on **Good enough reading** and Box 51; the section in Chapter 6 on **Documents**; and Chapter 8, particularly the section on **How to criticize**.

---

Documentary analysis involves the careful consideration of a range of related questions. These have been summarized in Box 101. Some examples of the process of analysing documents are given in Box 102.

Two key points come out the list of issues in Box 101, and the examples and quotations given in Box 102 and the text:

• Documents, whatever their nature (statistics or words, official or unofficial, public or private), cannot be taken at face value. They are artificial and partial accounts, which need to be critically assessed for research purposes.

---

**Box 101: Issues in documentary analysis**

For each document you are analysing, ask yourself:

• Who are the authors?
• What is their position?
• What are their biases?
• Where and when was the document produced?
• Why was the document produced?
• How was it produced? For whom?
• In what context was the document produced?
• What are its underlying assumptions?
• What does the document say, and not say?
• How is the argument presented?
• How well supported and convincing is its argument?
• How does this document relate to previous ones?
• How does this document relate to later ones?
• What do other sources have to say about it?

---

**Box 102: Examples of documentary analysis**

1  The original analysis of Summerland [the fire at the Summerland Leisure Centre in the Isle of Man] was based upon data drawn entirely from the official public inquiry into the incident . . . I worked paragraph by paragraph through this report, as I did for all of the accident reports published between 1965 and 1975. I asked, for each paragraph, what names or 'labels for ideas' I needed to identify those elements, events or notions which were of interest to me in my broad and initially very unfocused concern to develop a theory of disaster preconditions. I then recorded each name or concept label on the top of a 5" by 8" file card, together with a note of the source paragraph, and added further paragraph references to the card as I encountered additional instances of the concept identified. Eventually for my whole study I ended up with 182 of these cards, which had to be sifted, sorted and juggled into a coherent theoretical model. I produced general definitions for each of the categories which recurred, looking for causal and other links and moved gradually towards a theoretical pattern which helped to explain the range of data which I had about accidents.

(Turner 1994: 198)

2  Every copy of a trade union journal for a ten-year period was collected and examined. The analysis was both quantitative, in terms of content, and qualitative, based on selective reading and inference. The contents of the journal were classified into categories, with the number of contributions in each category counted and the contents of each article described. Conclusions were drawn about the relationship of the union to its membership, with suggestions about how this channel of communication could be used as an instrument of debate.

(Warran 1992)

3  Using data collected through the British and American components of the International Social Survey Programme, an analysis was carried out of gender role attitudes. A series of hypotheses were drawn up. Comparisons were made between the percentages of respondents endorsing 'egalitarian' as opposed to 'traditional' positions regarding role conflict, segregation and combination. These three indices were themselves created through a factor analysis of the data.

(Scott and Duncombe 1992)

---

• Much of the significance and interest in documents is revealed when they are considered in relation to each other. We develop our understanding of the ideas, issues and policies with which documents deal through a comparative analysis.

If you doubt these points, try Exercise 54.

Documentary analysis proceeds, therefore, by abstracting from each document those elements which we consider to be important or relevant, and by

---

**Exercise 54: Doing documentary analysis**

As an adult, or as a researcher, you will probably attend many meetings. Set yourself the task, at one of these meetings, of taking a note ('the minutes') of what took place and what decisions were reached. If you seldom or never attend meetings, you could take notes of a television programme instead.

Once you have finished, look at the document you have produced, and consider these questions:

- How full a summary of what was said, and what took place, have you produced?
- What did you leave out, and why?
- How have you organized your account?
- What biases are there in it?
- What other documents would help you to understand better the events described in your notes or minutes?
- How does the account presented in those documents differ from that which you have produced?

A variant of this exercise involves recording the same event with someone else: then you can compare the documents that you have produced.

---

grouping together these findings, or setting them alongside others which we believe to be related. What you see or read in documents will be a product of your viewpoint, discipline or focus.

## ☐ Analysing interviews

The analysis of data collected from focus group interviews can be long-winded and difficult. The data is not 'cold'. It has been collected within a certain interactive context, or a variety of different ones . . . and must be analysed with that in mind. Care must be taken that comments are not lifted or quoted outside that context or out of sequence. Conclusions arrived at under such conditions can be premature and misleading. The same participants in another forum may come to different conclusions.

(Williams 1994: 20)

We separated out the sections of the interview that were designed to yield specific scores based on the theoretical and empirical work of Perry, Kohlberg, and Gilligan. These sections were scored independently by coders who were 'blind' to (unaware of) the women's age, ethnicity, social class, institutional base, and other factors.

(Belenky *et al.* 1986: 14)

---

**Box 103: Examples of interview analysis**

1 Abramson and Mizrahi describe the use of a 'grounded theory' approach in the analysis of the transcripts of interviews which had focused on social worker–physician collaborations. They identify three phases of data collection and analysis:

- *Open coding*: the preliminary phase of analysis. Ten transcripts were reviewed to identify provisional concepts. These concepts were then modified and added to, leading to a redirection of the sampling strategy and improvements in interview techniques. The categories devised from this initial analysis were then applied to another round of data to see if they fitted.
- *Axial coding*: to seek connections between the categories identified. 'We had evolved from a simple enumeration of tasks (what social workers do) to a grouping of like properties (spheres in which they carry out their roles).'
- *Theoretical coding*: the evolution of a paradigm and a conditional matrix.

> We identified underlying uniformities (from the original set of categories and their properties), and formulated theoretical ideas from a set of concepts. We moved back and forth between inductive and deductive thinking, checking propositions about collaboration against the data. As we immersed ourselves further, patterns of collaborative behaviour and attitudes emerged.
>
> (Abramson and Mizrahi 1994, quotes from p. 38)

2 *An orderly person spreads out her interview records in the garden*

Hester was working on the records of the interviews she had carried out with a sample of students. Each record contained her typed up shorthand notes made during the interview, and a summary of the student's background. Each consisted of several pages, including direct quotations. She first went through the interview notes, analysing them 'question by question'. This meant having all the records spread out at once. She wanted her analysis to be both 'professional' and 'scientific', without losing the personal touch. She preferred an orderly approach:

> I tried breaking up all the scripts, question by question. I sat with the scripts and got out my pad, and went through each script and each question and noted down the similarities and dissimilarities. First of all I looked for common themes, and then I went through each script again noting which themes had come up.

---

Two examples of the process of analysing interviews are given in Box 103. These two examples usefully illustrate both some of the different approaches possible and some of the commonalities in the analysis of interview data.

The first example, involving two more experienced researchers, applied an established methodology, grounded theory. This approach was first developed in the 1960s by two American sociologists, Glaser and Strauss, though it built, of course, on existing practices. Thus, grounded theory involves the coding of the interview transcript – and/or other data collected – in terms of key concepts, which are mainly developed during the work itself. Coding may be carried out by individual researchers, alone, comparatively or together. Grounded theory also builds upon a cyclical or spiral perception of the research process, with concept development, data collection and data analysis taking place in close conjunction, and feeding into each other. As the research process unfolds, winding on and around itself, a clearer identification and understanding of the concepts of relevance is reached.

The second example in Box 103 involved a novice researcher who was not consciously following any particular approach to the analysis of the data she had collected. Nevertheless, the account of her analysis shows strong similarities to a grounded theory approach, though it was not as cyclical or extensive. The examination of interview transcripts question by question, and the comparison of the answers to specific questions given by a range of interviewees, is also analogous to the general approach to documentary analysis outlined in the previous section.

There are, of course, other approaches to the analysis of interviews. You may not produce a transcript, but analyse the tape recordings direct. You may not have recorded the interviews, but be working from your notes. You may input your data to a computer and use a software program for analysis (see the previous section in this chapter on **Computer-based analysis**). The process of looking for significant statements, and comparing what was said in different interviews, will, however, be similar.

## ☐ Analysing observations

A small sales and marketing team from a shoe manufacturing company were sent on a tour of the Pacific region to assess market potential. The marketing manager received two early reports. One read, 'The majority of the population are not wearing shoes: excellent marketing opportunity!' The other read, 'Most of the people do not wear shoes: poor marketing opportunity.'

As this (apocryphal) anecdote suggests, it is possible for two people to analyse the same observation data and come to very different, indeed diametrically opposed, conclusions. It is also possible, as the examples of the process of analysing observations given in Box 104 and the examples given in the previous chapter indicate, to focus on either a more quantitative or a more qualitative form of analysis.

> You might like to refer back to Box 88 at this point.

Based on the various examples which have been given, a number of key points may be made about the analysis of observations in social science research:

**Box 104: Examples of observation analysis**

1 This hierarchy is graphically demonstrated in the seating arrangements in registrars' chambers. In one court studied in the research, for example, there are two tables arranged in a 'T' shape. The registrar sits in the middle of the horizontal part of the T, looking down the vertical part. Everyone else sits along the vertical part: the barristers sit opposite one another nearest to the registrar; the solicitors sit next to them; and the clients sit beside them, furthest from the registrar.

Registrar

| Barrister | Barrister |
| Solicitor | Solicitor |
| Client | Client |

(Collins 1994: 184)

2 A simple chart, as in the example below, can be given to parents to help them think about the factors that trigger the problem as well as the consequences of the behaviour.

| Setting conditions | Behaviour | Consequences |
| --- | --- | --- |
| Checkout of supermarket | Screaming and struggling for sweets | Give him sweets to keep him quiet |

Other types of charts can record the incidence of the problem to see how often it occurs or whether there is any pattern in the day.

| Behaviour | 7.00 | 8.00 | 9.00 | 10.00 | 11.00 | 12.00 |
| --- | --- | --- | --- | --- | --- | --- |
| tantrums | ++ | | | | ++ | ++ |
| hitting | + | + | + | | ++ | |

(Douglas 1988: 135)

- quantified forms of observation lend themselves to fairly routinized forms of data collection and analysis, which can be very powerful in getting across particular issues in tabular or diagrammatic form;
- the collection and analysis of observation data, as with that of other research techniques, occurs as much in parallel as in sequence;
- observation, again like other research techniques, is very often used in conjunction with other methods, both to contextualize and to extend the analysis being carried out.

---

**Box 105: Mixing observation with other techniques**

I    By linking the everyday slogans, comments and anecdotes of the strike to material deriving from newspaper archives, company and trade union documents, letters and richly detailed minutes of trade union–management meetings, I was able to develop a longitudinal/processual analysis. This demonstrated how the contemporary beliefs, values and attitudes of the workforce, and the mutual feelings of animosity and distrust between employees and management, were shaped by a sequence of historical events stretching back over 20 years.

(Waddington 1994: 115)

2    While my approach was partisan, 'camera sociology' was not the method employed in the study. The policing of the Miners' Strike and the striking community's perceptions of it were situated within their historical, political, and economic contexts. In addition, the views of striking miners, while remaining the focus of the study, were not examined outside the context of the perceptions of other groups within the mining community. Picketing strikers were contrasted with non-picketing strikers, women, and working miners.

(Green 1993: 109)

---

The last of these points is further illustrated by the two examples reported in Box 105, both of which are at the 'participant comprehension' rather than the 'unobtrusive observation' end of the observation spectrum.

---

This distinction is made in the quote at the beginning of the section on **Observations** in Chapter 6.

---

These extracts both relate to studies of strikes, in one case the national miners' strike in 1984–5, in the other a brewery strike in 1981. Both researchers made considerable use of documentary and interview evidence alongside their observations. They 'lived' their research for the period of their projects; they were participant observers with their own political views on the events they were witnessing and researching.

The studies briefly reported in Box 105 make clear one further point about the analysis of observation data, namely that it is both selective and partisan. This is, however, true of all social research. While it seems obviously so in the examples quoted, and indeed is made manifestly apparent by the researchers concerned, these characteristics are present in other research projects as well. Being select-ive and partisan is inevitable in research, and it is healthy to recognize and discuss this within your project report or dissertation.

---

**Box 106: Examples of questionnaire analysis**

1 The following are some basic rules for coding:

    1 Codes must be mutually exclusive . . .
    2 Codes must be exhaustive . . .
    3 Codes must be applied consistently throughout.

  Five steps in the coding process are identified:

    • Developing the coding frame for both pre-coded and open questions.
    • Creating the code book and coding instructions.
    • Coding the questionnaires.
    • Transferring the values to a computer.
    • Checking and cleaning the data.
                        (Fielding 1993, quotes from pp. 225, 220)

2   [A]ssessing the degree of association between individual characteristics (such as sex or activity status) and learning status can be a complex process. The fact, for instance, that women are more likely than men to work part-time complicates exploration of the individual relationships between, first, sex and learning status, and, secondly, part-time employment and learning status. In order to address this problem more sophisticated statistical tools are required than those used in the previous chapter. The next two sections are based upon the results of analyses carried out using logistic regression. This multivariate technique constructs statistical models through which it identifies key characteristics (or variables) of use when attempting to predict an individual's learning status. This process subsequently allows the calculation of the estimated probability of an individual with certain characteristics being a learner.

                                          (Park 1994: 30)

---

## ☐ Analysing questionnaires

Some examples of the process of analysing questionnaires are given in Box 106.

The data collected by questionnaires may, of course, be either qualitative or quantitative. Alternative strategies for analysing qualitative data have been suggested and discussed in the preceding sections. Questionnaires do, however, lend themselves more to quantitative forms of analysis. This is partly because they are designed to collect mainly discrete items of information, either numbers or words which can be coded and represented as numbers. This emphasis is also partly owing to the larger scale of many questionnaire surveys, and their common focus on representation, which encourages a numerical or quasi-numerical summary of the results.

The discussion in this section focuses, therefore, on quantitative forms of analysis. This necessarily calls for some consideration of statistics, which is another

---

**Box 107: Levels of quantitative analysis**

*Descriptive statistics*
Variable frequencies, averages, ranges.

*Inferential statistics*
Assessing the significance of your data and results.

*Simple interrelationships*
Cross-tabulation or correlation between two variables.

*Multivariate analysis*
Studying the linkages between more than two variables.

---

of those terms which some readers may find very off-putting or threatening. Quantitative analysis may be used, however, at a number of levels, and the simplest of these may be the most useful in your case (see Box 107).

Many small-scale research studies which use questionnaires as a form of data collection will not need to go beyond the use of descriptive statistics and the exploration of the interrelationships between pairs of variables. It will be adequate to say that so many respondents (either the number or the proportion of the total) answered given questions in a certain way; and that the answers given to particular questions appear to be related. Such an analysis will make wide use of proportions and percentages, and of the various measures of central tendency ('averages') and of dispersion ('ranges') (see Box 108).

You may, however, wish or need to go beyond this level of analysis, and make use of inferential statistics or multivariate methods of analysis. There are

---

**Box 108: Descriptive statistics**

*For nominal or ordinal data*

• Proportions.
• Percentages.
• Ratios.

*For interval or ratio data*

Measures of central tendency

• Mean: total sum of values divided by the number of cases.
• Median: the value of the middle case.
• Mode: the most frequently occurring value.

Measures of dispersion

• Range: the difference between the highest and lowest values.
• Standard Deviation: the square root of the mean of the squared deviations from the mean.

---

---

**Box 109: Examples of inferential statistics**

*Chi-square*

- Function: to compare sets of values.
- Assumptions: random sampling, nominal data.

*Kolmogorov–Smirnov*

- Function: to compare two samples.
- Assumptions: random sampling, ordinal data.

*Student's t-test*

- Function: (a) single sample test of mean; (b) two sample test of means.
- Assumptions: random sampling, interval data, normal distribution.

---

dozens of inferential statistics available: three commonly used examples are outlined in Box 109. The functions of these statistics vary, but they are typically used to compare the measurements you have collected from your sample for a particular variable with another sample or a population, in order that a judgement may be made on how similar or dissimilar they are. It is important to note that all these inferential statistics make certain assumptions about both the nature of your data (see Box 110) and how they were collected, and should not be used if these assumptions do not hold.

Multivariate methods of analysis may be used to explore the interrelationships among three or more variables simultaneously. Commonly used examples include multiple regression, cluster analysis and factor analysis. While you do not need to have an extensive mathematical knowledge to apply these techniques, as they are all available as part of computer software packages, you should at least have an understanding of their principles and purposes.

See also the earlier section in this chapter on **Computer-based analysis.**

One key point to be aware of when carrying out quantitative analyses is the question of causality. One of the purposes of analysis, we have argued, is to seek explanation and understanding. We would like to be able to say that something is so because of something else. However, just because two variables of which you have measurements appear to be related, this does not mean that they are. Statistical associations between two variables may be a matter of chance, or due to the effect of some third variable. In order to demonstrate causality, you also have to find, or at least suggest, a mechanism linking the variables together.

---

**Box 110: Types of quantitative data**

*Nominal*
Numerical values are assigned to categories as codes.
For example, in coding a questionnaire for computer analysis, the response 'male' might be coded as '1', and 'female' as '2'.
No mathematical operations can be performed on the resulting codes. No ordering is implied.

*Ordinal*
Numerical values are assigned in accordance with a qualitative scale.
For example, in coding a questionnaire, the responses 'very satisfactory', 'satisfactory', 'neither satisfactory nor unsatisfactory', 'unsatisfactory' and 'very unsatisfactory' are coded '5', '4', '3', '2' and '1' respectively.
The ordering of the responses is retained in the coding.

*Interval*
Measurements are made on a quantitative scale, in which the differences between points are consistently of the same size but the base point is arbitrary.
For example, dates. The year AD 2000 occurs 1500 years after the year AD 500.
The ordering of, and distance between, values is given. Addition and subtraction can be used, but not multiplication or division.

*Ratio*
Measurements are made on a quantitative scale, in which the differences between points are consistently of the same size and there is a 'true zero'.
For example, people's ages, countries' population.
All basic mathematical operations – addition, subtraction, multiplication and division – may be applied.

---

## ☐ Interpretation

In 1951, Oscar Lewis published his *Life in a Mexican Village: Tepoztlan Revisited*. This was a study of communities previously studied by Redfield in the 1930s. Redfield had seen Tepoztlan as a society in which there was little change, a strong sense of belonging together and a homogeneity among the inhabitants. Lewis, in re-studying the community, was not trying to prove Redfield wrong, but looking for the type of errors that could be made in community studies. To Lewis, Tepoztlan manifested individualism not cooperation, tensions, fear and distrust rather than Redfield's picture of contentment and a sense of community.

(Shipman 1988: 71)

After presenting a lecture on the book's findings, I was approached by a member of the public who quietly and authoritatively explained:

'It's all bollocks, no offence mind, but it's bollocks. You make us all like fucking wallies, they must be them dopey ones who fuck up everything, but us no. Like me, I'm a face, East End face. I own two houses. I'm her landlord, yeah, the student she pays me rent. I could pull up £250k if I had to. I'm a face. No offence, but all these people in this book they must be fucking backward. I know a good champagne, Bollinger I always drink. I'm not the only one, there's lots like me, all my mates we're all like it, all got a few bob. The Pakis they come in, all this about capitalism and the docks, we moved out 'cos the Pakis. That's why we all vote for Maggie, fucking Labour won't let you buy your Council house. We got money all of us.'

    *D.H.:* 'Have you read the final section in the chapter on entrepreneurship?'

    'No, I just had a look at some of her notes, all these silly fucking stories so I thought I'd come and front you with it.'

(Hobbs 1993: 60–1)

Interpretation is the process by which you put your own meaning on the data you have collected and analysed, and compare that meaning with those advanced by others.

**Your own perspective**

We have emphasized at a number of places in this book how important it is to recognise, and make explicit, your own role and position within your research. This is partly about asserting ownership, and partly about recognizing the possible limitations, influences and biases of your own perspective. A critical element of the data analysis process is arriving at your own assessment of what the results mean, and how they relate to other relevant research and writing in your subject area. What do you think is significant? What do you think this suggests? Where and how do you think this kind of study might be developed further? These are the kinds of questions you should be asking yourself, and doing so, at least initially, without any direct reference to other authorities.

---

*Hint:* Try explaining it to a non-specialist again. See the section on **Focusing** in Chapter 2.

---

**Distancing yourself from your data sources**

At the same time as recognizing and asserting your own perspective on your data and their analysis, it is important not to get too embedded and bound up in this view. Researchers generally have a commitment to their projects, their methods, their data and their interpretations. It is healthy, therefore, to stand back for a time and attempt to view your research from the more dispassionate perspective of an outsider. Of course, it is impossible to do this in any absolute sense, given the personal commitment which any researcher makes to research. But it is possible to achieve some distance, though the ways in which you might do this will probably vary. Possible strategies include:

- the management of your data, through the processes of coding, annotating, labelling and so on, as discussed in an earlier section in this chapter, can reduce their immediacy and make them appear as if they have been put together by someone else;
- taking some time out, perhaps a week or two, before you come back to your analysis can increase the strangeness or foreignness of your data, and lead to a livelier interpretation (this is not a bad idea, if you have the time and are not afraid that you will lose your purchase, at any stage of your research);
- analysing your data alongside a similar set may lead you to focus on the similarities and dissimilarities, rather than just on your own findings and interpretations.

### Shared understandings

Having recognized, and begun to develop, your own perspective on what your research indicates, it becomes important to review these views in the light of those of others. To what extent do your findings, and your interpretation of them, agree or disagree with those of other authorities or researchers? Confirmatory or supportive results can be extremely useful in advancing general understanding. Such shared understandings can also be generated, by, for example, reporting on your findings in a seminar, workshop, conference or paper, and debating with others on their significance or interpretation.

### How to handle different accounts

As well as recognizing and building upon shared understandings, you will need to be able to accept and work from alternative perspectives. This can occur in at least two major ways: different accounts within your own data, and differences between your interpretations and those of others. Both are to be expected, welcomed and acknowledged. There is no reason, given our lack of comprehensive understanding of the world we live in, together with the varied perspectives held by different individuals, why our views and behaviours should always be common and shared. An important part of the interpretation of research is, therefore, the recognition of the diverging patterns within the data collected, and the attempted explanation of these. Similarly, you should not be unduly concerned if your findings appear to diverge from those of other researchers in your field; but you should look for reasons why this might be so, and/or argue the relevance of your interpretation against those of others.

### The value of data that don't fit

The preceding discussion suggests the importance of the observation that doesn't fit your general interpretation, or 'the exception that proves the rule'. This saying may, of course, be taken at least two ways. One, the most literal reading, suggests that a single exception is a rogue piece of data which should in effect be ignored. The other reading, perhaps the more relevant to the research process, would be that data which don't fit should not be ignored, but accepted, reported and cherished. It is not uncommon for accepted interpretations to be challenged and eventually demolished. Do not cast aside pieces of data which may be the basis for doing this!

## What does it all mean?

Unless your interpretation is to be a one-off and wholly personal exercise, you will have to engage in a more general consideration of the relevance and usefulness of your work. Such a consideration will bring you into touch with four related concepts: significance, generalizability, reliability and validity. All competent researchers need to have an understanding of what these concepts mean, and need to be able to review and defend their own work in this light (see Box 111).

---

**Box 111: Significance, generalizability, reliability and validity**

*Significance*
The concept of significance has both a specific, statistical meaning and a more general, common-sense interpretation. In statistical parlance, it refers to the likelihood that a result derived from a sample could have been found by chance. The more significant a result, the more likely that it represents something genuine. In more general terms, significance has to do with how important a particular finding is judged to be.

*Generalizability*
The concept of generalizability, or representativeness, has particular relevance to small-scale research. It relates to whether your findings are likely to have broader applicability beyond the focus of your study. Thus, if you have carried out a detailed study of a specific institution, group or even individual, are your findings of any relevance beyond that institution, group or individual? Do they have anything to say about the behaviour or experience of other institutions, groups or individuals, and, if so, how do you know that this is the case?

*Reliability*
The concept of reliability has to do with how well you have carried out your research project. Have you carried it out in such a way that, if another researcher were to look into the same questions in the same setting, they would come up with essentially the same results (though not necessarily an identical interpretation). If so, then your work might be judged reliable.

*Validity*
Validity has to do with whether your methods, approaches and techniques actually relate to, or measure, the issues you have been exploring.

---

---

**Exercise 55: The general applicability of your research project**

Consider the research project you have been carrying out, or which you plan to carry out, in the light of the discussion of significance, generalizability, reliability and validity in Box 111.

How significant, generalizable, reliable and valid do you think that your research and its findings are (or will be)? Does this matter to you?

---

Having looked at Box 111, you might like to try Exercise 55.

In the end, your interpretation of your findings is, however, limited by the methods you have used and the sample you have studied:

> some of the seeming polarity in the debate around home-based work can be explained by the differing methodologies and sampling procedures. For instance, the evidence collected by local homeworking research projects, officers and campaigns on the incidence and persistence of extremely low-paid, arduous, manufacturing, home-based work in the UK had often only been possible after building of trust between project workers and home-based workers . . . but because these surveys have been conducted largely in inner cities they have had little to say about non-manual homeworkers and whether the latter face particular problems.
>
> (Phizacklea and Wolkowitz 1995: 19)

Small-scale research has its limitations, therefore, but is also able to make a significant contribution in less studied areas.

## ☐ Summary

Having read this chapter, you should:

- have an appreciation of the different forms of data, and the kinds of analysis appropriate to them;
- be aware of the interleaving processes of data management, analysis and interpretation which are involved in making sense of your data collection;
- have an understanding of the different approaches which you might take to the analysis of documents, interviews, observations and questionnaires;
- be able to assess the significance, generalizability, reliability and validity of your research and findings.

## ☐ Further reading

In this section, we list a selection of books which are of particular relevance to the topics discussed in this chapter, together with an indication of their contents.

Argyrous, G. (2000) *Statistics for Social and Health Research, with a Guide to SPSS.* London: Sage.
The six sections of this comprehensive text cover univariate descriptive statistics, bivariate descriptive statistics, inferential statistics (for one sample, two or more independent samples and two dependent samples) and multivariate descriptive statistics.

Babbie, E. R. and Halley, F. (1995) *Adventures in Social Research: Data Analysis Using SPSS for Windows.* London: Pine Forge.
Designed for students, this text introduces SPSS through Windows. The text includes activities to aid learning.

Bryman, A. and Burgess, R. G. (eds) (1994) *Analysing Qualitative Data.* London: Routledge.
This edited collection explores the practice and processes of qualitative analysis through first-hand accounts. Examples include the use of computers, discourse analysis, the linkage between qualitative and quantitative data. Discussions of projects conducted by single researchers and teams are included and the contexts of research comprise fieldwork with gypsies and stepfamilies, media, women's economic lives, adult kin relationships, education and health.

Bryman, A. and Cramer, D. (2000) *Quantitative Data Analysis with SPSS Release 10 for Windows,* 2nd edn. London: Routledge.
A step-by-step guide, with examples, to the use of the various quantitative analysis procedures available with SPSS.

Champney, L. (1995) *Introduction to Quantitative Political Science.* New York: HarperCollins.
An introduction to the computation and interpretation of statistics, and to key concepts of social scientific enquiry. Includes both academic and practical applications, together with examples of research articles and reports with accompanying critiques.

Coffey, A. and Atkinson, P. (1996) *Making Sense of Qualitative Data.* Thousand Oaks, CA: Sage.
This text focuses on the processes of analysing and writing in qualitative research. The chapters include discussion of concepts and coding, narratives and stories, meanings and metaphors, and writing and representation. Particular attention is paid to the use of computer-aided analysis.

Coxon, A. P. M. (1999) *Sorting Data: Collection and Analysis.* Thousand Oaks, CA: Sage.
Part of an extensive series of short books on 'quantitative applications in the social sciences'. Includes chapters on the collection, description and comparison, and analysis of free sorting data.

Cramer, D. (1997) *Basic Statistics for Social Research: Step-by-step Calculations and Computer Techniques Using Minitab.* London: Routledge.
An introduction to the use of a range of statistical techniques with the Minitab package. Topics covered include measurement, statistical significance, tests of difference and association for different kinds of data, regression, reliability and agreement.

Cramer, D. (1998) *Fundamental Statistics for Social Research: Step-by-step Calculations and Computer Techniques Using SPSS for Windows.* London: Routledge.
Explains how and why to apply a range of common statistical procedures to social science research, using SPSS for Windows.

Cramer, D. and Bryman, A. (1996) *Quantitative Data Analysis with Minitab.* London: Routledge.
Designed as a non-mathematical introduction for social scientists, explains the use of statistical tests in non-technical language.

Dale, A. and Davies, R. B. (eds) (1994) *Analyzing Social and Political Change: A Casebook of Methods*. London: Sage.
The problems and possibilities of analysing change over time are presented in this edited collection. A number of techniques are outlined, including event history, time series analysis, multilevel and log-linear models.

Dey, I. (1993) *Qualitative Data Analysis*. London: Routledge.
This text is mainly concerned with the use of computers for analysing field data, although in detailing the steps the text contains more generalizable discussion in relation to qualitative analysis. Mapping across cases, linking data, splitting and slicing are all dealt with.

Feldman, M. S. (1994) *Strategies for Interpreting Qualitative Data*. London: Sage.
Four different strategies to analysing qualitative data are presented in this text. These are ethnomethodology, semiotics, dramaturgy and deconstruction. Each of these is applied to a single data set and the different results are presented.

Field, A. (2000) *Discovering Statistics Using SPSS for Windows: Advanced Techniques for the Beginner*. London: Sage.
Covers data exploration, correlation and regression, logistic regression, comparing means, analysis of variance and factor analysis. A CD-ROM containing SPSS data sets and examples is included.

Fielding, J. L. and Gilbert, G. N. (2000) *Understanding Social Statistics*. London: Sage.
The three sections of the book focus on preliminary issues (including the use of computers), univariate analysis (e.g. frequencies, percentages, measures of central tendency, the normal curve) and bivariate analysis (e.g. correlation and regression, sampling and inference, modelling data).

Foster, J. J. (1998) *Data Analysis Using SPSS for Windows*. London: Sage.
Following an introductory overview of statistical analysis, 20 chapters set out what can be done with SPSS, illustrated stage by stage. Topics covered include *t*-tests, analysis of variance, correlation and regression, non-parametric techniques, reliability analysis and factor analysis.

Gahan, C. and Hannibal, M. (1998) *Doing Qualitative Research Using QSR NUD*IST*. London: Sage.
A practical guide to using the NUD*IST package for the analysis of unstructured data such as text from interviews, historical or legal documents, or non-textual material such as videotapes.

Hinde, A. (1998) *Demographic Methods*. London: Arnold.
Describes and explains the methods used to analyse population data. Covers basic methods, as well as parity progression ratios, survival analysis and birth interval analysis. Includes exercises, plus access to data sets on the publisher's website.

Hinton, P. R. (1995) *Statistics Explained: A Guide for Social Science Students*. London: Routledge.
Written for psychology and other social science students, this text takes the reader through the principles of statistical analysis. Indicative contents are: descriptive statistics, hypothesis testing, sampling, significance, variance, ANOVA, chi-square and using statistics programs on computers. The text includes an appendix of statistical tables.

Howarth, D. (2000) *Discourse*. Buckingham: Open University Press.
A comprehensive overview of the different conceptions and methods of discourse analysis, and of the traditions of thinking (structuralist, post-structuralist, post-Marxist) from which these have emerged.

Hoyle, R. H. (ed.) (1999) *Statistical Strategies for Small Sample Research*. Thousand Oaks, CA: Sage.

The methods and issues considered include randomized designs, bootstrapping, categorical and non-parametric data, dynamic factor analysis and structural equation modelling.

Josselson, R. and Leiblich, A. (eds) (1995) *Interpreting Experience: The Narrative Study of Lives*. Newbury Park, CA: Sage.

Narrative analysis forms the framework of this book and is applied to career biography.

Kelle, U. (ed.) (1995) *Computer Aided Qualitative Data Analysis*, London: Sage.

An edited collection which discusses the role of the computer for analysis and theory building.

Keren, G. and Lewis, C. (eds) (1993) *A Handbook for Data Analysis in the Behavioural Sciences: Methodological Issues*. Hillsdale, NJ: Lawrence Erlbaum.

This text comprises a collection of papers which deal with statistical analysis in psychology. The emphasis is as much on the understanding of, and creativity in the use of, statistics as technical competences. The text is divided into four parts, dealing with models and measurement, methodological issues, intuitive statistics, hypothesis testing, power and effect size.

Langford, D. (1994) *Analysing Talk: Investigating Verbal Interaction in English*. Basingstoke: Macmillan.

An introduction to the structure of talk, this text uses a series of exercises to support readers' understanding. Topics include patterns of speech activities, turn-taking, the organization and patterns of talk and transcribing talk.

Levitas, R. and Guy, W. (eds) (1996) *Interpreting Official Statistics*. London: Routledge.

Critical guide to the use and interpretation of British official statistics, including data on households, unemployment, social class, health, manufacturing safety, working women, ethnicity, disability and crime.

Lewis-Beck, M. A. (ed.) (1993) *Experimental Design and Methods*. London: Sage.

Volume 3 in the *International Handbook of Qualitative Applications in the Social Sciences* series, this text is an introduction to experimental approaches. Discussion includes focusing on issues of design and analysis, emphasizing the quantitative approach.

Lewis-Beck, M. A. (ed.) (1993) *Basic Statistics*. London: Sage.

This introductory text is composed of five parts: central tendency and variability, understanding significance testing, analysis of nominal data, analysis of ordinal data, measures of association.

Lewis-Beck, M. A. (ed.) (1993) *Regression Analysis*. London: Sage.

This text is written for those, particularly non-experimentalists, who are interested in developing their competence in the techniques of regression analysis. The text is composed of five chapters which build on each other in terms of levels of difficulty.

Miles, M. B. and Huberman, A. M. (1994) *Qualitative Data Analysis: An Expanded Sourcebook*. London: Sage.

Over 300 pages of techniques, ideas and references, this text has been written to aid researchers in all fields of social research and at all levels. The contents of the book have been drawn from literature searches and through a snowball sample of researchers who were asked for specific examples from their own work.

Persell, C. H. and Maisel, R. (1995) *How Sampling Works*. London: Pine Forge.

An introduction to statistical sampling and inferences, this text aims to be non-mathematical in approach.

Psathas, G. (1994) *Conversation Analysis: The Study of Talk-in-interaction*. London: Sage.

This text outlines the procedures and strengths for those interested in conversation analysis.

Rose, D. and Sullivan, O. (1996) *Introducing Data Analysis for Social Scientists*, 2nd edn. Buckingham: Open University Press.

Five sections cover the logic and language of social research, from data collection to computer, descriptive data analysis, inferential data analysis and multivariate analysis. Includes an introduction to the use of computers and SPSS, exercises and a data disk.

Solomon, R. and Winch, C. (1994) *Calculating and Computing for Social Science and Arts Students: An Introductory Guide*. Buckingham: Open University Press.

Part I of this text begins at the level of basic arithmetic (fractions, multiplication, division) and takes the reader through modes, medians, means, regression and *t*-tests. Part II discusses the jargon associated with computing (RAM, WIMP, viruses), and steps in learning wordprocessing, the use of spreadsheets, databases and using the computer to aid analysis.

Traub, R. E. (1994) *Reliability for the Social Sciences: Theory and Application*. Thousand Oaks, CA: Sage.

Concerned with outlining the principles of reliability theory, this text indicates the ways in which measurement can be improved. The text also aims to promote understanding, and consequent implications, of the error associated with measurement and observation in the production of quantitative data. The text includes questions for students at the end of each chapter.

Wasserman, S. and Galaskiewicz, J. (eds) (1995) *Advances in Social Network Analysis: Research in Social and Behavioural Sciences*. London: Sage.

For those interested in the ways in which social networks can be studied and analysed, this text includes discussion of the applicability of social network analysis and specific contexts for the study of social networks. These include inter-organizational relations, the spread of disease in epidemiology and social influence.

Weitzman, E. A. and Miles, M. B. (1995) *Computer Programs for Qualitative Data Analysis*. Thousand Oaks, CA: Sage.

The authors ask 'Do you want to start, extend or update your use of computer software for qualitative data analysis?' If so, this text has been designed for you. The book reviews over 20 programs, as well as giving guidance on choice of computer in relation to potential research plans.

Wolcott, H. F. (1994) *Transforming Qualitative Data: Description, Analysis and Interpretation*. London: Sage.

Using examples from his own work, Wolcott takes the reader through the processes of description, analysis and interpretation.

Wright, D. B. (1997) *Understanding Statistics: An Introduction for the Social Sciences*. London: Sage.

This book begins by examining the theoretical relationship between statistics and research, then examines the use of *t*-tests, regression, analysis of variance, two variable tests and more advanced techniques.

# 8

# WRITING UP

## ☐ Introduction

Research without writing is of little purpose. There are, of course, other ways of communicating your research and its findings, most notably through oral presentation, but writing them up remains of paramount importance in most areas of research. The research report, thesis or dissertation, the journal article, academic text and conference paper remain the major means by which researchers communicate with each other, and with other interested parties, across space and time. The rapid development of new information and computer technologies may have changed the speed and scope of such communication, but it has not altered the importance of writing as the means for communicating.

It is something of a contradiction or paradox, therefore, that many researchers, both novice and experienced, are extremely reluctant or fearful of committing their ideas to paper. This is perfectly understandable in the case of the new or relatively inexperienced researcher, who may have little idea of the potential readership or what might be expected. That it is common among older and more experienced researchers would seem to indicate a distaste for the writing experience, partly due, no doubt, to a preference for other aspects of the research process, as well as a continuing lack of confidence in their abilities.

Writing up is not just a critical, but also a continuing, part of the research process, which should start soon after the commencement of the research project, and continue to and beyond its completion. So don't be misled by this being the penultimate chapter: writing up begins as soon as you start thinking about and reading around your research.

The purposes of this chapter, then, are to encourage early and regular writing, to identify the different skills and issues involved in writing up research and to build up confidence by confronting the concerns commonly encountered in writing up.

This chapter has the following sections:

* **Drafting and redrafting**. How to progress your writing up.
* **How to argue**. The organization and structure of your writing.
* **How to criticize**. Placing your work in the context of that of others.
* **Who am I writing for?** Writing appropriately for your audience.
* **Grammar, punctuation and spelling**. Some hints and tips.
* **Using tables, diagrams and other illustrations**. When and when not to.
* **Panics**. Common worries encountered in writing up research.

## ☐ Drafting and redrafting

The matter of typing reveals in part the whole philosophy for the research paper. The key words in this philosophy are organisation, discipline and convention . . . in my experience, students tend to carry over into the realm of the research paper attitudes and aims, formed in the field of creative writing, that have no place in research . . . Organisation is necessary for the efficient allocation of one's time and effort, and for the presentation of a paper whose internal structure is balanced and sound, and whose argument proceeds along logical lines. Discipline is central to the long labour of sifting authorities, and adding one's own critical comments only when these authorities have been fully assimilated. Conventions are vital in a context where one writes not for oneself, but for a critical public.

(Berry 1994: 2–3)

I realised that I was trying to ensure that my ideas were 'right', so that I could be sure when voicing them, and not expose myself to either undue praise or criticism. I despaired of achieving this, especially given some of the thorny, long-running questions in the area (such as whether men and women are *really* the same or different), and the many committed camps of theorists. I envied the makers of films such as 'Thelma and Louise', who seemed to be able to present multi-faceted explorations of gender-related issues without taking the mincing steps of academic debate. Happily I woke one morning with a revelatory insight – that I would never get it right, that seeking to do so was a futile waste of energy, that I should proceed with this 'truth' in mind and allow myself to be more playful in my explorations.

(Marshall 1995: 28–9)

Writing up your research should start early and become a regular and continuing activity. It is also likely to be an iterative or cyclical process. That is, you will draft a section or chapter, then move on to some other activity, and return one or more times to redraft your original version. This is partly because as the totality of the research thesis or report takes shape, what you have written in subsequent sections affects what you wrote earlier and necessitates changes in it. It is also the case that as your research proceeds you find out more, read more and change your mind about some things.

Two key skills here are, therefore: recognizing when you need to redraft your report or thesis, or part of it; and knowing when you have done enough drafting, and it is time to present your report or thesis, and then move on to something else. Writing up, like other aspects of research, is at root a set of pragmatic skills, honed through experience.

---

The importance of recognizing when you have done enough is the subject of the next chapter, **Finishing off**.

---

### How to recognize procrastination and what to do about it

What do you do if you just don't know how or what to write, or you don't feel like writing? We have all, at one time or another, sat in front of a blank screen or sheet of paper. You may be suffering from any of the 20 forms of procrastination listed in Box 112, or from some other unmentioned version. At such times, the suggestion that you just start by writing anything seems trite and

---

**Box 112: Twenty forms of procrastination**

1  I just can't get started.
2  There are too many words to write.
3  There are too few words to play with.
4  I've never written an academic thesis before.
5  I've never written a work report before.
6  I'll do it tomorrow.
7  I'm not in the mood.
8  I'd rather be surfing.
9  It's too noisy to concentrate.
10  I can't type.
11  My wordprocessor has broken down.
12  It's all been done already.
13  What's the point?
14  The oven needs cleaning.
15  It's too difficult.
16  I'm no good at writing.
17  I've only got half an hour.
18  I wish I'd never started.
19  I don't feel very well.
20  The children will be home soon.

---

**Box 113: Twenty suggestions for overcoming procrastination**

1 Make notes on what you have read.
2 Make notes on interviews you have conducted.
3 Make notes on your last discussion with your supervisor or manager.
4 Draft your contents page.
5 Type out your references or bibliography.
6 Draft the structure for a section or chapter.
7 Type out the quotations you think you may use.
8 Note down the points you think you will refer to.
9 Set yourself a target for writing a given number of words each day, week or month.
10 Speak your ideas out loud, tape record and then transcribe them.
11 Write anything so that you dirty your page or screen.
12 Work out how many words you will devote to each chapter, section or sub-section.
13 Write up to your word limit, and then edit what you have written.
14 Give yourself a treat, but then come straight back.
15 Think about all the other time you procrastinated, and what you did about it then.
16 Don't allow yourself to do anything else until you have written something.
17 Give someone else the responsibility to oversee your writing.
18 Talk it through with somebody else.
19 Try writing at a different time of day, or time of the week.
20 Just write anything.

---

unhelpful. You might find some comfort and assistance in Box 113, which contains 20 practical suggestions for overcoming procrastination.

Whatever your reasons for procrastination, the basic advice has to be to do something, whatever works, to get you writing something, and preferably something which will be of use to you. What you write is unlikely to come out straight away as a polished and finished piece of work, however good and experienced at research writing you are. The point is to aim to produce some writing as regularly as you can, and then work from that. It is likely to get somewhat easier as you progress, though there will be more and less difficult times throughout.

Most of the problems and suggestions contained in Boxes 112 and 113 are dealt with, directly or indirectly, later in this chapter. The remainder of this section tackles three of the most common issues encountered in drafting and redrafting your writing.

### Editing and reworking your writing

Once you have written something – anything – the writing up process becomes in part a process of rewriting what you have already written. You will need to rewrite in order to:

- bring in new material, ideas and thinking;
- reduce the length of what you have written;
- revise old sections to refer to newly drafted material;
- alter the structure of what you have written;
- respond to the suggestions made by your readers;
- remove any inadvertent repetitions.

Redrafting is a normal event. It does not mean that your original draft is useless, merely that the writing process takes place over a period of time, during which you do what you can to make your report or thesis as effective as possible.

The process of redrafting is made a lot easier if you are writing on a wordprocessor or computer. This will enable you to access easily those sections you wish to change or update, to move sections of text around, to make simple alterations throughout the text, to check your spelling, and may even produce a contents page and index for you. If you don't have a wordprocessor, you will still need to do these kinds of things, but it will take a little longer manually.

You may want to refer back to the section in Chapter 5 on **Using wordprocessors and computers**.

One question often posed about redrafting is how often to do it. This depends partly on your own preferences, and partly also on the length of your project in both time and words. The longer the project, the more likely it is that you are going to want to redraft at a number of stages, and your work is likely to benefit from this. For relatively small-scale projects, including those lasting less than one year, it may be best first to draft all the chapters or sections individually, though not necessarily sequentially, and have a single redraft near to the end of the project. Either way, it is good practice to make notes on earlier drafts, as you go along, as to where and how you intend to make changes.

*Hint:* It is a good idea to meet with your supervisor, mentor or manager before (and after) you produce your final draft.

### Writing to the appropriate length

The need to reduce the length of what you have written has already been highlighted as one of the reasons for redrafting material you have already drafted. You might also, though this is probably less likely, need to increase the length of what you have written.

---

**Box 114: How to contract your writing**

1 Remove unnecessary, qualifying or repetitive words, and perhaps clauses, from sentences.
2 Summarize two or more sentences, perhaps whole paragraphs, in one sentence.
3 Delete references and quotations which are not essential to your discussion.
4 Replace lengthy descriptions by tables or charts where possible.
5 Remove whole sections, or perhaps even chapters, where these are not central to your argument.

---

Writing to the appropriate length is not easy. You may have a specific limit, perhaps both a maximum and a minimum, set on the number of words and/or pages which your report or thesis can comprise. Or you may have general guidance, or perhaps no guidance at all, in which case it could be a good idea to set your own limit, and then check this out with your likely readers.

There are two basic approaches which you can then adopt for writing to a given length:

• the *planned* approach, where you sketch out the contents of your report or thesis in some detail, allocate a given number of words or pages to each sub-section and then endeavour to keep to those lengths as you draft;
• the *slash and burn* approach, where you initially draft without reference to any length constraints, and then subsequently cut down or extend your drafts as necessary.

Whichever combination of these approaches you use – it is unlikely that you will be able to rely solely on the first approach – you will probably need to employ a range of simple techniques for getting your initial drafts to the appropriate length in the redrafting process.

To contract your writing, you might use any or all of the five techniques outlined in Box 114. These techniques avoid the use of artificial and self-defeating methods, such as reducing your print size, increasing the size of your page or placing more material in appendices outside of the main text. All researchers have to engage in editing their work at some time; most have to do it repeatedly. It is both a courtesy to your readers, to reduce the amount of time they have to spend in getting to the nub of your argument, and a means of helping to ensure that you have more readers.

The need to expand what you have written is a less obvious skill in writing up, but all researchers have to face it when they first begin to turn their outline into the finished report or thesis. It may also be necessary at a later stage when you, your supervisor or manager detect imbalances or omissions in your work. You can't assume that your readers know all that you know, so there may be a need to put in more explanatory material. To expand your writing, you might use the five methods listed in Box 115.

---

**Box 115: How to expand your writing**

1 Look for more references and quotations on the subjects or issues which you are writing about.
2 Build individual sentences up into paragraphs by developing your argument.
3 Add new sections, or even chapters, of relevant material.
4 Integrate appendices within the main text.
5 Take more space to discuss your methodology, and how well it worked.

---

## Coping with interruptions

[W]hen I came to write, there were very few material obstacles in my way. Writing was a reputable and harmless occupation. The family peace was not broken by the scratching of a pen. No demand was made upon the family purse . . . You have only got to figure to yourselves a girl in a bedroom with a pen in her hand. She had only to move that pen from left to right – from ten o'clock to one.

(Woolf 1995: 1–2)

You may not be so fortunate! Most researchers, particularly those carrying out work-based projects and those who are studying part-time, have to learn to cope with interruptions. This can be particularly irritating when they occur during the process of writing up, since then the need for peace and quiet can seem to be particularly strong.

The obvious way of coping with this problem, if possible, is to confine your writing to times and places when you are unlikely to be interrupted. Do it at lunch time, after working hours, when the children are at school or when they have gone to bed. Do it in a separate study, in a library, in a quiet room, away from home and work if necessary.

If these suggestions are impractical in your case, you might be best advised to do your writing up in a very planned way. That is, outline what you are going to write in considerable detail, so that you can then do it bit by bit or sub-section by sub-section. This way, you are less likely to lose the thread of what you are writing when you are interrupted, or, if you do, will need to spend less time to recover it.

---

*Hint:* When you stop writing for a period, write a note for yourself on what you planned to do next. Map out your plans several steps ahead if you can. This should be very useful in getting you back into writing quickly next time.

## ☐ How to argue

### Organization

Writing up your research, whether in the form of a work report or an academic thesis, requires particular skills and forms of organization. The extent to which you make use of these will vary depending on the size and scope of your research project.

However, in organizational terms, your report or thesis is likely to include, as a minimum:

1 An introduction, at the beginning, and a set of conclusions, at the end. These may be supplemented or perhaps replaced by, respectively, a summary and a series of recommendations.
2 A series of distinct sections or chapters, which may be further divided into sub-sections or sub-chapters. Each section or chapter may have its own introductory and concluding passages.
3 References to existing research and publications, possibly illuminated by selected quotations. A list of the material referred to will be included, probably at the end of the report or thesis, possibly in the form of a bibliography.

In addition, your report or thesis may include:

4 Tables, diagrams, charts and other forms of illustrations (the use of these is discussed in more detail later in this chapter).
5 A number of prefatory sections, such as a preface, abstract, dedication and acknowledgements; and/or supplementary sections, in the form of appendices.

> The use of prefatory sections and appendices is discussed in the section on **Added extras** in Chapter 9.

### Argument

These organizational elements are the bare bones of any research report or thesis. To put them together to make a successful and effective argument requires four things:

• a context;
• one or more themes;
• some ordering;
• linkages.

> You may like to refer back to the section in Chapter 2 on **Focusing**, which discusses related issues at an earlier stage of the research process.

The *context* for your report or thesis, and for your research project as a whole, consists of your broader understanding of the area within which you are researching. This may operate at least at three levels:

- In terms of your disciplinary background; thus, if you are a sociologist, this will be sociology and sociological writings.
- In terms of your field of study; for example, the sociology of the family, transport economics, 16–19 educational policy.
- In terms of the methodology you are employing; for example, questionnaire surveys or participant observation.

Your report or thesis may not refer to all these levels, but it is likely to include some reference to at least two of them if you are to provide an adequate contextualization of your study for your readers. This contextualization is likely to form an important part of the early sections or chapters of your work, with some reference back to it towards the end.

The *themes* of your report or thesis are the key issues, concepts or questions you identify as being of relevance and interest. These will both inform the research you undertake, so will be evident in your contextual discussion, and help to structure your analysis and findings. They are the aspects of your field of study or discipline to which your research is contributing. They could include, for example, development theory, gender relations at work, the spatial structure of the city, the effectiveness of different forms of staff training or measures of monetary supply.

These themes are likely to be introduced early on in your report or thesis, forming part of its context. They will then be referred to throughout the main body of your discussion, as the running thread holding it all together. A significant part of the concluding sections will probably be devoted to reflecting on what your research has told you about these themes, and how they might be explored further in future. Exercise 56 is designed to help you to identify the context and themes for your writing.

The *ordering* of your report or thesis relates to how you set out your argument in stages, and how you break it down into manageable chunks for the reader. We have already indicated some aspects of this ordering, by referring to the use of introductory and concluding sections, and suggesting an early contextualization and a later discussion and reflection. Some further suggestions as to what a typical academic thesis or work report might look like are given in the next sub-section.

---

### Exercise 56: Context and themes

Note down the context and themes for your research report or thesis. If your context is complex, as it is quite likely to be, or you have several themes, draw a diagram or chart to make clear the linkages involved. What does this suggest for the organization and argument of your writing?

See also Exercise 10 in Chapter 2.

---

*Linkages* have to do with how you aid readers in finding their way through your report or thesis. They may take the form of regular references to the themes you have identified. They are also likely to be made apparent through cross-references between chapters, sections or pages. The aim is to present a coherent whole to the reader, however the report or thesis may be structured and organized. When done effectively, readers should be able to make sense of your work quickly, whichever page they start reading from.

## What an academic thesis or work report might look like

Boxes 116 and 117 offer suggestions of what academic theses and work reports, based on a small-scale research project, might actually look like in terms of organization and structure.

It should be emphasized at once that these are just examples, albeit common ones. The indications as to chapter or section titles, and as to the relative proportion of the overall report or thesis which they would comprise, are meant only as guidelines. There are many other, and much more innovative and interesting, ways of putting together a report or thesis. Every individual case is likely to

---

**Box 116: Possible forms for an academic thesis**

1    A dissertation is far more than a passive record of your research and generally involves presenting an argument or point of view. In other words, it must 'say' something and be substantiated with reasoned argument and evidence. If you want it to be interesting as well as academically convincing, you will need to raise intriguing issues and discuss them, besides presenting your outcomes.

(Barnes 1995: 100)

2   The 'classic' dissertation structure is:

- contents;
- abstract;
- introduction (10 per cent of words or space);
- review of the background literature (20 per cent);
- design and methodology of the research (10 per cent);
- implementation of the research (15 per cent);
- presentation and analysis of data (15 per cent);
- comment and critique of the outcomes or findings (20 per cent);
- summary and conclusion (10 per cent);
- references;
- bibliography;
- appendices.

'[A]cademics . . . say they enjoy innovative structures devised by their students, but they also warm very positively to this classic model.'

(Barnes 1995: 130)

---

---

**Box 117: Possible forms for a work report**

1 *Executive summary*
A one-page synopsis of the research, focusing on its practical implications (5 per cent).

*Aims and objectives*
As specified by the funder or researcher (5 per cent).

*Context*
A discussion of the organization and its work, and of the reasons for undertaking the research (30 per cent).

*Results*
An account of what the research discovered (50 per cent).

*Recommendations*
A list of actions to be taken (10 per cent).

2 There are other formats for writing research reports . . . There is the *psychological format* where the logical approach is reversed. The conclusions and recommendations come first (after the introduction) and the findings are presented later. This is an arrangement widely used in what might be called *popular reports*, e.g. for business clients. Typical contents of a popular report would be:

- title-page,
- list of contents,
- research project objectives,
- methods used,
- conclusions and recommendations,
- findings,
- appendices.

This style is simple, clear and free of jargon and complicated statistics.
(Bennett 1983: 188–9)

---

differ, not least in terms of varying disciplinary practices, and of the titles and sub-titles used. It would be excessively boring for the readers of research if all reports or theses were arranged in this fashion.

*Health warning:* Remember to check on any regulations or expectations which might affect what your thesis or report should look like.

By comparison with academic theses, work reports tend to be more brief (otherwise they are never read) and to focus more clearly on the practical applications of the research undertaken. Research is rarely undertaken in the work setting for the sake of it. However, as in the case of the academic thesis, the bulk

---

**Exercise 57: Organizing your argument**

Having looked at the suggestions in Boxes 116 and 117 as to what an academic thesis or work report might look like, draw up a chart of how you propose to organize your argument, giving chapter or section titles and summary contents. How much space might you allocate to each of your chapters and sections?

---

of the work report is likely to be devoted to a discussion of the context for the research and of the results uncovered.

Three further differences may be noted. First, the work report is much less likely to include a separate section of references. Fewer works will typically be mentioned, and they will tend to be detailed in the text itself. Second, the work report is quite likely to be presented in terms of numbered sections and paragraphs, rather than chapters. Third, it may contain an executive summary at the beginning.

Exercise 57 invites you, in the light of these suggestions, to consider how you will organize your research report or thesis.

## ☐ How to criticize

The most common motives which govern academic writing are these:

- AGREEING WITH, ACCEDING TO, DEFENDING or CONFIRMING a particular point of view;
- PROPOSING a new point of view;
- CONCEDING that an existing point of view has certain merits *but* that it needs to be QUALIFIED in certain important respects;
- REFORMULATING an existing point of view or statement of it, such that the new version makes a better explanation;
- DISMISSING a point of view or another person's work on account of its inadequacy, irrelevance, incoherence or by recourse to other appropriate criteria;
- REJECTING, REBUTTING or REFUTING another's argument on various reasoned grounds;
- RECONCILING two positions which may seem at variance by appeal to some 'higher' or 'deeper' principle;
- RETRACTING or RECANTING a previous position of one's own in the face of new arguments or evidence.

(Taylor 1989: 67)

Where it is not explicit, criticism is implicit within research writing. Since you are always writing within the context of existing research and understanding, your research also constitutes your evaluation of others' work and beliefs. This is the essence of criticism: placing your work within the context of that of others; acknowledging the deficiencies of that work, both yours and theirs; and then moving the debate forward.

---

You may like to refer back to the section in Chapter 4 on **Good enough reading**, particularly Boxes 50 and 51.

---

### Criticizing is not rubbishing

Criticizing others' research and writing does not mean rubbishing them. You may, in certain extreme cases, feel that this is justifiable, but it is unlikely to achieve much. By the same token, the blind acceptance of others' data, arguments and conclusions, just because they have been published, or because they are widely accepted, is ill advised. Even the most reputable authors may benefit from a little measured criticism.

Criticism is evaluation. It should be careful, considered and justified. It should also be even-handed, recognizing that you are capable of error, and may change your mind in time. Anything may be criticized: underlying assumptions, arguments, methodologies, the accuracy of data collected, the interpretation of that data. You may also use your own research to assess that of others critically, where you feel these are in disagreement.

Criticism is about joining in a wider research debate with others you may never meet. Research is never perfect. It could always have been done differently or better. By joining in a critical debate, you can help to improve future research and understanding.

### Using your sources

At the heart of critical writing is your use of your sources, your response to them and your written account of this. Much depends, therefore, on the reading you have undertaken, a theme dealt with in Chapter 4. Your sources cover more than just all the published or unpublished materials which you may have accessed and studied in the course of your research project. They also include your broader engagement with ideas through discussion with others, as well as your own research data and your interpretation of this.

You should make full use of this range and variety of sources in your writing, where it is relevant to, or illustrative of, the argument you are putting forward. Thus, you will probably use selected sources:

- to build up the context for your own research, demonstrating existing thinking and practice;
- to exemplify and justify the methodology you adopted;
- to complement, or contrast with, your findings and interpretations.

You will be likely to have a mixture of positive and negative comments to make about these sources.

### Establishing your argument

Do not, however, get swamped by your sources. Even if your aim is just to provide a synopsis of the literature, it is your argument and your interpretation that should be at the forefront of your writing. You need to control your sources, therefore, rather than have them control you. You will provide the summaries and the linkages; you will determine the order in which you introduce and comment on your sources; you will decide what else to add and how to progress the argument of your research.

This will involve establishing your voice and your argument early on in your report or thesis; maintaining it as the key thread running through your work; and returning to a fuller evaluation of it at relevant points.

### Going back to the literature

As well as returning to your argument, it is common to return to a discussion of existing research and understanding towards the end of your thesis or report. Having introduced and critically discussed a selection of this material early on, you can then relate it to your own research findings once these have been presented and discussed. You may wish to re-evaluate your earlier thinking and criticism at this point.

As this suggests, the whole process of criticism, like that of research as a whole, is cyclical and iterative. As a researcher, you are engaged in a continuing round of evaluation and re-evaluation.

### ☐ Whom am I writing for?

'Research' is a process which occurs through the medium of a person – the researcher is always and inevitably present *in* the research. This exists whether openly stated or not; and feminist research ought to make this an open presence. To paraphrase a slogan once current in the gay movement, researchers must 'come out' in their writings.

(Stanley and Wise 1983: 179)

### Voice and style

When you start to write up your research, there are two related issues which you will need to address, whether explicitly or implicitly, early on. These are the issues of voice and style:

- *style* relates to how you write up your research, which may be determined by the requirements of your audience, by your own predelictions or by a mixture of the two;
- *voice* has to do with how you express yourself and tell the story of your research, and is something you are likely to develop further as you write and research.

## Box 118: Writing styles

Middleton's paper is written in two columns. It has been deliberately structured in this way to indicate the links between theory and 'lived reality' which can be generative of theoretical construction. It is also a response to, and demonstration of, postmodernist writing techniques. Middleton says 'This is an experimental piece of writing, which transgresses conventional academic forms in order to expose their constructedness.' An extract from the article is given below. The left-hand column is written in conventional academic form and is concerned to draw out the implications of 'postmodern theory for feminist pedagogy in education courses'. The right-hand column describes the 'location and circumstances in which the left hand column was written'.

### TOWARDS A FEMINIST PEDAGOGY FOR TEACHER EDUCATION

Academic papers normally begin, as Dorothy Smith has described it,

from a position in the discourse as an ongoing process of formally organized interchange. We begin from a position within a determinate conceptual framework which is identified with the discipline. ... and by virtue of our training and of what it means to do the professional work in our discipline, we begin from outside ourselves, to locate problematics organized by the sociological, the psychological, the historical discourse (Smith, 1979: 146).

Postmodernism is becoming increasingly influential within feminist educational theory. Post-modernists have rejected the monolithic categories upon which previous feminisms have rested - 'the rationally autonomous individual' (liberalism); the 'essential feminine' (radical feminism); and the class-differentiated gender groups of Marxism. Post-modernist theories are based on a scepticism about the possibility or desirability of attempting to produce totalizing

### INTERRUPTIONS

It is the last day of the Winter term. Tomorrow the August study break begins. Winter sun beckons me through my office window. I shall go home early - snatch this afternoon to write my proposal for AERA. I want to reflect on the experience of being a feminist academic writer - to write about the rhythms, and the fragmentations, of our lives. The harmonies, dissonances, and disruptions...

The phone shrieks. A breathless voice asks, "Dr Middleton - have you noted the change in date for the meeting of the Administrative Committee? It will now be at 9.00 on the first morning of the study break?"... I hadn't...The relevant agenda surfaces from the cascades of papers on my desk. I place it in my canvas carry bag and dig deeper under the piles of unopened brown envelopes for my copy of the conference paper instructions...

This office is seldom my space for academic writing. It is the place where I compose memoranda, file minutes of meetings, write letters in response to the contents of brown envelopes... It is also the space where I meet with students. I have made it as 'safe', as 'like home' as possible. The bureaucratic flooring is covered with a large rug - earth-colours -ochre red, gold, beige, black. There is an old armchair in one corner. The cream walls are hidden behind shelves of books. Above the smaller book-cases are pictures - a poster from Queensland; a batik from Kenya. Near the door is a sketch which my daughter, Kate, drew several years ago for a social studies project. Hippies - beads, flowers, banners... A 1960s protest march.

Like many of today's feminist teachers and writers I attended university during the 1960s and began paid work (in my case secondary school teaching) in the early 1970s - times of full employment and hope. Today, as an educator in the 1990s, I watch my students and my daughter moving into adulthood in times of economic recession and despair. The kinds of feminism and progressive educational theories which offered possibilities to my generation may seem to today's students irrelevant and quaint anachronisms. How can we, middle-aged and older teachers of women's studies

*Source:* Middleton (1995, quotes from pp. 87 and 88, extract from p. 89)

---

**Exercise 58: Voice and style**

Look at the quotes at the beginning of the section on **Drafting and redrafting**. Now look at the extract from an article in Box 118.

What are the issues that come to your attention in relation to:

(a) writing styles you are comfortable with;
(b) appropriateness for your audience?

Practise writing in different ways for exploratory purposes. Discuss your findings with your mentor, manager or supervisor.

---

It is a good idea to study a variety of examples of research writing to get some guidance on both the range of possibilities and how you might approach your own writing. Box 118 contains extracts from an article which deliberately counterposed two very different forms of writing. Exercise 58 invites you to reflect upon styles and voices in writing. Box 119 suggests some good reasons why you might want to experiment with alternative forms of writing.

One of the key distinctions here is whether to write impersonally in the third person (e.g. 'it appears') or in the first person (e.g. 'I found'). Writing impersonally is standard for much research, and conveys an impression, whether justified or not, of considered and distanced objectivity. The first person comes across as more immediate, personal and committed, and does not deny any inherent subjectivity. Whether you use the first or third person will depend upon your discipline, your politics, your purpose and your audience.

## Representing reality

Another key factor to be borne in mind during your writing up is that you are in the process of fashioning and presenting a representation of reality. You are, in other words, telling a story, and need to be aware of the different techniques which you might make use of in so doing. Indeed, it has been suggested that constantly asking 'What's the main story here?' (Strauss 1987: 35) is a useful tool for data analysis. Your research participants and sources may be seen as the characters in this story, and will need to be introduced and developed as they would be in a novel.

This is not to imply that your research has been made up, or is arbitrary or wholly subjective. You will probably have devoted a lot of time and consideration to collecting data, assessing their reliability and then interpreting what you have found. Yet, however much work you have done, you are highly unlikely to have exhausted your research topic, and you will not be in a position to write the last word on it. You will have partial and incomplete information, and should be aware of its deficiencies as well as its strengths.

---

**Box 119: Alternative forms of writing**

As more attention has been given to the connections between writing in the social sciences and writing in the humanities, there has been a growing interest in alternatives to traditional forms of writing. There are some very good reasons why researchers may want to experiment with different writing styles:

- Engaging in experimental forms of writing allows the researcher to nurture her or his voice. This is important because it presents a counterbalance to a problem for many new, and established, researchers when they are over-reliant on the voices of others. For example, a poem does not require citations. You are freed up to create your new knowledge without feeling that you have to know everything that has been written on the topic.
- Experimental forms of writing are explicit attempts to engage the emotions of the writer and the reader. This can be either positive or negative. For example, Richardson (1992) describes how writing her data as poems enabled her to engage with the subject of her research in a much more intensive and joyful way. Alternatively, some readers may reject data-led poems because they do not conform to traditional expectations.
- Experimental forms of writing can give greater recognition to how readers create their own meanings. A common method for reporting research is one where the researcher's main aim is to guide the reader through the 'facts' of the research in a linear or cumulative way. The data are used as evidence of the findings. However, some researchers try to disrupt the idea that the researcher has all the knowledge. They want to leave more space for readers to come to their own conclusions. Using different forms of writing is one way in which researchers try to do this. For example, the lines of a standard text are dense and often crammed on to the page. A short poem will have a much less cluttered appearance. The idea is that as the clutter diminishes, so the potential for thinking and feeling around, within and through the words and lines grows. In the poem's refusal to run common phrases together, we are caused to pay attention and to notice that which we mostly skim over. And, while we may be tempted to speed read a poem, as is common in academic work, why bother? Their point is to open up the potential for new and unexpected ways of knowing.

---

## Different audiences and conventions

The different demands posed by writing your research up for your employer and for academic credit are discussed in the section on **How to argue** earlier in this chapter. Each of these approaches has its own varying set of conventions and particular styles, as well as similarities. Whichever you are writing, it is critical – as we repeatedly emphasize throughout this book – that you are aware of, and adhere to, any and all regulations or expectations concerning your writing up.

### Safe and risky writing

Even if you take note of any and all regulations or expectations affecting your writing, there are still safer and riskier strategies for writing up. When in doubt, as when you are a novice researcher and you are unsure of the likely response to what you are writing, it is almost certainly in your best interests to adopt a safe strategy in writing up. If you are rather more experienced, think you are on to something, want to give yourself an extra challenge or simply can see no other way of doing it, you may choose to write up your research in a less standard and hence more risky fashion.

You might, for example, opt to write in the first person, and perhaps in an autobiographical style. You might use a chapter or section structure very different from those suggested in this book. You might include poems or fictional elements in your report or thesis. You might present your work in terms of a dialogue or a play. All these strategies can work very well, and can further illuminate the representational elements and issues involved in doing research. You would be well advised, though, to do some sounding out among your assessors or likely readers in advance.

What you want to avoid is a strong reaction against, or rejection of, your report or thesis purely on the basis of the way in which it has been written up and presented. You don't want to have to do it all again, reworking your writing to a more conventional or acceptable style. So don't take the risk unless you really have the freedom and know what you are doing.

### Non-discriminatory writing

Beyond any formal regulations, there is now a general expectation that all writing will strive to be non-discriminatory. To do otherwise would make you likely to offend your readers, at the very least. You may actually be provided with, or recommended to, a style guide by your institution or employer. If not, the references at the end of this chapter contains some helpful sources.

The basic principle involved is writing in a way that does not denegrate or exclude particular groups of people on the basis of what may be fairly arbitrary characteristics, such as sex, age, race, religion, physical and mental abilities or sexual orientation.

### References or bibliography?

Another question you may face in writing up your research is whether to include a bibliography or just a set of references. The difference may be very small in practice:

- a set of references contains details of all the books, articles, reports and other works you have directly referred to in your thesis or report;
- a bibliography contains details of all, or a selection of, the books, articles, reports and other works of relevance you have consulted during your research, not all of which may be directly referred to in your text.

Whether you provide references or a bibliography may already have been determined for you. Alternatively, restrictions on the space you have available for writing up may lead you to restrict yourself to just essential references or a select bibliography. In other cases, you will have to decide for yourself which is the most appropriate strategy. It is very unlikely, and probably inadvisable on grounds of space and repetition, that you will wish to include both references and a bibliography.

*Hint:* Check your file of regulations and expectations, and follow the conventions of your discipline and institution.

Whichever you do use, you should make sure that you include full details of all the works you refer to, so that your readers can themselves track them down and examine them if they so wish. Exercise 59 offers you a chance to test the thoroughness of your referencing practice.

See the section in Chapter 4 on **Recording your reading**, particularly Box 54.

**Exercise 59: What is wrong with these references?**

Bearing in mind the strictures on accurate and full referencing made in the text, what errors or omissions can you detect in the following list of references?

Hoyte, R. 'How I Got my First in Human Communication'. pp. 25–30 in Arksey H. (ed) *How to Get a First Class Degree: recent graduates disclose how they got their 'first' at university.* Lancaster, University of Lancaster, Unit for Innovation in Higher Education.
Hughes, C., and Tight, M. (1996) 'Doughnuts and Jam Roly Poly: sweet metaphors for organisational researchers'. *Journal of Further and Higher Education*, 20, 1.
Hulton, P. (1990) *Survey Research for Managers: how to use surveys in management decision-making* (2nd edition) Basingstoke, Macmillan.
Jones, L. (ed) (1983) *Keeping The Peace.* The Woman's Press.

To check your views, have another look at the section in Chapter 4 on **Recording your reading**. Or check with the list of references at the end of this book.

**Being consistent**

Above all, whatever audience you are writing for, it is important to be consistent in terms of style and organization. Switching between styles is usually confusing for all concerned, and hence inadvisable, except in exceptional and/or carefully handled circumstances. Thus, if you have written your thesis or report in the third person, and in a measured style, it is unwise to begin using the first person suddenly. The main exception to this is what you write in prefatory sections, such as a preface or acknowledgements, which lie outside of the main content of your thesis or report.

> The use of prefatory sections is discussed in the section on **Added extras** in Chapter 9.

## ☐ Grammar, punctuation and spelling

Many researchers, even experienced ones, have problems with grammar, punctuation and spelling when they are writing up. This is not unusual and should not be a cause for shame. Many of us may not have had a particularly good initial education, or were more interested in other matters at the time. For others, English is not their first language. However, once you begin to write up your research for consideration and assessment, as a report or as a thesis (and particularly if you are thinking of publishing some or all of it), your use of 'correct' grammar, punctuation and spelling becomes very important. Your readers are likely to be irritated, amused or put off by errors. They will detract from your ability to get your ideas across.

There is not enough scope in a book of this nature to provide detailed guidance on this subject, but Box 120 suggests a number of general points to bear in mind.

---

**Box 120: Some tips on grammar and punctuation**

- Try to avoid long sentences. The sense of what you are saying gets lost, whereas a series of shorter, punchy sentences can advance the argument in a much better way.
- Avoid one-sentence paragraphs. Paragraphs should contain a number of sentences on the same subject, and then lead on to the next paragraph, which will move the discussion on.
- Avoid beginning sentences with 'joining' words, such as 'but', 'and' or 'because'. These should normally be used to link clauses within sentences.
- Avoid incorporating lengthy lists of material in your text. Your writing should read as a flowing piece of text, not as a summary or precis. If you need lists, they are probably better placed separately from the main text in tables or figures.
- Understand and make use of the full range of standard punctuation forms; including, in particular, the colon (:), semi-colon (;), comma (,) and full stop (.).
- Use quotation marks (" and ') consistently.

Beyond this basic guidance, there is a range of useful existing publications which you could turn to. Some of these are listed in the annotated bibliography.

If you are writing your research up on a wordprocessor, you might want to make use of the facilities which much software has for checking your spelling and grammar, and for suggesting alternative words to use. These can be very useful for checking drafts, but remember that they will not recognize many specialist words or names, and, perhaps most importantly, that they often use American English spelling.

---

See the section in Chapter 5 on **Using wordprocessors and computers**.

---

## ☐ Using tables, diagrams and other illustrations

It can be a good idea to include tables, diagrams and other illustrations in your research report or thesis, providing that these are both permitted and relevant. Such illustrations may serve to illuminate, break up, extend and confirm your writing. Their impact and intelligibility can be heightened further if you have access to a colour printer.

Tables may be used to summarize information, usually in a numerical format, and to indicate the relationships between the different variables under consideration. Diagrams are also useful for indicating relationships and structures: they can convey ideas much more effectively than lengthier textual explanations.

While tables and diagrams are the most common and popular means for illustrating research reports or theses, many other kinds are used. Maps may be used to illustrate relative locations, and are common in geographical research. Graphs show relations in linear form between pairs of variables, as in the case of time series or correlations. Photographs have their uses, particularly for observational or case studies. Line drawings can be employed in a similar fashion. In all cases, these illustrations may be reproduced or original to the research.

---

*Hint:* Many computer programs contain facilities for producing tables. See the section on **Computer-based analysis** in Chapter 7.

---

The question then arises: when should you use such illustrations, and when are they better left out? Box 121 offers some general guidance.

## ☐ Panics

The process of writing up, like many aspects of doing research, is likely to give rise to a number of common worries, particularly among relatively new

---

**Box 121: When to use illustrations**

- Where the illustration replaces a substantial piece of text (i.e. a paragraph or more), use it but do not keep the text as well.
- Where the illustration serves to make a point which would be difficult to make, justify or support otherwise, use it.
- Don't use the illustration if it is copyright and you do not have appropriate permission.
- Always refer to illustrations individually in the text. If you don't, there is no reason for the reader to examine them. They are there to be used as an essential part of your argument.
- In most cases, illustrations are better split up, and spread throughout the text close to where they are referred to. If they are gathered together, at the end of chapters or sections, or in an appendix, they are less likely to be consulted by the reader.
- Normally, the text should be the driving force of the research report or thesis. The reader will expect to encounter a near continuous text, interspersed with relevant illustrations. Large clutches of illustrations, or a text dominated by them, are likely to be off-putting.
- Don't use the illustration unless it is clear, unambiguous and well reproduced.

---

researchers. We end this chapter, therefore, by considering four of the most common reasons for panics:

- If it's new to me, is it original?
- I've just discovered someone has written this before.
- It's all a load of rubbish.
- Conflicting advice.

### If it's new to me, is it original?

---

See also the section in Chapter 1 on **What is original?**

---

The answer to the question, as posed, is, we would suggest, 'yes'. Unless you have totally replicated someone else's research, using the same literature, methodology, sample and analytical framework – a circumstance which is almost unimaginable unless you set out deliberately to do so – your research will be to some extent original.

You may have used the same methodology and analytical framework, and explored much the same literature, to study a different sample, and come up with much the same conclusions. This is still original research, however, in that you have used a different sample. It could also be very valuable, as replication research may confirm, deny or modify the conclusions of earlier studies.

Unless you are studying for a doctoral degree, trying to build up your research reputation or developing an invention for patenting, originality in research is unlikely to be that important. Highly original research is, as we said in Chapter 1, very unusual. So don't worry, and get on with your writing up.

### I've just discovered someone has written this before

This is an observation quite often made by new researchers to their supervisors, mentors or managers, but it is never literally true. If it were, you would be guilty of some kind of amazing subconscious plagiarism. What is usually meant is that the researcher has just come across a book or article which makes many of the points the research has raised, or which has studied much the same issues or area. While it is preferable if the book or article has only been recently published, or has been difficult to get hold of, because this suggests that you have carried out a reasonably competent literature review, neither of these findings is cause for despair.

The most appropriate response is to add the book or article to your literature review, explain the circumstances of its discovery, assess its argument critically and then adjust your own report or thesis accordingly. It can actually be very useful to have a similar piece of research with which to confirm and contrast your own approach, argument and findings. It's also quite legitimate to start out with this deliberately in mind. While it may be disappointing to find that you are not first in the field, this is a common enough occurrence in research, and you are almost certain to find something in your own research project which adds to what has already been published.

### It's all a load of rubbish

Again, this is a comment frequently made by researchers as they begin to engage with writing up. It usually means one or more of three things:

- you're bored;
- the writing up is not going as well as you think it might;
- you have become so familiar with a group of ideas and theories that they appear to you now to be no more than common sense.

These feelings strike all researchers at some time, and affect most of us with disturbing regularity.

There is no simple and foolproof response. You have to learn to find your own way around this problem, as it is endemic to research (and many other activities). You might, for example:

- take a break or give yourself a treat;
- seek someone else's opinion on what you have written;
- remind yourself of how far you have travelled on your intellectual journey;
- use some of the suggestions given in the section on **Drafting and redrafting** earlier in this chapter.

Research and writing are, in part, about becoming more self-aware.

**Conflicting advice**

As a researcher, you are bound to encounter conflicting advice sooner or later, most probably sooner. This is because research is about conflict. We research to understand our world better. Because we do not currently fully understand our world (otherwise we would not be researching), it is likely that our developing understandings will be at least partially conflictual. This state of affairs is, to some extent, encouraged by the way research and research careers are structured. Put simply, one good strategy for getting ahead and being noticed as a researcher is to disagree with the findings of existing research.

Every time you submit your research work for consideration or assessment by more than one other person, you are likely to get more than one view: on your reading, on your methodology, on your findings, on your interpretation of those findings. This may occur even when you only have one advisor, since they are quite likely to disagree with your views and change their own. So you will get conflicting advice. And some people's advice will count for more than that of others, because they are an authority or have influence over the progress of your research.

The problems which power relations can cause are considered further in the section of Chapter 9 on **The process of assessment**.

Probably the best way to cope with this, if you find it unsettling, is to teach yourself to consider it as a strength. In your reading, you should already have come across conflicting views. You are adding to these through your research. Your advisors, and their conflicting views, are helping you to do so. They are giving you the opportunity to respond, in your drafting and redrafting, to some of the range of opinions of relevance to your area of research. The greater the range of the views you are exposed to as you are writing up, the better your report or thesis is likely to be, because it will have to have addressed many of the issues and questions which would otherwise have only been raised after it had been completed.

Conflicting advice is, therefore, to be welcomed, challenged and responded to.

## ☐ Summary

Having read this chapter, you should:

- appreciate the need to begin writing as soon as possible, and to revisit and revise what you have drafted;
- understand what is meant by critical writing;
- have a greater awareness of whom you are writing for, and the alternative writing styles and voices which may be open to you to use;
- have a clearer idea of the structure and organization of your research thesis or report.

# ☐ Further reading

In this section, we list a limited selection of books which are of particular relevance to the topics discussed in this chapter, together with an indication of their contents.

Berry, R. (2000) *The Research Project: How to Write It*, 4th edn. London: Routledge.
  A concise guide to the elements of writing a dissertation, research project or paper. The chapters include discussions of using a library, the Internet, preparing a bibliography, taking notes and composing the paper. The text contains an appendix listing some popular search engines.
Brause, R. S. (2000) *Writing Your Doctoral Dissertation: Invisible Rules for Success*. London: Falmer Press.
  Organized in three main sections. 'Getting a sense of the terrain' explores the meaning of the dissertation and the processes involved in writing one. 'Preparing for your study' looks at choosing your topic and the role of supporters. 'Doing your study' considers the work involved in collecting, analysing and presenting your data.
Coley, S. M. and Scheinberg, C. A. (2000) *Proposal Writing*, 2nd edn. Thousand Oaks, CA: Sage.
  A basic guide to proposal writing, dealing with the context, the different elements of the proposal, and budgeting.
Creme, P. and Lea, M. R. (1997) *Writing at University: A Guide for Students*. Buckingham: Open University Press.
  Includes consideration of titles and key words, the role of reading in writing, organization and shaping, academic writing and putting it all together on time.
Collinson, D., Kirkup, G., Kyd, R. and Slocombe, L. (1992) *Plain English*, 2nd edn. Buckingham: Open University Press.
  Designed to be user-friendly and to meet the needs of all students who wish to improve their writing skills, this book contains both advice and exercises on punctuation, spelling, grammar, style and references.
Ellis, C. and Bochner, A. (eds) (1996) *Composing Ethnography: Alternative Forms of Qualitative Writing*. Walnut Creek, CA: Altmira Press.
  This text explores the borders between the social sciences and the humanities through a focus on a variety of forms of ethnographic writing. The text is divided into three sections, dealing with autoethnography, sociopoetics and reflexive ethnography.
Ely, M., Vinz, R., Downing, M. and Anzul, M. (1997) *On Writing Qualitative Research: Living by Words*. London: Falmer Press.
  A comprehensive guide to, and analysis of, the processes of, and approaches to, writing. Successive chapters examine the purposes of writing, different narrative forms, analytic and interpretive modes of writing, negotiating, collaborating and responding, and the effects of writing on the writer and readers.
Hertz, R. (ed.) (1997) *Reflexivity and Voice*. Thousand Oaks, CA: Sage.
  An array of contemporary ethnographers grappling with the problems and new conventions of ethnographic writing. Chapters discuss topics such as communication problems in intensive care units, fieldwork strategies in cloistered and non-cloistered communities, gender and voice, writing, the limits of informants and interactive interviewing.
Locke, L. F., Spirduso, W. W. and Silverman, S. J. (2000) *Proposals that Work: A Guide for Planning Dissertations and Grant Proposals*, 4th edn. Thousand Oaks, CA: Sage.
  The three parts cover: writing the proposal (function, content, style, presentation); getting money for research; four examples of specimen proposals.

Lowe, R. (1993) *Successful Instructional Diagrams*. London: Kogan Page.
This book is designed to introduce the elements of desktop publishing and diagram design. The text includes examples, step-by-step instructions and advice.

Mannan, J. van (ed.) (1995) *Representation in Ethnography*. Thousand Oaks, CA: Sage.
This text explores the literary and textual elements of writing ethnography. The chapters contain discussions of the relationships between ethnography and other forms of writing, issues of voice in the text and the potential for less orthodox ways of writing research accounts. Topics covered include narrative, humour and performativity.

Modern Humanities Research Association (1996) *MHRA Style Book: Notes for Authors, Editors and Writers of Theses*, 5th edn. London: Modern Humanities Research Association.
A guide to producing a manuscript with advice on the use of abbreviations, referencing, quotations, footnotes, spelling and punctuation.

Punch, K. F. (2000) *Developing Effective Research Proposals*. London: Sage.
Considers the function and context of the proposal, the complexity of contemporary social research methodology and the issues arising from this, the evaluation of proposals and the process of their development.

Schwartz, M. (1995) *Guidelines for Bias-free Writing*. Bloomington: Indiana University Press.
This text gives advice on bias-free writing in relation to gender, 'race', ethnicity, citizenship, nationality, religion, disabilities, medical conditions, sexual orientation and age.

Thomson, A. (1996) *Critical Reasoning: A Practical Introduction*. London: Routledge.
Containing many exercises and summaries, this text deals with the identification of reasoning and assumptions, the evaluation of reasoning and recognizing its implications. The practical skills involved are identified and helpful suggestions given for their development.

Winter, R., Sobiechowska, P. and Buck, A. (1999) *Professional Experiences and the Investigative Imagination: The Art of Reflective Writing*. London: Routledge.
Explains and demonstrates how creative writing can be used successfully in the context of professional education.

Woods, P. (1999) *Successful Writing for Qualitative Researchers*. London: Routledge.
Considers all aspects, including getting started, organizing your work, coping with problems and blockages, style and format, editing, writing alone and in a team, approaching publishers and getting published.

# 9

---

# FINISHING OFF

---

## ☐ Introduction

For the new researcher, and even many of those with considerable experience, finishing off can be as difficult as getting started. There is a common reluctance to let go, to present the completed work and then to get on with something else. This is perfectly understandable, of course. If you have spent a long time on a particular task, and have gained something from it, you may not be aware that you have finished. You may be a perfectionist, or think that there is so much more that needs doing.

The purpose of this chapter, then, is to help you to finish off your research project. We are assuming that you will be writing up your work for the consideration of others, in many cases for academic credit.

The chapter tackles the following issues:

- **Planning to finish?** Avoidable and unavoidable reasons for not finishing your research project on time.
- **The penultimate and final drafts**. Checking the presentation of your work.
- **Added extras**. When, and when not, to include prefaces or appendices.
- **The process of assessment**. What others may do with your thesis or report.
- **What do I do now?** Building on and looking beyond your research project.

---

**Box 122: Twenty good reasons for not handing your report or thesis in on time**

1 My hard disk crashed.
2 My car broke down.
3 My funder has refused to allow publication.
4 My mother has just died.
5 I've won the lottery.
6 My informants won't talk to me any more.
7 My informants want to talk to me some more.
8 My supervisor won't talk to me.
9 I forgot the deadline.
10 I have too many other things to do.
11 It isn't finished yet.
12 There was an oil blockade.
13 I've lost it.
14 It must have got lost in the post.
15 I got a job.
16 I decided to get married/have a baby.
17 I haven't got enough data.
18 It isn't good enough.
19 I've not been very well.
20 The other members of my research group haven't finished their bits yet.

---

## ☐ Planning to finish?

There are just so many reasons – and there always have been – for not finishing off and handing in your report or thesis. If you doubt this, look at the list in Box 122. As you will see from the 20 suggestions made, some reasons are old while some are new.

If you have been thinking ahead, however – that is, if you have read some or all of this book – you should be able to recognize that:

- some reasons are simply unavoidable, and are connected with life crises over which you have no control;
- some reasons could have been avoided, if you had planned ahead, allowed yourself sufficient time and been strict with yourself;
- some reasons lie in between the avoidable and the unavoidable, e.g. perhaps it's your bad luck that they cropped up, but you might also have anticipated something of this sort.

You might, particularly if you are planning ahead or feel that it would be useful to review your experience at this point, like to try Exercise 60. The message is that planning ahead is indispensable.

**Exercise 60: Avoidable and unavoidable delays**

Look at the list of reasons given in Box 122 for not finishing off and handing in your report or thesis on time. Add to them from your own and others' experience.

Which of these reasons do you think were:

- avoidable;
- unavoidable;
- bad luck?

What implications does this have for your management of your research project?

## ☐ The penultimate and final drafts

Writing up your research project was the subject of Chapter 8. As part of that process, you will probably have drafted and redrafted the contents of your report or thesis a number of times. Here, our concern is with getting you from a full and near-final draft of your work – the penultimate draft – to the final draft itself. This is basically a matter of checking your presentation, and of making any essential or desirable corrections before you run off, copy and bind the final version. This section provides a simple checklist of points you may need to address. These are summarised in Box 123.

### Checking the title page

What have you called your research report or thesis? Does this title accurately reflect the contents? You may have changed your topic or approach significantly since you began your research, so now could be a good time to revise your title as well if you have not already done so.

---

**Box 123: Checking your penultimate draft**

1 Have you put the title, your name, the date and any other information required on the title page?
2 Are all the pages there?
3 Are they all numbered consecutively?
4 Are all your chapters and/or sections numbered consecutively?
5 Have you checked for spelling and grammatical errors?
6 Have you allowed adequate margins, and double-spaced if required?
7 Are all the materials referred to in the text listed in the references or bibliography?
8 Have you provided full details for all your references?
9 Have you checked your text against the regulations?

---

> The issues involved in choosing a good title are also considered in the
> section on **What to do if you can't think of a topic** in Chapter 2.

Is your title too unwieldy? If it is to engage the reader, it should be relatively short and pithy. If you want to locate your research specifically, you might consider having a short title and a longer sub-title. The following book titles illustrate this approach:

*Access to privilege: patterns of participation in Australian post-secondary education.*

*Paradise dreamed: how utopian thinkers have changed the modern world.*

*The rise of professional society: England since 1880.*

This is, however, very much a matter of taste and style. If you have a good, accurate, short title, don't feel that you have to embroider it.

The title is, of course, not the only thing to go on the title page. You should also add your name – it is surprising how commonly people forget to do this – the date, so that readers know when you wrote it, and perhaps your institution or job title, together with anything else you are required to include.

Most research reports or theses, unless they are very short, will usually also contain a contents page. This should list your chapters or sections, together with the page or paragraph numbers where they start.

**Checking the contents**

Are they all there? Are any pages, or anything else, missing? Are they of the appropriate length (in terms of words and/or pages)?

Are all the pages consecutively numbered? You may start your numbering with arabic numerals (i.e. 1, 2, 3 etc.) literally from your title page. Or you may opt to start the numbering on the first page of your first chapter or section, and either leave the title and contents pages, and any other preparatory material, unnumbered, or number them separately using roman numerals (i, ii, iii etc.). Unless you have specific guidance, do what you feel most comfortable with.

Are all your chapters or sections (and perhaps also paragraphs) numbered consecutively? What about any tables, diagrams or figures? Are they all labelled and numbered appropriately?

Have you checked for spelling and grammatical errors? And how about read-ability and intelligibility? Here, you might find it very useful to get a friend or relative, who need not know anything about the subject of your research, to read through your penultimate draft.

Is the layout as required or appropriate? Have you double-spaced? Have you left wide enough margins for binding, if your report or thesis is going to be bound? If you do not do this, you may find that part of your text, on the left hand side of the page, either disappears when it is bound or becomes very difficult to read.

## Checking the references

Are they all there? Are they in alphabetical order? You will probably have put together the penultimate draft over a period of time, so some sections or chapters, and their associated references or bibliographies, will have been put together well before others. In the process, it is possible that you may have forgotten to add some references, or that some may still be included which are no longer referred to in the text.

You should check two things at this stage:

- Have you provided all the details required for each individual reference, so that your readers can themselves trace them and read them if they so wish?

> If you are in doubt about referencing, see the section on **Recording your reading** in Chapter 4.

- Are all the materials referred to in your text included in your references or bibliography? If you are listing just references rather than a wider bibliography, check that there are no references listed which are not referred to in your text.

> You might like at this stage to refer back to the section in Chapter 8 on **Who am I writing for?** This makes clear the differences between these two approaches.

## Checking the regulations

If you have been carrying out a research project for academic credit, there will, as has been pointed out a number of times in this book, be a set of regulations which you have to satisfy.

> You might like to refer back to the section in Chapter 2 on **Choosing a topic.**

Even if you are not producing a thesis for academic examination, there will probably still be a series of expectations you need to address.

You may think that you know the appropriate regulations by heart, and that you have been religiously following them throughout your research, but it is still a good idea to check them now. Similarly, you will probably find it useful to think about the expectations of those people who are going to read your thesis or report, and perhaps make a few amendments if this seems advisable. This important point is discussed in the section on **The process of assessment** later in this chapter.

## ☐ Added extras

In addition to the basic components of almost any research report or dissertation – a title page, a contents page, a series of chapters or sections, a set of references or a bibliography – there are a number of additional or optional elements which you might wish to include. These could include acknowledgements, a preface, a dedication, an abstract and one or more appendices. The basic question to be addressed here is: do you really need any of these? On balance, if they are not required or necessary, we would recommend doing without all of them, for two related reasons.

First, they add to the length of your report or thesis. This may be a critical factor if you have a word or page limit, but should be an important consideration whatever your situation. Think of your readership, and of your own experience as a reader: do you really want your readers to have to wade through, and probably ignore, page after page of material at the beginning or end of your work? Second, if what is contained in this supplementary material is so important to your report or dissertation, shouldn't it be contained within the main body of the work itself, where it will be given proper attention?

However, there may be good reasons why you want or need to include one or more of these 'added extras'. Let us consider them individually.

### Acknowledgements

> How spouses and families react to the researcher's absence in the field – or, alternatively, constrain his or her presence in the setting – would make an interesting study that might contrast considerably with the obligatory, and often sickening, gratitude to domestic partners displayed in acknowledgements. Americans are particularly obsequious in this respect, although a perusal of their dedications can reveal that the source of affection has changed between publications. I still find it difficult to forgive missing an exciting and dramatic police raid on a Chinese gambling den in Amsterdam because my wife imposed a curfew on my fieldwork, which was backed with chilling sanctions.
>
> (Punch 1986: 8–9)

The usual purpose of acknowledgements is to give credit to people or organizations that were particularly helpful to you in carrying out your research. In some cases, they may be used critically, as when those who have not been as helpful as you might have liked or expected are damned with faint praise; but that is probably best avoided.

Including a list of acknowledgements on a separate page at the front of your report or thesis can be a pleasant way of paying your dues. Those who might be mentioned could include your sponsor (mention of whom may be a mandatory requirement), supervisor, colleagues, family and friends, secretary or typist, as well as any fellow researchers. The list might also include those who gave you access, and even your research subjects, but bear in mind any requirements of confidentiality here. You may, of course, wish to give copies of your report or dissertation to some of those you mention.

## Prefaces

A preface is a form of writing which falls outside of the conventions of the main body of your text, and for that reason should not say anything which adds materially to the content of the main text. Prefaces are most typically used to say something about the author's personal experience of carrying out the research and/or writing it up. Where the research has been a group activity, they might locate the individual's work within the larger whole. They often include a list of acknowledgements at the end.

## Dedications

Dedications are largely a matter of personal taste. They can be a nice way to ritualize the ending of a significant piece of work, and, at the same time, to link this to someone you respect or love. Thus, you might want to dedicate your report or dissertation to your partner or lover, to your children or parents. Alternatively, you might name it for someone who has been particularly influential or helpful to you in carrying out the research. The recipient of your dedication may be alive or dead, and you may never have met them. You might, though, at least in some cases, wish to check before you put your dedication in print, or to send the dedicatee a copy of the completed text.

Dedications, like acknowledgements and prefaces, can be quite interesting and fun to write and to read, if you have the inclination. A small selection is included in Box 124.

## Abstracts

Of all the 'added extras' we have identified, an abstract is without doubt likely to be the most useful. It may also be a mandatory requirement. The 'executive summary', so beloved of business and commerce, may be seen as roughly equivalent. The function of the abstract or executive summary is to summarize briefly the nature of your research project, its context, how it was carried out and what its major findings were. Ideally, it should require no more than one page of text, and will typically be restricted to 200 to 300 words or less (i.e. no more than one page).

---

**Box 124: Dedications we have known**

Once again I am indebted to Paul Atkinson for his detailed attention to my work. I am lucky to have a critic in the house, especially one who exorts me to keep redrafting and restructuring until the text says what I mean. As previous books have been dedicated to John Corlett, the late Jocelyn Cadbury, my grandmother Irene Kimber, my mother Lisa Delamont, my father Dean Delamont, my 'A' level teachers, the late Professor Gillian Powell and the pupils of 'St Lukes', it is high time I dedicated this one to Paul.

(Delamont 1992)

To Rama, for space, love and support, and to our first child, for whom we've got some surprises.

(Coolican 1990)

For students – who want meaning and lives in research.

(Riessman 1994)

To C.

(Barnes 1995)

For Georgia, is that all there is?, and in loving memory of Jean.

(House and Howe 1999)

This book is dedicated to the memory of John L. Martin (1954–1992).

(Renzetti and Lee 1993)

For Sue and Sarah – again.

(Bryman 1988)

For my parents and parents-in-law (as well as Sue and Sarah, as usual).

(Bryman 1989)

For my educated sister.

(Arksey 1992)

This volume is dedicated to Leela Dube, who was one of the first anthropologists to consider seriously the relationship between gender and ethnography.

(Bell et al. 1993)

---

Abstracts are extremely useful to the potential reader, and for this reason are commonly published in specialist journals which carry nothing but abstracts. An abstract can help the potential reader to decide quickly whether it is worth looking at a publication more closely. Many of your readers will probably do no more than look at the abstract, so it is important that you get it right.

Abstracts can also be helpful to writers, by forcing them to distil their wisdom as briefly as possible. They may assist you in restructuring and putting together the final draft. They are, however, quite difficult to write well. You may find it useful to refer back to Chapter 4, particularly Exercise 27. If you would like some practice at writing abstracts, try Exercise 61.

---

**Exercise 61: Writing an abstract**

Select a book or an article which you have found useful in your research. Write an abstract of it, using no more than 200 words. You should aim to summarize the subject of the book or article, its context, methodology and conclusions. Take no more than half an hour.

This exercise may be particularly useful if the book or article you have selected already contains an abstract. In that case, you should produce your own without consulting the existing abstract, and then compare the results.

---

## Appendices

Researchers, and not just novice ones, are often tempted to include all kinds of material in the form of appendices at the end of their reports or dissertations. These may include copies of letters and questionnaires, transcripts of interviews, summaries of case studies, reproductions of institutional documents and so forth.

While all this material is, in some sense, relevant to your research, it is questionable whether you should aim to include any or all of it in your report. You are highly unlikely to be able to include all the original material you have collected or generated during the course of your project. Much, therefore, has to be summarized or left out and, to a certain extent, taken on trust.

There are considerable advantages in minimizing, or omitting altogether, the use of appendices. It can be very irritating for the reader who is working through the main body of your text to be directed to one appendix after another for more details. Too often, the temptation will be not to bother, and the appendices you have so carefully put together will be ignored.

So if you have to include some material which you have thought of putting in appendices, you might consider instead including this in the main body of your text. Or, alternatively, you might place your appendices at the end of the sections or chapters in which they are referred to, rather than at the end of your report or dissertation as a whole.

Remember to keep all these added extras short and to the point.

## ☐ The process of assessment

Once you have completed what you consider to be the final draft of your thesis or report, it is time, of course, to type or print it out; check again that everything is there and in the right order; make the requisite number of copies you and/or others require; get it bound or stapled together; and hand it to your supervisor, manager or readers.

If you have undertaken your research in an academic context, your dissertation or thesis will now be assessed by one or more examiners. The actual arrangements and regulations will vary from institution to institution, so you will need to check these individually.

If you have been researching as part of your work role, or out of personal interest, your final report may not be assessed in an academic way, but it is still going to be read and 'judged' by others. The criteria on which this judgement is made may vary, but the process will be analogous to that which takes place in an academic setting.

There are a series of common issues which arise during this process:

- How will your work be received?
- What are the roles of your supervisor, examiner, manager, mentor, colleagues, funders or prospective publishers?
- What specific events are associated with the process of assessment?
- How do you cope with criticism, referral or rejection?

### How will your work be received?

> 'You draw something', he said, 'and you get nothing. Then you do the same thing again, but this time you get a star and are praised, how come?'
>
> 'It's something to do with time', she said. 'You got a star because you had spent more time on the second drawing. And spent the time in a particular way. We think they have a plan, and that it has to do with time.'
>
> 'So the second one wasn't any better?'
>
> 'There's no such thing as better', she said. 'The second one just fitted better with their plan.'
>
> (Hoeg 1995: 77)

The period after you have completed your thesis or report can be one of considerable anti-climax. It may take months for the process of assessment to be completed. You may never receive any extended comments on your work. It can feel as if you have worked hard for a long time to no great purpose, as if no one is particularly interested in what you have done or what you have found, or as if everyone who is not indifferent is highly critical of what you have done. If doing research is a risky business, writing up that research for assessment makes these risks doubly visible. To the individual participant, the whole process of assessment can seem to be an astonishingly arbitrary business.

It is natural to be concerned about how your work will be received, whether by your examiners, your colleagues, your family, the subjects of your research or other readers. There is a whole range of techniques which you might use in order to try to reduce any stress this may be causing you. There is relatively little you can do, however, to hurry up the process, and you may need to exercise a considerable amount of patience and self-restraint. The middle of the process of assessment is probably not a good time to ask supervisors or managers whether your work was good enough. It may be out of their hands, or they may not be in a position to tell you.

There are, though, plenty of things you can do once an initial assessment has been reached, and these are discussed in the sections which follow.

**What are the roles of your supervisor, examiner, manager, mentor, colleagues, funders or prospective publishers?**

Understanding the roles of those who may be involved in the process of assessment is an important, though usually avoided or overlooked, part of being a researcher. Two key aspects of these roles are not that widely appreciated:

- The process of assessment can be as much an assessment of those doing the assessing as it is of the person(s) being assessed. The judgement of your assessors may be called into question, just as the quality of your work may be found wanting. So the process can be a stressful one for all concerned. Remember, research can be very threatening.
- The assessments of your report or thesis made by your assessors may not be consistent. They may be quite at liberty to disagree with each other, so the process of assessment may be largely about resolving those disagreements.

You may find it useful to refer back to the discussion on 'Conflicting advice' in the section on **Panics** in Chapter 8.

While the assessment process may differ widely from institution to institution, and from case to case, there are certain features which tend to be common. You should make it your business, if you do not already know, to find out as much as you can in advance about how the practices affecting you will differ.

If your thesis or dissertation is being assessed for academic credit, there should be considered and written regulations which apply to your case. Get hold of a copy and make sure that you understand them. While university and college practices vary, much also depends upon the level of degree you are studying for, e.g. first degree, masters degree, doctoral degree (see Box 125).

If your research report is being assessed in the work setting – as well as, or instead of, by a university or college – the process may be broadly analogous, but the emphases are likely to differ (see Box 126). However, assessment of research in the work setting is much less likely to be bound by regulations, or perhaps even established practices. It is, correspondingly, much more likely to focus on the practical changes or applications which might stem from your research.

**What specific events are associated with the process of assessment?**

The special event most likely to be associated with the process of assessing a research report or thesis is some kind of presentation, perhaps a seminar if the research has been carried out in a work setting, or a viva if it has been completed for academic credit. In many, probably most, cases, however, particularly if you have been carrying out a relatively small-scale piece of research, or have not been studying for a research degree, there is unlikely to be a formal presentation involved; unless you choose, and are able, to arrange one yourself, that is.

---

**Box 125: Common academic assessment practices**

The higher the level of qualification involved, the more likely it is that:

- your assessment will no longer be largely a matter for the members of the department you have been studying in (internal examiners), but will involve a substantial input by academics from one or more other institutions (external examiners);
- your academic supervisor will have less direct involvement in these processes;
- you will be assessed on your own, rather than at the same time as others who have been studying for the same qualification;
- the assessment will involve you in making a presentation to, and answering questions from, your examiners (this is considered further in the next sub-section);
- your work will be referred back for some further work, probably relatively minor in nature (this slightly worrying, but common, experience is considered further in the next but one sub-section).

---

**Box 126: Common work assessment practices**

Depending on the size and importance of the work you have been carrying out at your organization, and your own status within that organization, the process may involve:

- a simple report in writing to your immediate superior, or a substantial, glossy and widely circulated (at least internally) publication;
- a brief meeting with your immediate superior, a seminar to a section or group of managers, or a presentation to the board or to the leader of the whole organization;
- little or no follow up of the work itself, or a large-scale dissemination and retraining exercise.

---

Research presentations may have a number of related purposes. At the simplest level, they are about you having the opportunity to present your work to an audience in summary form, perhaps focusing in particular upon your findings and conclusions, and the possible implications and applications of these. Beyond that, they are also concerned with giving you and your audience the opportunity to discuss your work together, perhaps with a particular emphasis on how it relates to their own work and concerns. This also implies, of course, that you may be put on the defensive, criticized and challenged (the subject of the next sub-section).

If your research has been carried out in a work setting, your presentation may involve close colleagues or superiors, those particularly concerned with your findings and in the best place to do something with them. The focus is likely to be on the extent to which your conclusions and recommendations fit with received wisdom and practices, or respond to particular felt needs or problems.

---

**Box 127: What to do before presenting your research**

Prepare as thoroughly as possible:

- find out who is going to be there, what their interests and backgrounds are;
- practise presenting the results of your research, using audio-visual aids if these are available and allowed;
- keep up to date with what has happened in your research area in the period between your finishing your report or thesis and its presentation;
- read and re-read your thesis or report so that you know it backwards, and can instantly find and respond to specific queries;
- practise with a friend or colleague responding to questions of a friendly or unfriendly nature;
- work out some questions which you would like to ask as part of the process;
- be prepared to enjoy and get something out of your presentation, though you may also find it a draining and stressful procedure;
- remember that you do have some measure of control: you know more about your particular piece of research than anyone else;
- be prepared to defend and promote your work, while recognizing its limitations and deficiencies.

---

There is likely to be less interest in how you actually did the research, and on any difficulties you may have encountered. The tenor of the meeting is likely to be fairly brisk and practical.

If, on the other hand, your research has been carried out for academic credit, your viva, if you have one, will probably only involve two or three people. One of these may be your supervisor, but you may have met none of them before. However, you may, if you have prepared wisely, be familiar with their work, and have read it and referred to some of it in your thesis.

One common characteristic of most presentations, whether in academic or work settings, is that you are likely to be, and feel, on your own. This is unlikely to be the case, of course, if you have been involved in a piece of group research, though you may still feel alone when you come to present your bit. If this is going to bother you greatly, it may be worth investigating whether you can take some kind of supporter along with you (a friend, your supervisor, a colleague), even if he or she can take no direct part in the process.

Box 127 offers some general advice if you are going to present your research.

### How do I cope with criticism, referral or rejection?

If your research project has been at all challenging and worthwhile, you are likely to meet some criticism. You may also meet referral, if you have carried out the work for academic credit, and possibly outright rejection. You may find these responses more or less difficult to cope with.

Criticism is, however, part of the process of doing research. Just as you have to be able, and are expected, to criticize other researchers and writers, so you

---

**Box 128: Responding to criticism**

After recovering from any initial disappointment:

* initially welcome and accept the criticism;
* evaluate the validity and implications of the criticism for your research;
* compare each criticism with the other responses your work has engendered;
* possibly modify your research findings or strategies;
* make a considered response to the criticism.

---

have to be able to handle and respond to criticism of your own work. The most positive way of handling it is to see it as something which itself contributes to your research, potentially making it a better piece of work. Seen from that perspective, responding to criticism may have a number of typical stages (see Box 128).

If at all possible, do not be pressurized into responding instantly to criticism, even if it is presented verbally during your presentation. Take your time. Criticisms may cause you to alter your report or thesis, usually to its benefit. They can also be misguided.

*Hint:* If under pressure to respond to criticism immediately, take a few deep breaths, then ask your critic to 'run that past me again', 'be more specific' or 'elaborate on your comments'. This will give you more time to think.

Referral is a common response to research work carried out for academic credit. It means that your work is not judged to be quite up to scratch for the qualification you are seeking, but you are being given a further opportunity to bring it up to scratch. As an alternative, you might be offered a lower level qualification than the one you were aiming for.

The modifications which your assessors suggest you make to your thesis will usually be fairly minor, but may be quite far-reaching. You should be given a specific time-scale in which to make the corrections or amendments, fairly detailed guidance about what needs changing and some further support from your supervisor during this process. Check the regulations, particularly those to do with appeals.

Let's make no bones about it. Referral is disappointing at best, depressing at worst. It places extra demands upon your time, and is likely to impose some additional costs. It is best avoided altogether, if at all possible, by making sure that you have done well enough before you submit your work for assessment. Even with the best intentions, however, this may not always be possible. You may have been poorly advised. Or you may have ignored the good advice you were given.

Referral can make you feel like giving up. It is probably best to think of it as a normal and common part of the academic assessment process, another hurdle to be got over, which will have some benefits for you and your research, and which will lead on to the desired end of qualification. Having been once referred, you are relatively unlikely to be referred or rejected again, always provided that you carefully follow the guidance which you should be given on how to improve your report or thesis.

If your research report or thesis is rejected, however, things look rather gloomier. In an academic setting, you may be able to appeal if, for example, you believe your assessors have not reached their decision fairly, or have done so in ignorance of relevant facts. In a work setting, this is likely to be difficult unless you have recourse to other influential contacts within your organization. In extreme cases, recourse to the law may be a possibility. Bear in mind, however, that if your work has been rejected, there are likely to be good reasons for this decision, even if you do not find them particularly palatable.

In the end, how you respond to rejection comes down to how committed you feel personally to the research you have carried out. You may be best advised to try to forget it and get on with the rest of your life. Or you could think in terms of dissemination and publication, or of further research (which are discussed in the next section).

## ☐ What do I do now?

OK, you've finished! Your research project has been completed, written up, submitted and assessed. You are likely to feel at least two things: on the one hand, a great sense of relief and release, as if a great weight has been removed from your shoulders; on the other hand, a sense of loss, of a gaping hole in your life which will need replacing in some way. What do you do now? The options are potentially limitless, restricted only by your resources, situation and imagination. Box 129 makes 20 more or less serious suggestions.

Three of these suggestions can be seen as part of the research process itself, namely:

• dissemination;
• publication;
• further research.

In other words, your research isn't really over when it has been written up and assessed. If it is of any potential interest or use to others, you owe it to yourself, your organization and the subjects of your research to let others know of it.

Dissemination is the process by which you communicate your research report or thesis, its findings and recommendations, to other potentially interested parties. You might think about presenting your work:

• within your organization;
• to meetings where people from similar organizations gather;

---

**Box 129: Twenty things to do now that you have finished your research**

1 Take a holiday.
2 Go to bed.
3 Stay in the sauna until you have forgotten it.
4 Celebrate with close family and friends.
5 Take the dog for more walks.
6 Try for promotion.
7 Organize seminars to disseminate your findings.
8 Plan what you are going to wear to your graduation.
9 Collect information about other courses of study.
10 Read a good book.
11 Burn your books.
12 Go on a diet.
13 Give some time to your family.
14 Write up and publish your research.
15 Write to us about how you used this book.
16 Get another job.
17 Implement your findings.
18 Have another drink.
19 Get yourself a life.
20 Do some more research.

---

- to your union branch;
- to professional associations;
- to a local adult education group;
- at national or international conferences.

There is also a range of different ways in which you might present your work: as a lecture (or series of lectures), as a seminar, as a workshop. You might think about presenting it in a written as well as a spoken form; that is, you may think about publication.

Publication, like dissemination in general, takes a variety of forms. It may be restricted to internal, and perhaps confidential, circulation within your organization or kindred bodies. It may be popular, professional or academic. It may be placed in mass market newspapers or magazines, or in small circulation specialist journals. It may be in the form of a book, and may be self-published and distributed.

Once you begin to publish or disseminate your work, it enters the public domain, and is liable to varied interpretation, criticism and use. One example of these reactions is summarized in Box 130.

The final option suggested in this section is that of engaging in further research. It is something of an in-joke in research circles that one of the main recommendations of any research project is always that 'further research is needed'. This is not simply a matter of trying to ensure further employment and

---

**Box 130: Research in the public domain**

[T]here is no evidence that shows women as a group to be less serious or committed to a career than their male colleagues, but plenty of evidence to suggest that they are believed to be and so denied access to promotion.

(Homans 1989: 23)

The report's findings, contextualized in primary and secondary data and literature surveys, were reported by the press on 4 May 1989 as follows:

Women key to averting NHS crisis

*(The Guardian)*

Sex bias could lead to NHS staffing crisis

*(The Times)*

Women hit by 'myths': carers hit by tales of 'leaving to have babies'

*(Morning Star)*

NHS 'prejudice': women held back by men

*(Daily Mail)*

Men 'spoil' NHS careers for women

*(Daily Telegraph)*

Now go back to Box 1!

---

funding. It is a characteristic of any research project that it almost always generates more questions than answers. Doing research is, therefore, and perhaps primarily, a very good method of determining what needs researching.

It is also a somewhat addictive process for many people. Once you have demonstrated to your own and others' satisfaction that you can do competent research, and that you enjoy and get something from the process, it is very tempting to go on to do more, even if it is not your job. So, if you want to, do some more research: it is not a sin, at least not a mortal one!

*Hint:* So now return to your original starting point. If our analogy of research as a spiral (see Box 6) works for you, you should be able to start your research again now, but your starting point will be different.

## ☐ Summary

Having read this chapter, you should:

- appreciate the importance of finishing the research project you are engaged in;
- understand the checking processes you will need to go through in preparing the final draft of your report or thesis;

- be aware of the uses and disadvantages of prefatory material and appendices;
- be forewarned of what might happen during the assessment of your report or thesis;
- know of the options for presenting your results, and for engaging in further research if you wish.

## ☐ Further reading

In this section, we list a limited selection of books and articles, together with an indication of their contents.

The selection given here is designed to provide a basis for further and often deeper or more theoretical reading in different areas of social research.

Alasuutari, P. (1995) *Researching Culture: Qualitative Method and Cultural Studies.* London: Sage.
  The qualitative traditions of sociological and anthropological research, including ethnography and symbolic interactionism, are considered, along with the main methods used in studying language and interaction: semiotics, narrative analysis, conversation analysis, discourse analysis. Attention is also given to the relevance of quantitative analysis.
Alvesson, M. and Skoldberg, K. (2000) *Reflexive Methodology: New Vistas for Qualitative Research.* London: Sage.
  Reflexivity is presented as an essential part of the research process, enabling field research and interpretations to be placed in perspective. Empiricism, hermeneutics, critical theory, poststructuralism and postmodernism are considered.
Arbnor, I. and Bjerke, B. (1997) *Methodology for Creating Business Knowledge,* 2nd edn. Thousand Oaks, CA: Sage.
  Discusses, in principle and application, three basic social scientific methodological approaches commonly applied in studying business: the analytical approach, the systems approach and the actor's approach. The links between basic presumptions, methodological approaches, methods or techniques, and the study of the field are also considered.
Bauer, M. W. and Gaskell, G. (eds) (2000) *Qualitative Researching with Text, Image and Sound.* London: Sage.
  The book is organized into four parts, examining different ways of collecting data and different types of data, the main analytic approaches, computer-assisted analysis and issues of good practice.
Becker, H. A. (1997) *Social Impact Assessment.* London: UCL Press.
  A practical guide to the associated techniques. Aimed at teachers and professional workers who need to assess social impact.
Bell, D., Caplan, P. and Karim, W. J. (eds) (1993) *Gendered Fields: Women, Men and Ethnography.* London: Routledge.
  Written for those with particular interests in anthropology and gender studies, this edited collection is international in scope. Its aim is to highlight the significance of gender to the conduct of social research. The text includes discussion of both feminist and masculinist perspectives.
Blaikie, N. (1993) *Approaches to Social Enquiry.* Cambridge: Polity Press.
  This text outlines the range of methodological frameworks used in research. It is divided into three parts: what kind of science is social science?; research strategies;

some methodological issues. The contents include reference to positivism, critical rationalism, interpretivism, critical theory, realism, structuration theory and feminism. Four basic research strategies are outlined. These are induction, deduction, retroduction and abduction.

Blaxter, L., Hughes, C. and Tight, M. (1998) *The Academic Career Handbook*. Buckingham: Open University Press.
For those who might be interested in moving into academic employment. Five main academic roles – networking, teaching, research, writing and managing – are explored, and the possible stages in an academic career are detailed.

Bollen, K. A. and Long, S. (eds) (1993) *Testing Structural Equation Models*. London: Sage.
With an emphasis on 'testing', this text looks at model building, specifications, power analysis and summarizing evidence.

Bowen, J. and Petersen, R. (eds) (1999) *Critical Comparisons in Politics and Culture*. Cambridge: Cambridge University Press.
Anthropologists and political scientists debate the problem of comparison, and critique conventional forms of comparative method. Abstract model building and ethnographically based approaches are discussed.

Burgess, R. G. (ed.) (1994) *Postgraduate Education and Training in the Social Sciences: Processes and Products*. London: Jessica Kingsley.
Not a methods book, but a set of papers based on researching the processes of postgraduate training. Read this for a 'researched' view of the experiences you may be having.

Chamberlayne, P., Bornat, J. and Wengraf, T. (2000) *The Turn to Biographical Methods in Social Science*. London: Routledge.
Examines the historical and philosophical origins of biographical research methods, and shows how such methods are currently useful and popular. Topics discussed include generational change and social upheaval, political influences on memory and identity, biographical work in reflexive societies and individual and researcher narratives.

Cohen, M. Z., Kahn, D. L. and Steeves, R. H. (2000) *Hermeneutic Phenomenological Research: A Practical Guide for Nurse Researchers*. Thousand Oaks, CA: Sage.
Hermeneutic phenomenology, the study of how people interpret their lives, is presented as ideally suited to nursing research. This book explains how to conduct such a research project, from writing the proposal, through sampling and data collection, to analysis and writing up.

Coulon, A. (1995) *Ethnomethodology*. London: Sage.
This text introduces the theoretical and methodological practices of ethnomethodology.

Denzin, N. K. and Lincoln, Y. S. (eds) (1994) *Handbook of Qualitative Research*. Thousand Oaks, CA: Sage.
A comprehensive volume of edited papers which aim to synthesize current activity and issues in qualitative research. Six parts cover: locating the field, major paradigms and perspectives, strategies for inquiry, methods of collecting and analyzing empirical materials, the art of interpretation, evaluation and presentation, the future of qualitative research.

Denzin, N. K. and Lincoln, Y. S. (eds) (1998) *The Landscape of Qualitative Research: Theories and Issues*. Thousand Oaks, CA: Sage.
Contains an introductory survey, plus three parts focusing on the location of the field (history, traditions, politics, ethics), major paradigms and perspectives (constructivist, interpretivist, critical, feminist etc.) and the future.

Ekegren, P. (1999) *The Reading of Theoretical Texts*. London: Routledge.
Contributes to methodological debates in the social sciences through an examination of developments in literary criticism, philosophy and critical theory.

Erlandson, D. A., Harris, E. L., Skipper, B. L. and Allen, S. D. (1993) *Doing Naturalistic Inquiry: A Guide to Methods*. London: Sage.
Designed for those interested in the constructivist paradigm, this book includes getting started, designing naturalistic research, data gathering and analysis.

Greig, A. and Taylor, J. (1999) *Doing Research with Children*. London: Sage.
A comprehensive and practical introduction to the issues involved. Three parts cover: the special nature of children in research, and appropriate theories and approaches; reviewing, designing and conducting research with children; and ethical and other issues.

Griffiths, M. (1998) *Educational Research for Social Justice: Getting off the Fence*. Buckingham: Open University Press.
A book for those educational researchers motivated by considerations of justice, fairness and equity. Due attention is given to both theoretical frameworks and practical possibilities.

Hack, V. (1997) *Targeting the Powerful: International Prospect Research*. London: Association for Information Management.
Explains how to conduct in-depth research into a person, company or charitable foundation, and how then to use this information to recommend a line of approach most likely to succeed. Includes a detailed list of books, on-line suppliers and websites for major countries worldwide.

Hammersley, M. (ed.) (1993) *Social Research: Philosophy, Politics and Practice*. London: Sage.
An edited collection which explores the values and practice of social research. Includes discussion of the relation between qualitative and quantitative methods, ethics, documentary analysis, feminist methodology and the production of statistics.

Hammersley, M. (1995) *The Politics of Social Research*. London: Sage.
This text examines arguments which suggest that research is essentially political and explores the importance of value neutrality.

Hammersley, M. (ed.) (1999) *Researching School Experience: Explorations of Teaching and Learning*. London: Routledge.
Twelve chapters report on research into, for example, the effects of audit accountability on primary teachers' professionality, the effects of recent educational reforms, the influences of parenthood on teaching, issues of gender in the classroom and learning about health risks.

Hammersley, M. (2000) *Taking Sides in Social Research*. London: Routledge.
Assesses debates about the inevitability of research being political in its assumptions. Includes a consideration of the contribution of 'founding fathers', such as Mills and Becker, and brings the debate up to the present day.

Hatch, J. A. and Wisniewski, R. (eds) (1995) *Life History and Narrative*. London: Falmer Press.
Chapters address issues such as linking emotion and reason through narrative voice, the audience and politics of narrative, life history and women's gender identity, the qualitative analysis of narrative data and narrative strategies for case reports.

Hine, C. (2000) *Virtual Ethnography*. London: Sage.
Includes chapters on the Internet as culture and cultural artefact, time, space and technology, authenticity and identity, and reflection.

Holcomb, E. L. (1999) *Getting Excited about Data: How to Combine People, Passion and Proof*. Thousand Oaks, CA: Corwin Press.

Designed for schoolteachers who want to be able to demonstrate how well their pupils are learning and achieving.

Hollway, W. and Jefferson, T. (2000) *Doing Qualitative Research Differently: Free Association, Narrative and the Interview Method.* London: Sage.

Argues for the centrality of narrative and an interpretive method which gives interviewees' free associations precedence over coherence. The use of this approach is then examined, with examples, through the phases of empirical research practice.

Homans, H. (1989) *Women in the National Health Service: Report of a Case Study into Equal Opportunities in Clinical Chemistry Laboratories.* London: HMSO.

Hood, S., Mayall, B. and Oliver, S. (eds) (1999) *Critical Issues in Social Research: Power and Prejudice.* Buckingham: Open University Press.

This book addresses the following questions. Whose interests are served by research? For whom is it undertaken? What research methods are appropriate? How can the researched find a voice in the research process? The groups researched that are explored include children, women, black people, elderly people, gay men and those with disabilities.

House, E. R. and Howe, K. R. (1999) *Values in Evaluation and Social Research.* Thousand Oaks, CA: Sage.

The three sections of this book consider value claims (facts and values, evaluative reasoning), critiques of other views (received, radical constructivist and postmodernist views) and deliberative democratic evaluation.

Hymes, D. (1996) *Ethnography, Linguistics, Narrative Inequality: Towards an Understanding of Voice.* London: Routledge.

Illustrates the contributions that ethnography and linguistics have made to education, as well as the contribution that education makes to linguistics and anthropology.

Jarvis, P. (1999) *The Practitioner-Researcher: Developing Theory from Practice.* San Francisco: Jossey-Bass.

This book is organized in five parts, considering the connections between research and practice, the nature of practice, research in practice, practice and theory, and the role of the practitioner-researcher. Designed to help all practitioners for whom research is a tool to help improve practice.

Josselson, R. and Lieblich, A. (eds) (1999) *Making Meaning of Narratives.* Thousand Oaks, CA: Sage.

Following an introductory review chapter, contributors focus on a range of narrative settings, including women in academic life, professional practice in a mental hospital and young girls' diaries. Issues discussed range from the transformation of meanings across generations to the transformational power of stories within organizations.

Layder, D. (1993) *New Strategies in Social Research: An Introduction and Guide.* Cambridge: Polity Press.

The aim of this text is to combine new perspectives in social research with the actual problems of research. The contents include discussion of theorizing, including grounded theory and middle range theory.

Layder, D. (1998) *Sociological Practice: Linking Theory and Social Research.* London: Sage.

Considers not just the relations between theory and research, but also practical ways in which research can be theoretically informed and theory can be empirically supported.

Lewis, A. and Lindsay, G. (eds) (1999) *Researching Children's Perspectives.* Buckingham: Open University Press.

Designed for researchers and graduate students in psychology, education, health, social work and law, addressing the issues and practicalities surrounding the obtaining of children's views.

Lieblich, A., Tuval-Mashiach, R. and Zilber, T. (1998) *Narrative Research: Reading, Analysis and Interpretation*. Thousand Oaks, CA: Sage.
Considers how to read, analyse and interpret life story materials. Four models of reading are presented: holistic-content, holistic-form, categorical-content and categorical-form. Two narratives are then introduced and analysed using these models.

McCulloch, G. and Richardson, W. (2000) *Historical Research in Educational Settings*. Buckingham: Open University Press.
A guide to theory, rationales and problems, as well as to the opportunities for research in the field.

Middlewood, D., Coleman, M. and Lumby, J. (1999) *Practitioner Research in Education*. London: Paul Chapman.
Drawing on the experience of participants in a university educational management programme, the text aims to show how research can make a difference in a wide range of educational contexts in several countries.

Morse, J. M. (ed.) (1993) *Critical Issues in Qualitative Research Methods*. London: Sage.
An edited collection with wide-ranging discussions of qualitative research. The text includes discussion of ethics, videotaping, theoretical development and how students learn to conduct qualitative research.

Moustakas, C. (1994) *Phenomenological Research Methods*. London: Sage.
This book outlines the theoretical underpinnings of phenomenology and offers a guide to the processes involved in conducting a phenomenological study.

Okeley, J. (1996) *Own or Other Culture*. London: Routledge.
Challenges the idea that fieldwork in familiar Western settings is easy, or that it discovers what is already 'known'. The subjects examined include British boarding schools, gypsies and feminism.

Ozga, J. (1999) *Policy Research in Educational Settings: Contested Terrain*. Buckingham: Open University Press.
Offers guidance on the theoretical and methodological resources available for those with an interest in doing research, and discusses some of the main issues and problems they may face.

Prosser, J. (ed.) (1998) *Image-based Research: A Sourcebook for Qualitative Researchers*. London: Falmer Press.
Eighteen chapters consider the theory, process and practice of image-based research in anthropology, sociology, psychology and education. The examples covered include film, photographs, cartoons, graffiti, maps, drawings, diagrams, signs and symbols.

Reason, P. (ed.) (1994) *Participation in Human Enquiry*. London: Sage.
An introduction to participatory methods where the emphasis is on working with and for, rather than on, people.

Reher, D. S. and Schofield, R. (eds) (1995) *Old and New Methods in Historical Demography*. Oxford: Oxford University Press.
A variety of techniques are discussed. These include demographic research related to population reconstruction and econometric behaviour, family reconstitution, event-history analysis and the use of simulation models.

Ribbens, J. and Edwards, R. (eds) (1998) *Feminist Dilemmas in Qualitative Research: Public Knowledge and Private Lives*. London: Sage.
The book is organized around the concept of voice, considering the issues involved in speaking, listening, hearing and representing different voices. Research topics covered include motherhood, sisters, childbirth, mature women students and the self.

Rose, D. (1998) *Researching Social and Economic Change*. London: Routledge.
An examination of the possibilities and pitfalls of panel studies, as used to analyse social change internationally.

Sage Publications/SRM (1995) *Database of Social Research Methodology on CD-ROM*. London: Sage.
A computerized database which can be used on your own PC with a facility to search for more than 34,000 references in social science methodology.

Scarborough, E. and Tanenbaum, E. (eds) (1998) *Research Strategies in the Social Sciences: A Guide to New Approaches*. Oxford: Oxford University Press.
Mainly focused on quantitative methods. Twelve chapters cover a range of topics from linear structural equation models and categorical data analysis through modelling space and time to game-theoretic models and discourse theory.

Scheurich, J. J. (1997) *Research Method in the Postmodern*. London: Falmer Press.
Considers how postmodernism can be applied to critiquing research approaches and to their reconceptualization. The book goes beyond the philosophical level to show the implications of postmodernism for research practice.

Schratz, M. and Walker, R. (1995) *Research as Social Change: New Opportunities for Social Research*. London: Routledge.
Aims to demystify research and integrate different forms of qualitative research, action research and case study methods within the ambit of professional practice in the workplace.

Scott, D. (2000) *Realism and Educational Research: New Perspectives and Possibilities*. London: Routledge.
Examines the complex issue of power in educational settings, how educational research is being technicized, and how educational researchers are being made accountable for their findings.

Shacklock, G. and Smyth, J. (eds) (1998) *Being Reflexive in Critical Educational and Social Research*. London: Falmer Press.
Thirteen contributions from sixteen authors provide personal, reflexive views of the issues and dilemmas involved in doing educational research. The topics addressed include ethnography, action inquiry, narrative, international development and multiculturalism.

Silverman, D. (1993) *Interpreting Qualitative Data: Methods for Analysing Talk, Text and Interaction*. London: Sage.
Covering the major philosophies of qualitative research, ethnography, symbolic interactions and ethnomethodology, this book focuses on issues of observation, analysis and validity. Uses examples and student exercises.

Smith, J. A., Harre, R. and Langenhove, L. van (eds) (1995) *Rethinking Methods in Psychology*. London: Sage.
Challenging psychology's traditional preoccupation with experiments, this text considers the application of a range of qualitative measures – such as semi-structured interviews, grounded theory and discourse analysis – as well as a reworking of quantitative methods.

Smith, L. T. (1999) *Decolonizing Methodologies: Research and Indigenous Peoples*. London: Zed Press.
This book challenges European epistemology, including emancipatory paradigms. Smith argues that social research methods need decolonizing, and shows how alternative research practices are associated with global indigenous movements.

Stanfield, J. H. and Dennis, R. M. (eds) (1993) *Race and Ethnicity in Research Methods*. Newbury Park, CA: Sage.

A range of methodological approaches to the study of 'race' and ethnicity are included in this edited collection. These include survey, demography, discourse analysis, testing and assessment, archival research and comparative methods. The text is divided into four parts: introduction and epistemological considerations, qualitative methods, quantitative methods, historical/comparative methods.

Truman, C., Mertens, D. C. and Humphries, B. (eds) (1999) *Research and Inequality.* London: Routledge.

Examines how issues such as ethnicity, sexuality, disability, gender, health and old age are addressed in research conducted among people who may be the objects of research but who have little control over what is said about them.

Van Maanen, J. (ed.) (1995) *Representation in Ethnography.* London: Sage.

As ethnography is deconstructed for its biases and literary devices, this volume explores the challenges of representationalism which have arisen. The contents include discussions of the relationship between ethnography and other forms of writing.

Walford, G. (ed.) (1998) *Doing Research about Education.* London: Routledge.

A compilation of accounts of research, including consideration of ethnographic approaches, researching gender and sexuality, longitudinal studies, international projects, directing a research centre, contract cultures and compulsive publishing.

Warren, C. A. B. and Hackney, J. K. (2000) *Gender Issues in Ethnography*, 2nd edn. Thousand Oaks, CA: Sage.

Discusses gender in relation to fieldwork relationships, interviewing and representation.

Webb, E. J., Campbell, D. T., Schwartz, R. D. and Sechrest, L. (2000) *Unobtrusive Measures*, rev. edn. Thousand Oaks, CA: Sage.

Reissue of a classic text first published in 1966. Considers the use of physical traces, running records, episodic and private records, simple and contrived observation.

Williams, F., Popay, J. and Oakley, A. (eds) (1998) *Welfare Research: A Critical Review.* London: UCL Press.

Offers a theoretical and methodological context for research into welfare, and provides examples of research using different concepts (stress, coping, social support and structural inequalities).

Yates, B. T. (1996) *Analyzing Costs, Procedures, Processes, and Outcomes in Human Services.* Thousand Oaks, CA: Sage.

Discusses the techniques of cost-effectiveness and cost–benefits analysis, and their application to mental health and other human services.

# REFERENCES

Abramson, J. and Mizrahi, T. (1994) 'Examining social work/physician collaboration: an application of grounded theory methods'. In C. Riessman (ed.) *Qualitative Studies in Social Work Research*. Thousand Oaks, CA: Sage, pp. 28–48.

Acker, S. (1981) 'No woman's land: British sociology of education 1960–1979'. *Sociological Review*, 29(1), 77–104.

Amer, A. (1993) 'Teaching EFL students to use a test-taking strategy'. *Language Testing*, 10(1), 71–7.

Arber, S. and Ginn, J. (1995) 'Gender differences in the relationship between paid employment and informal care'. *Work, Employment and Society*, 9(3), 445–71.

Arbnor, I. and Bjerke, B. (1997) *Methodology for Creating Business Knowledge*. London: Sage.

Arksey, H. (ed.) (1992) *How to Get a First Class Degree: Recent Graduates Disclose How They Got Their 'First' at University*. Lancaster: University of Lancaster, Unit for Innovation in Higher Education.

Atweh, B., Kemmis, S. and Weeks, P. (1998) *Action Research in Practice: Partnerships for Social Justice in Education*. London: Sage.

Baker, S. (1999) 'Finding and searching information sources'. In J. Bell (ed.) *Doing Your Research Project: A Guide for First-time Researchers in Education and Social Science*, 3rd edn. Buckingham: Open University Press.

Barker, E. (1984) *The Making of a Moonie: Choice or Brainwashing?* Oxford: Blackwell.

Barnes, R. (1995) *Successful Study for Degrees*, 2nd edn. London: Routledge.

Bateson, M. (1990) *Composing a Life*. New York: Plume.

Belenky, M., Clinchy, B., Goldberger, N. and Tarule, J. (1986) *Women's Ways of Knowing: The Development of Self, Voice and Mind*. New York: Basic Books.

Bell, D., Caplan, P. and Karim, W. (eds) (1993) *Gendered Fields: Women, Men and Ethnography*. London: Routledge.

Bennett, R. (1983) *Management Research: Guide for Institutions and Professionals*. Geneva: International Labour Office, Management Development Series No. 20.

Berry, R. (1994) *The Research Project: How to Write It*, 3rd edn. London: Routledge.

Bowling, A. (1997) *Research Methods in Health: Investigating Health and Health Services*. Buckingham: Open University Press.

Bowman, W. (1992) *The Ascent of Rum Doodle* and *The Cruise of the Talking Fish*. London: Pimlico (first published 1956, 1957).

Brannen, J., Meszaros, G., Moss, P. and Poland, G. (1994) *Employment and Family Life: A Review of Research in the UK (1980–1994)*. Sheffield: Employment Department, Research Series No. 41.

Bruce, C. (1994) 'Research students' early experiences of the dissertation literature review'. *Studies in Higher Education*, 19(2), 217–29.

Bryman, A. (1988) *Quality and Quantity in Social Research*. London: Routledge.

Bryman, A. (1989) *Research Methods and Organisation Studies*. London: Routledge.

Burgess, R. (1993) *Research Methods*. Walton-on-Thames: Nelson.

Burns, R. (2000) *Introduction to Research Methods*. London: Sage.

Cansino, C. (1995) 'Party government in Latin America: theoretical guidelines for an empirical analysis'. *International Political Science Review*, 16(2), 169–82.

Cockburn, C. (1991) *In the Way of Women: Men's Resistance to Sex Equality in Organisations*. London: Macmillan.

Cohen, L. and Manion, L. (1995) *Research Methods in Education*, 4th edn. London: Routledge.

Collins, H. (1984) 'Research spoonbending: concepts and practice of participatory fieldwork'. In C. Bell and H. Roberts (eds) *Social Researching: Politics, Problems, Practice*. London: Routledge and Kegan Paul, pp. 54–69.

Collins, J. (1994) 'Disempowerment and marginalisation of clients in divorce court cases'. In S. Wright (ed.) *Anthropology of Organisations*. London: Routledge, pp. 181–95.

Coolican, H. (1990) *Research Methods and Statistics in Psychology*. London: Hodder and Stoughton.

Corder, N. (1992) 'On the margin: a study of staff development, training and tutor support of part-time adult education tutors in Buckinghamshire'. Unpublished MEd thesis, University of Warwick, Department of Continuing Education, Coventry.

Crotty, M. (1998) *The Foundations of Social Research: Meaning and Perspective in the Research Process*. London: Sage.

Delamont, S. (1992) *Fieldwork in Educational Settings: Methods, Pitfalls and Perspectives*. London: Falmer Press.

Denzin, N. and Lincoln, Y. (eds) (1994) *Handbook of Qualitative Research*. Thousand Oaks, CA: Sage.

Dey, I. (1993) *Qualitative Data Analysis: A User-friendly Guide for Social Scientists*. London: Routledge.

Dillon, J. (1990) *The Practice of Questioning*. London: Routledge.

Douglas, J. (1988) 'Behaviour disorders: principles of management'. In N. Richman and R. Lansdown (eds) *Problems of Preschool Children*. Chichester: John Wiley, pp. 131–49.

Edwards, R. (1993) *Mature Women Students: Separating or Connecting Family and Education*. London: Taylor & Francis.

Edwards, A. and Talbot, R. (1994) *The Hard Pressed Researcher: A Research Handbook for the Caring Professions*. Harlow: Longman.

Field, J. and Spence, L. (2000) 'Informal learning and social capital'. In F. Coffield (ed.) *The Necessity of Informal Learning*. Bristol: Policy Press, pp. 32–42.

Fielding, J. (1993) 'Coding and managing data'. In N. Gilbert (ed.) *Researching Social Life*. London: Sage, pp. 218–38.

Finch, J. (1986) *Research and Policy: The Uses of Qualitative Methods in Social and Educational Research*. Lewes: Falmer.

Fink, A. (1998) *Conducting Research Literature Reviews: From Paper to the Internet*. Thousand Oaks, CA: Sage.

Flick, U. (1998) *An Introduction to Qualitative Research*. London: Sage.

Francis, J. (1976) 'Supervision and examination of higher degree students'. *Bulletin of the University of London*, 31, 3–6.

Frankenberg, R. (1993) *The Social Construction of Whiteness: White Women, Race Matters*. London: Routledge.

Galton, M. (1988) 'Structured observation techniques'. In J. Keeves (ed.) *Educational Research, Methodology and Measurement: An International Handbook*. Oxford: Pergamon, pp. 474–8.

Glucksmann, M. (1994) 'The work of knowledge and the knowledge of women's work'. In M. Maynard and J. Purvis (eds) *Researching Women's Lives from a Feminist Perspective*. London: Taylor and Francis, pp. 149–65.

Green, A., Owen, D. and Winnett, C. (1994) 'The changing geography of recession: analyses of local unemployment time series'. *Transactions of the Institute of British Geographers*, 19(2), 142–62.

Green, P. (1993) 'Taking sides: partisan research in the 1984–1985 miners' strike'. In D. Hobbs and T. May (eds) *Interpreting the Field: Accounts of Ethnography*. Oxford: Clarendon Press.

Greenwood, D. and Levin, M. (1998) *Introduction to Action Research: Social Research for Social Change*. Thousand Oaks, CA: Sage.

Griffiths, M. (1998) *Educational Research for Social Justice: Getting off the Fence*. Buckingham: Open University Press.

Guba, E. and Lincoln, Y. (1994) 'Competing paradigms in qualitative research'. In N. Denzin and Y. Lincoln (eds) *Handbook of Qualitative Research*. Thousand Oaks, CA: Sage.

Hack, V. (1997) *Targeting the Powerful: International Prospect Research*. London: Association for Information Management.

Hammersley, M. (1984) 'The researcher exposed: a natural history'. In R. Burgess (ed.) *The Research Process in Educational Settings: Ten Case Studies*. Lewes: Falmer, pp. 39–68.

Hampson, L. (1994) *How's Your Dissertation Going? Students Share the Rough Reality of Dissertation and Project Work*. Lancaster: University of Lancaster, Unit for Innovation in Higher Education.

Hart, C. (1998) *Doing a Literature Review: Releasing the Social Science Research Imagination*. London: Sage.

Hart, E. and Bond, M. (1995) *Action Research for Health and Social Care: A Guide to Practice*. Buckingham: Open University Press.

Hendry, C., Jones, A., Arthur, M. and Pettigrew, A. (1991) *Human Resource Development in Small to Medium Sized Enterprises*. Sheffield: Employment Department, Research Paper No. 88.

Hobbs, D. (1993) 'Peers, careers and academic fears: writing as fieldwork'. In D. Hobbs and T. May (eds) *Interpreting the Field: Accounts of Ethnography*. Oxford: Oxford University Press, pp. 45–66.

Hoeg, P. (1995) *Borderlines*. London: Harvill Press.

Holland, J. and Ramazanoglu, C. (1994) 'Coming to conclusions: power and interpretation in researching young women's sexuality'. In M. Maynard and J. Purvis (eds) *Researching Women's Lives from a Feminist Perspective*. London: Taylor & Francis.

Hollway, W. (1989) *Subjectivity and Method in Psychology: Gender, Meaning and Science*. London: Sage.

Hollway, W. and Jefferson, T. (2000) *Doing Qualitative Research Differently: Free Association, Narrative and the Interview Method*. London: Sage.

Honigman, J. (1982) 'Sampling in ethnographic fieldwork'. In R. Burgess (ed.) *Field Research: A Sourcebook and a Field Manual*. London: George Allen and Unwin.

hooks, b. (1989) *Talking Back: Thinking Feminist, Thinking Black*. London: Sheba.

House, E. R. and Howe, K. R. (1999) *Values in Education and Social Research*. Thousand Oaks, CA: Sage.

Hoyte, R. (1992) 'How I got my first in human communication'. In H. Arksey (ed.) *How to Get a First Class Degree: Recent Graduates Disclose How They Got Their 'First' at University*. Lancaster: University of Lancaster, Unit for Innovation in Higher Education, pp. 25–30.

Hughes, C. and Tight, M. (1996) 'Doughnuts and jam roly poly: sweet metaphors for organisational researchers'. *Journal of Further and Higher Education*, 20(1), 51–7.

Hutton, P. (1990) *Survey Research for Managers: How to Use Surveys in Management Decision-making*, 2nd edn. Basingstoke: Macmillan.

Jones, L. (ed.) (1983) *Keeping the Peace*. London: The Women's Press.

Kane, E. (1985) *Doing Your Own Research*. London: Marion Boyars.

Lee, R. (2000) *Unobtrusive Methods in Social Research*. Buckingham: Open University Press.

Lewis-Beck, M. (ed.) (1993) *Experimental Design and Methods*. London: Sage.

Lipson, J. (1991) 'The use of self in ethnographic research'. In J. Morse (ed.) *Qualitative Nursing Research: A Contemporary Dialogue*. Newbury Park, CA: Sage, pp. 73–89.

McGuinness, K. and Short, T. (1998) *Research on the Net*. London: Old Bailey Press.

Mann, C. and Stewart, F. (2000) *Internet Communication and Qualitative Research: A Handbook for Researching On-line*. London: Sage.

Marshall, J. (1995) *Women Managers Moving On: Exploring Career and Life Choices*. London: Routledge.

Mason, J. (1996) *Qualitative Researching*. London: Sage.

Mason, J. (1999) *Inheriting Money: Kinship and Practical Ethics*. Leeds: University of Leeds, Centre for Research on Family, Kinship and Childhood.

May, T. (1993) *Social Research: Issues, Methods and Process*. Buckingham: Open University Press.

Middleton, S. (1995) 'Doing feminist educational theory: a postmodernist perspective'. *Gender and Education*, 7(1), 87–100.

Mikkelsen, B. (1995) *Methods for Development Work and Research: A Guide for Practitioners*. New Delhi: Sage.

Miles, J. (1994) 'Defining the research question'. In J. Buckeldee and R. McMahon (eds) *The Research Experience in Nursing*. London: Chapman and Hall, pp. 17–29.

Miles, M. and Huberman, A. (eds) (1994) *Qualitative Data Analysis*, 2nd edn. Thousand Oaks, CA: Sage.

Miles, M. and Weitzman, E. (1994) 'Choosing computer programs for qualitative data analysis'. In M. Miles and A. Huberman (eds) *Qualitative Data Analysis*, 2nd edn. Thousand Oaks, CA: Sage, pp. 311–17.

Morley, L. (1996) 'Interrogating patriarchy: the challenges of feminist research'. In L. Morley and V. Walsh (eds) *Breaking Boundaries: Women in Higher Education*. London: Taylor and Francis.

Morse, J. (ed.) (1991) *Qualitative Nursing Research: A Contemporary Dialogue*, rev. edn. Newbury Park, CA: Sage.

Morton-Cooper, A. (2000) *Action Research in Health Care*. Oxford: Blackwell.

Nixon, H. (2000) 'Mediascopes, technoscapes and ideoscapes: educational conundrums for Australian educators'. Paper given at the British Educational Research Association conference, Cardiff, September.

Oakley, A. (1999) 'People's way of knowing: gender and methodology'. In S. Hood, B. Mayall and S. Oliver (eds) *Critical Issues in Social Research: Power and Prejudice*. Buckingham: Open University Press, pp. 154–77.

O'Brien, O. (1993) 'Sisters, parents, neighbours, friends: reflections of fieldwork in North Catalonia (France)'. In D. Bell, P. Caplan and W. Karim (eds) *Gendered Fields: Women, Men and Ethnography*. London: Routledge, pp. 234–47.

Orna, E., with Stevens, G. (1995) *Managing Information for Research*. Buckingham: Open University Press.

Papps, F., Walker, M., Trimboli, A. and Trimboli, C. (1995) 'Parental discipline in Anglo, Greek, Lebanese and Vietnamese cultures'. *Journal of Cross-cultural Psychology*, 26(1), 49–64.

Park, A. (1994) *Individual Commitment to Lifetime Learning: Individuals' Attitudes. Report on the Quantitative Survey*. Sheffield: Employment Department, Research Series No. 32.

Parry, O. (1992) 'Making sense of the research setting and making the research setting make sense'. In R. Burgess (ed.) *Learning about Fieldwork*. Greenwich, CT: JAI Press, pp. 63–87.

Peelo, M. (1994) *Helping Students with Study Problems*. Buckingham: Open University Press.

Phillips, E. M. and Pugh, D. (2000) *How to Get a PhD: A Handbook for Students and Their Supervisors*, 3rd edn. Buckingham: Open University Press.

Phizacklea, A. and Wolkowitz, C. (1995) *Homeworking Women*. London: Sage.

Poland, F. (1990) 'The history of a "failed" research topic: the case of childminders'. In L. Stanley (ed.) *Feminist Praxis: Research, Theory and Epistemology in Feminist Sociology*. London: Routledge.

Punch, M. (1986) *The Politics and Ethics of Fieldwork*. Beverley Hills, CA: Sage.

Punch, M. (1998) *Introduction to Social Research: Quantitative and Qualitative Approaches*. London: Sage.

Renfrew, M. and McCandlish, R. (1992) 'With women: new steps in research in midwifery'. In H. Roberts (ed.) *Women's Health Matters*. London: Routledge, pp. 81–98.

Renzetti, C. and Lee, R. (eds) (1993) *Researching Sensitive Topics*. Newbury Park, CA: Sage.

Richardson, L. (1992) 'The consequences of poetic representation: writing the other, re-writing the self'. In C. Ellis and M. Flaherty (eds) *Investigating Subjectivity: Research on Lived Experience*. Newbury Park, CA: Sage, pp. 125–140.

Riessman, C. K. (ed.) (1994) *Qualitative Studies in Social Work*. Thousand Oaks, CA: Sage.

Rosier, M. (1988) 'Survey research methods'. In J. Keeves (ed.) *Educational Research, Methodology and Measurement: An International Handbook*. Oxford: Pergamon, pp. 107–13.

Rowntree, D. (1991) *Learn How to Study: A Guide for Students of All Ages*, 4th edn. London: Sphere.

Rudestam, K. and Newton, R. (1992) *Surviving Your Dissertation: A Comprehensive Guide to Content and Process*. Newbury Park, CA: Sage.

Sargant, N. (1991) *Learning and Leisure: A Study of Adult Participation in Learning and Its Policy Implications*. Leicester: National Institute of Adult Continuing Education.

Schatzman, L. and Strauss, A. (1973) *Field Research: Strategies for a Natural Sociology.* Englewood Cliffs, NJ: Prentice Hall.

Scott, J. and Duncombe, J. (1992) 'Gender-role attitudes in Britain and the USA'. In S. Arber and N. Gilbert (eds) *Women and Working Lives: Divisions and Change.* London: Macmillan, pp. 36–53.

Sherman, R. and Webb, R. (eds) (1988) *Qualitative Research in Education: Forms and Methods.* Lewes: Falmer Press.

Shipman, M. (1988) *The Limitations of Social Research,* 3rd edn. Harlow: Longman.

Siegler, R. (1995) 'How does change occur?' *Cognitive Psychology,* 28(3), 225–73.

Skeggs, B. (1997) *Formations of Class and Gender.* London: Sage.

Slim, H. and Thompson, P. (1993) *Listening for a Change: Oral Testimony and Development.* London: Panos.

Stanley, L. and Wise, S. (1983) *Breaking Out: Feminist Consciousness and Feminist Research.* London: Routledge and Kegan Paul.

Stein, B. (1986) 'The experience of being a refugee: insights from the research literature'. In C. Williams and J. Westermayer (eds) *Refugee Mental Health in Resettlement Countries.* Washington, DC: Hemisphere.

Stevens, P., Schade, A., Chalk, B. and Slevin, O. (1993) *Understanding Research: A Scientific Approach for Health Care Professionals.* Edinburgh: Campion Press.

Strauss, A. (1987) *Qualitative Analysis for Social Scientists,* Cambridge: Cambridge University Press.

Suzuki, Y. (1995) *'On-the-job training: a case study of on-the-job training and informal learning in a British manufacturing firm'.* Unpublished MA dissertation, University of Warwick Department of Continuing Education, Coventry.

Taylor, G. (1989) *The Student's Writing Guide for the Arts and Social Sciences.* Cambridge: Cambridge University Press.

Thomson, A. (1996) *Critical Reasoning: A Practical Introduction.* London: Routledge.

Tight, M. (2000) 'Reporting on academic work and life: a year of *The Times Higher Education Supplement*'. In M. Tight (ed.) *Academic Work and Life: What It Is to Be an Academic, and How This Is Changing.* New York: Elsevier Science, pp. 371–406.

Tizard, B. and Hughes, M. (1991) 'Reflections on *Young Children Learning*'. In G. Walford (ed.) *Doing Educational Research.* London: Routledge.

Townsend, P. (1996) 'The struggle for independent statistics on poverty'. In R. Levitas and W. Guy (eds) *Interpreting Official Statistics.* London: Routledge, pp. 26–44.

Turner, B. (1994) 'Patterns of crisis behaviour: a qualitative inquiry'. In A. Bryman and R. Burgess (eds) *Analysing Qualitative Data.* London: Routledge.

University of Warwick Graduate School (1999) *Guidelines on Responsibilities for the Supervision of Research Degree Students.* Coventry: University of Warwick.

Waddington, D. (1994) 'Participant observation'. In C. Cassell and G. Symon (eds) *Qualitative Methods in Organisational Research: A Practical Guide.* London: Sage.

Walford, G. (1991) 'Researching the City Technology College, Kingshurst'. In G. Walford (ed.) *Doing Educational Research.* London: Routledge, pp. 82–100.

Walkerdine, V. and Lucey, H. (1989) *Democracy in the Kitchen: Regulating Mothers and Socialising Daughters.* London: Virago.

Walter, T. and Siebert, A. (1993) *Student Success: How to Succeed at College and Still Have Time for Your Friends,* 6th edn. Fort Worth, TX: Harcourt Brace Jovanovich College Publishers.

Warran, R. (1992) 'Trade union communications'. *The Industrial Tutor,* 5(6), 5–24.

Weitzman, E. and Miles, M. (1995) *Computer Programs for Qualitative Data Analysis.* Thousand Oaks, CA: Sage.

White, B., Cox, C. and Cooper, C. (1992) *Women's Career Development: A Study of High Fliers.* Oxford: Blackwell.

Whyte, W., Greenwood, D. and Lazes, P. (1991) 'Participatory action research: through practice to science in social research'. In W. Whyte (ed.) *Participatory Action Research.* Newbury Park, CA: Sage, pp. 19–55.

Williams, S. (1994) 'The HITECC experience and the transfer to higher education'. Unpublished MA dissertation, University of Warwick Department of Continuing Education, Coventry.

Witmer, D., Colman, R. and Katzman, S. (1999) 'From paper-and-pencil to screen-and-keyboard: toward a methodology for survey research on the Internet'. In S. Jones (ed.) *Doing Internet Research: Critical Issues and Methods for Examining the Net.* Thousand Oaks, CA: Sage, pp. 145–61.

Woolf, V. (1995) *Killing the Angel in the House.* Harmondsworth: Penguin (the quote is from a lecture given in 1931).

Yin, R. (1993) *Applications of Case Study Research.* Newbury Park, CA: Sage.

# INDEX

# openup

ideas and understanding
in social science

## www.**openup**.co.uk

**Browse, search and
order online**

**Download detailed
title information and
sample chapters***

*for selected titles

www.**openup**.co.uk